Robert Schwandl

SUBWAYS & LIGHT RAIL in den / in the U.S.A.

Band 2: Westen | Vol. 2: The West

Berlin 2012

Robert Schwandl

SUBWAYS & LIGHT RAIL in den in the U.S.A.

Band 2: Westen
Vol. 2: The West

Seattle, Tacoma, Portland, Sacramento, San Francisco, San Jose, Los Angeles, San Diego, Honolulu, Las Vegas, Phoenix, Tucson, Salt Lake City & Denver

Mein Dank für ihre Hilfe geht an | My sincere thanks are due to:

Aleksandr Prodan, Mark Kavanagh, Ryan Park, Seth Morgan, Jack May, Bernhard Kußmagk, Norbert Reulke, Felix Thoma, Hildegard Schweitzer-Thoma as well as to Yuri Popov for checking the California maps!

Thanks also to MTS (San Diego), VTA (San Jose), UTA (Salt Lake City), TriMet (Portland) and Portland Streetcar for their help.

... und natürlich an alle, die Fotos beigetragen haben!
... and, of course, to all those who have contributed some of their photographs!

Robert Schwandl Verlag
Hektorstraße 3
D-10711 Berlin

Tel. 030 - 3759 1284 (0049 - 30 - 3759 1284)
Fax 030 - 3759 1285 (0049 - 30 - 3759 1285)

www.robert-schwandl.de
books@robert-schwandl.de

1. Auflage, 2012

Text & Netzpläne | Text & Network Maps © Robert Schwandl
Fotos ohne Vermerk | Photos without credits © Robert Schwandl

English Text by Robert Schwandl & Mark Davies

Druck: Ruksaldruck, Berlin

ISBN 978-3-936573-35-0

VORWORT

Nach dem Besuch aller städtischen Schienennahverkehrsmittel im amerikanischen Nordosten im ersten Band dieser Reihe* möchte ich Sie nun in den Westen mitnehmen, denn auch diese Region bietet ein überaus vielfältiges Programm. Neben dem „Urban Rail"-Paradies San Francisco, wo es fast alles gibt, was man sich unter einem städtischen Schienenverkehrsmittel vorstellen kann, entstanden hier in den letzten 30 Jahren zahlreiche Stadtbahnsysteme (*Light Rail*), oft unter Einbeziehung ehemaliger Eisenbahnstrecken. Als neuer Trend gilt die Wiedereinführung der klassischen Straßenbahn (*Streetcar*) zur Feinerschließung der Innenstädte. Einst gab es in allen Großstädten weitreichende Straßenbahnnetze, auf diese näher einzugehen, würde allerdings den Rahmen dieses Buchs sprengen. Abgesehen von der metro-ähnlichen BART im Großraum von San Francisco ist jedoch auch im Westen der USA der Regionalverkehr weiterhin sehr unterentwickelt, auch wenn es vereinzelt gute Ansätze gibt. Allgemein kann man beobachten, dass sogar im autofreundlichen Westen die neuen Bahnen stets gut angenommen werden, weshalb auch in den nächsten Jahren ein Ausbau der diversen Netze zu erwarten ist.

Durch die zahlreichen Farbfotos, die auf zwei längeren Reisen 2008 und 2012 entstanden, sowie die detaillierten Netzpläne bekommen auch Sie sicher Lust, diese Gegend selbst zu erkunden. Oder Sie waren schon dort, dann wird das Buch bestimmt die eine oder andere Erinnerung wecken.

Berlin, im November 2012

Robert Schwandl

FOREWORD

After visiting all the urban rail systems in the American Northeast in the first volume of this series*, I would now like to take you to the West, a region which also has a very diverse urban rail scene waiting to be explored. Besides the urban rail paradise of San Francisco, which boasts almost anything you can imagine in this field, many new light rail systems have emerged in this region over the last 30 years, often taking advantage of disused railway corridors. The latest trend is the re-introduction of the classic streetcar (tram) in the downtown areas. There used to be extensive streetcar systems in all the major cities, but to give them the necessary coverage would be beyond the scope of this book. Apart from the metro-like BART system in the San Francisco Bay Area, regional rail services remain rather underdeveloped in the West, although there have been a few promising examples. Generally speaking, the new urban railways have all been very successful, even in the car-friendly West, and their further expansion can therefore be expected.

With numerous colour photos taken during two trips in 2008 and 2012 as well as detailed network maps, you may just want to start planning your own visit to the area. If, on the other hand, you have already been there, then hopefully the book will bring back some pleasant memories.

Berlin, November 2012

Robert Schwandl

Inhalt | *Contents*

* Der dritte Band (Mittlerer Westen & Süden) soll 2014/2015 erscheinen (siehe Seite 158).
The third volume (Midwest & South) is expected in 2014/2015 (see page 158).

Pioneer Square – Stadtbahn im von Bussen mitbenutzten Innenstadttunnel | *Light rail train in the downtown tunnel shared with buses*

SEATTLE, WA

Seattle ist die nordwestlichste Großstadt in den USA, rund 160 km von der kanadischen Grenze entfernt und etwa gleich weit vom Pazifischen Ozean, mit dem es jedoch durch den Puget Sound und die Salish Sea verbunden ist, weshalb Seattle einer der wichtigsten Seehäfen des Landes ist. Die eigentliche Stadt (217,2 km²) hat rund 620.000 Einwohner. Im Großraum, der größtenteils im King County liegt, leben rund 2,7 Millionen Menschen, bei zunehmender Tendenz. Die Metropolregion (3,5 Mio.), zu der auch die Stadt Tacoma gehört, erstreckt sich 120 km in Nord-Süd-Richtung von Marysville bis Olympia, die Hauptstadt des Bundesstaats Washington.

Mit der Bahn ist Seattle mit dem Rest des Landes durch den Amtrak-Zug „Empire Builder" über Minneapolis/St. Paul nach Chicago und den „Coast Starlight" über Portland, Sacramento, Oakland und San Jose nach Los Angeles verbunden. Die Strecke zwischen Seattle und Portland wird außerdem mehrmals täglich durch „Cascades"-Züge bedient, von denen einige nach Süden bis Eugene in Oregon oder nach Norden bis Vancouver in Kanada durchgebunden werden.

Der städtische Schienenverkehr von Seattle bietet vier verschiedene Arten von Bahnen: Stadtbahn, Straßenbahn, Einschienenbahn und Pendlerbahn. Das vielfältige Angebot wird durch ein großes Obusnetz ergänzt. Was Seattle weltweit einzigartig macht, ist die gemeinsame Nutzung eines ÖPNV-Tunnels mit mehreren Stationen durch Stadtbahnen und Busse.

Located in the northwestern corner of the U.S., Seattle lies some 160 km from the Canadian border and about the same distance from the Pacific Ocean, to which it is linked, however, by the Puget Sound and the Salish Sea, making it one of the country's busiest seaports. The city proper (217.2 km2 land area) has a population of some 620,000, with some 2.7 million (and rising) in the urbanised area, most of which lies in King County. The larger metropolitan region (3.5 mil.) extends some 120 km in a north-south direction from Marysville to Olympia, Washington's state capital, and includes the City of Tacoma.

As far as rail goes, Seattle is linked to the rest of the country by Amtrak's "Empire Builder" to Chicago via Minneapolis/St. Paul, and the "Coast Starlight" to Los Angeles via Portland, Sacramento, Oakland and San Jose. The corridor between Seattle and Portland is also served several times a day by "Cascades" trains, some of which continue south to Eugene in Oregon, or north to Vancouver in Canada.

Seattle's urban rail system includes no less than four different types of train: light rail, streetcar, monorail and commuter rail. This manifold offer is complemented by a large network of trolleybus routes. What makes Seattle unique in the world is its transit tunnel with several stations shared by light rail trains and buses.

Seattle's various trains and buses are operated by different companies, and unfortunately, fare integration only par-

Pacific Place (Westlake Hub) – Straßenbahnendstelle | *streetcar terminus*

tially exists. There is no day pass suitable for visitors, although the ORCA smartcard, introduced in 2009, can be used on many trains and buses in the entire Puget Sound region, and offers free transfers within a 2-hour period. Within the City of Seattle, most diesel and all electric buses, as well as the streetcar line, are operated by King County Metro, whereas the Link Light Rail and regional express buses are run by Sound Transit.

Die verschiedenen Bahnen und Busse werden allerdings von verschiedenen Unternehmen betrieben und eine tarifliche Integration ist leider nur teilweise vorhanden. Es gibt keine für Besucher praktische Tageskarte, auch wenn die ORCA-Smartcard, die im Jahr 2009 eingeführt wurde, in vielen Bahnen und Bussen in der gesamten Puget Sound-Region verwendet werden kann und innerhalb von zwei Stunden kostenloses Umsteigen erlaubt. Innerhalb der Stadt Seattle werden die meisten Diesel- und alle elektrischen Busse sowie die Straßenbahn von *King County Metro* betrieben, während die Stadtbahn (Link Light Rail) und die regionalen Express-Busse in der Verantwortung von *Sound Transit* liegen.

Broadway & Olive Way – Seattle besitzt auch ein großes Obusnetz. *Seattle also has an extensive trolleybus network.*

Westlake Center – Monorail-Haltestelle im zweiten Obergeschoss des Einkaufszentrums | *monorail station on the second floor of the shopping mall*

SEATTLE

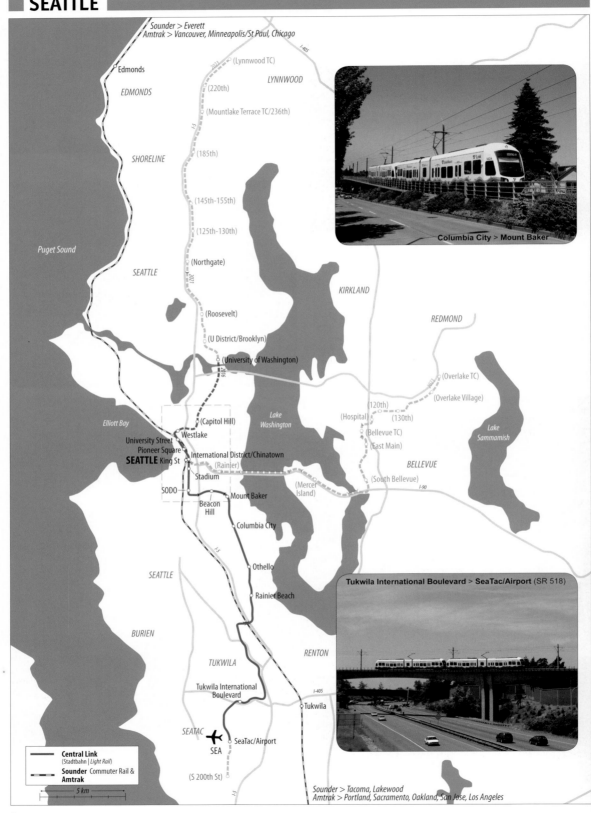

Sounder > Everett
Amtrak > Vancouver, Minneapolis/St Paul, Chicago

Edmonds

EDMONDS

2023 (Lynnwood TC)

LYNNWOOD

(220th)

(Mountlake Terrace TC/236th)

SHORELINE

(185th)

(145th-155th)

(125th-130th)

Puget Sound

SEATTLE

(Northgate)

2021

KIRKLAND

(Roosevelt)

REDMOND

(U District/Brooklyn)

(University of Washington)

2016

(Overlake TC)

(Overlake Village)

(120th)

(Hospital)   (130th)

(Bellevue TC)

(East Main)

BELLEVUE

Lake Washington

(Capitol Hill)

Elliott Bay

Westlake

University Street

Pioneer Square

SEATTLE King St

International District/Chinatown

(Rainier)

Stadium

SODO

(Mercer Island)

(South Bellevue)

Mount Baker

Beacon Hill

Columbia City

Lake Sammamish

I-90

Columbia City > Mount Baker

SEATTLE

Othello

Rainier Beach

BURIEN

Tukwila International Boulevard > SeaTac/Airport (SR 518)

TUKWILA

RENTON

I-405

Tukwila International Boulevard

Tukwila

SEATAC

SEA

SeaTac/Airport

(S 200th St)

Sounder > Tacoma, Lakewood
Amtrak > Portland, Sacramento, Oakland, San Jose, Los Angeles

Central Link
(Stadtbahn | *Light Rail*)

Sounder Commuter Rail &
Amtrak

5 km

Taylor Ave N
Aurora Ave N
Westlake Ave N
Lake Union
Fairview & Campus Drive
I-5
70
47

Lake Union Park
Roy St
Mercer St
5th Ave
Broad St
Westlake & Mercer
Terry & Mercer
Tram Depot

Seattle Center
Denny Way
Broad St
4th Ave
3rd Ave
2nd Ave
1st Ave
I-2·25·13
I-2·5·13
Westlake & Thomas
Terry & Thomas
Westlake & 9th
Westlake & Denny
Westlake Ave
Virginia St
Stewart St
70
Bellevue Ave E
Summit Ave E
E Olive Way
49
Broadway E
2016
12
23rd Ave E
01
43
E Thomas St
E John St
Denny Way
(Capitol Hill)
12th Ave

Westlake & 7th
Convention Place
Olive Way
Pacific Place Pine St
Westlake Center
Westlake
Pike St 10·47·43·49
Boren Ave
E Pine St
E Pike St
10
(Broadway & Pike)
Broadway
E Union St
2
23rd Ave

University Street
Seneca St
Spring St
Madison St
Boren Ave
2
2014
(Broadway & Marion/
Seattle University)
E Cherry St
E Jefferson St
3
3·4
(Broadway & Terrace)
12th Ave
10·72
Marion St
4th Ave
5th Ave
I-5

Pioneer Square
1st Ave
2nd Ave
3rd Ave
James St
Jefferson St
E Yesler Way
(Yesler/10th)
Boren Ave S
(14th & Washington)
14

Main St
(Jackson & 1st)
SEATTLE
King Street
International District/
Chinatown
(Jackson & 7th) 7·14·36
(Jackson & 13th)
Rainier Ave S
S Jackson St
23rd Ave S

Elliott Bay
Alaskan Way Viaduct

Tram Depot
I-90
I-90
12th Ave S
15th Ave S
S Dearborn St
P·01
P·01
(Rainier)
Martin Luther King Jr Way S

Stadium
Airport Way S
12th Ave S
15th Ave S
Beacon Ave S
36
S Holgate St
S Plum St
S Walker St
S College St

SODO
1st Ave S
SODO Busway
S Lander St
Light Rail Depot
Beacon Hill
I-5
Beacon Ave S
15th Ave S
23rd Ave S
Rainier Ave S
Mount Baker

Rainier Beach (Martin Luther King Jr. Way South) – ebenerdiger Stadtbahnabschnitt | *at-grade light rail section*

🚦 LINK LIGHT RAIL

Seattles einzige Stadtbahnlinie gehört zur zweiten Generation der modernen Stadtbahnen in den USA, denjenigen, die von Anfang an mit Niederflurfahrzeugen betrieben wurden. Sie ist Teil von *Sound Transit*, einem Unternehmen, das für die Planung, den Bau und den Betrieb von Express-Bussen, Stadtbahn und Vorortbahnen in den städtischen Bereichen des King, Pierce und Snohomish County zuständig ist. Die Stadtbahn fährt Montag bis Samstag von 5:00 bis 1:00 Uhr, und an Sonn- und Feiertagen von 6:00 bis 24:00 Uhr, alle 7 ½, 10 oder 15 Minuten, je nach Tageszeit. Einzelfahrten kosten je nach Strecke von 2,00 $ bis 2,75 $. Ein besetzter Fahrkarten- und Info-Schalter befindet sich im U-Bahnhof Westlake, ansonsten sind Fahrscheine an Automaten erhältlich. Eine Fahrt vom Flughafen bis Westlake in der Innenstadt von Seattle dauert 38 Minuten. Auf der 27,8 km langen Strecke gibt es 13 Stationen, von denen fünf typische Stadtbahnhaltestellen sind, während die anderen acht als richtige U-Bahn-Stationen bezeichnet werden können. Wie in Mexiko tragen alle Stationen sowohl einen Namen als auch ein Bildsymbol!

Anders als bei den meisten Light Rail-Systemen fährt die Stadtbahn in Seattle nicht ebenerdig durch die Innenstadt, sondern nutzt einen schon länger existierenden ÖPNV-Tunnel. Die Strecke beginnt daher unterirdisch am U-Bahnhof Westlake mitten im Einkaufsviertel der Stadt. Hier kann man zur Monorail, zur Straßenbahn und zu zahlreichen Stadtbussen umsteigen. Nach zwei weiteren U-Bahnhöfen, University Street und Pioneer Square entlang der 3rd Avenue, erreicht die Stadtbahn International District/Chinatown, eine teilweise nach oben offene Tiefstation in unmittelbarer Nähe des Hauptbahnhofs von Seattle, King Street Station. Ein paar hundert Meter weiter südlich trennt sich die Stadtbahn von den Bussen und fährt auf einem eigenen Gleiskörper Richtung Süden weiter.

Seattle's only light rail line belongs to the second generation of modern light rail systems in the U.S., those which have been operated with low-floor vehicles from the beginning. It is run by Sound Transit, an agency responsible for planning, building and operating express bus, light rail and commuter train services in the urban areas of King, Pierce and Snohomish Counties. Link trains run from 05:00 to 01:00 Mon-Sat and from 06:00 to 24:00 on Sundays and holidays, every 7 ½, 10 or 15 minutes depending on the time of the day. Adult fares range from $2.00 to $2.75, depending on the distance travelled. A staffed ticket and information counter is located inside Westlake station, although elsewhere tickets have to be bought from vending machines. A ride from the Airport to Westlake in downtown Seattle takes 38 minutes. On the 27.8 km line there are 13 stations, five of which are typical light rail stops, whereas the other 8 can be classified as full metro stations. Like in Mexico, each station can be identified by its name as well as a pictorial symbol!

Unlike most other such systems, Seattle's light rail does not run at grade through the city centre, but instead uses a previously existing transit tunnel. The route therefore starts underground at Westlake in the heart of the city's shopping

SEATTLE Link Light Rail

27.8 km (+ 5.0 km im Bau | *under construction*)
13 Haltestellen | *stations* (+ 2 i.B. | *u/c*)

20 July 2009: Westlake – Tukwila International Boulevard
19 Dec 2009: Tukwila International Boulevard – SeaTac/Airport
2016: Westlake – University of Washington

Westlake – Bus im Stadtbahntunnel | *bus in the light rail tunnel*

Westlake – moderne Kunst in sonst klassischem U-Bahnhof – *modern artwork in otherwise classic underground station*

Der Bau des sog. „**Downtown Seattle Transit Tunnel**" begann im März 1987. Das Hauptziel dieses Projekts war es, die wie in Manhattan engen Straßen vom übermäßigen Busverkehr zu entlasten. Die beiden Tunnelröhren folgen weitgehend der 3rd Avenue und biegen dann um 90 Grad in Richtung Osten unter die Pine Street ab und enden an einem Portal an der 9th Avenue. Direkt außerhalb des Tunnels liegt die Busstation Convention Place, wo die Busse wenden, auf städtischen Straßen weiterfahren oder direkt auf den HOV-Spuren der I-5 (für Busse und Privatfahrzeuge mit mehreren Insassen reservierte Fahrspuren) als Express in die nördlichen Vororte fahren können. Das südliche Ende der beiden Röhren befindet sich direkt nördlich der Station International District/Chinatown. Als der 2,1 km lange Tunnel am 15. September 1990 in Betrieb ging, wurde er mit Duo-Bussen (Diesel/elektrisch) befahren, d.h. die Busse wechselten an der Tunneleinfahrt auf Obusbetrieb. Das unterirdische Obusnetz war nicht mit dem oberirdischen verbunden. Im Tunnel waren sogar Schienen für einen eventuellen künftigen Stadtbahnbetrieb verlegt worden.

Nach 15 Jahren Busbetrieb wurde der Tunnel am 24. September 2005 geschlossen, um ihn für den Einsatz von modernen Stadtbahnen, die Seattle mit dem rund 25 km südlich der Innenstadt gelegenen Flughafen verbinden sollten, umzubauen. Die ursprünglich vorgesehenen Gleise erwiesen sich nach heutigen Maßstäben als ungeeignet und mussten ersetzt werden. Gleichzeitig wurde die Fahrbahn in den Stationen abgesenkt, um Niedrigbahnsteige zu erhalten, an denen sowohl Bahnen als auch neue Busse halten sollten. Der Obusbetrieb wurde nicht wieder aufgenommen, als der Tunnel am 24. September 2007 wiedereröffnet wurde, stattdessen kommen nun

area. Here, transfer is available to the Monorail, the Streetcar and numerous city bus lines. After serving two more underground stations along 3rd Avenue, University Street and Pioneer Square, trains arrive at International District/Chinatown, a partly covered subsurface station within walking distance of Seattle's main railway station King Street. A few hundred metres south of International District/Chinatown station, the light rail tracks separate from the bus lanes to continue south on their own right-of-way.

The construction of the **Downtown Seattle Transit Tunnel** began in March 1987. The main goal of this project was to relieve the narrow Manhattan-like city streets of excessive bus traffic. The twin-tube tunnels follow 3rd Avenue before turning 90 degrees east to continue under Pine Street to a portal at 9th Avenue. Just outside the tunnel is Convention Place bus station, where buses can turn around, continue on urban roads, or enter the I-5 HOV lanes directly to run express to the northern suburbs. The southern end of the tube tunnels is located just north of International District/Chinatown station. When the 2.1 km tunnel was brought into service on 15 September 1990, it was served by dual-mode buses (diesel/electric) which switched to trolleybus operation before entering the tunnel. The underground trolleybus system was not linked to the existing surface network. The underground busway was even fitted with rail tracks in provision for future light rail operation.

After 15 years of bus operation, the Transit Tunnel was closed on 24 September 2005 to be upgraded for use by modern light rail vehicles serving Seattle's first line to SeaTac Airport some 25 km south of the city centre. The tracks origi-

Westlake – derzeitiger Endpunkt der Stadtbahn | *current light rail terminus*

University Street – U-Bahnhof im Bankenviertel | *CBD station*

International District/Chinatown – nach oben großteils offener U-Bahnhof
– *mostly uncovered subsurface station*

neue Hybridbus-Busse von New Flyer mit einem Akku auf dem Dach zum Einsatz, wohl weil das eher kleine Röhrenprofil von 5,50 m die Installation von zwei parallelen Fahrleitungen nicht erlaubte. Das hybride Allison-System bewirkt, dass der Bus bei niedriger Geschwindigkeit weitgehend elektrisch angetrieben wird und somit keine Abgase in den Tunnel abgibt.

Das Tunnelausbau-Projekt umfasste auch den Bau eines Tunnelstutzens unter der Pine Street, wo die Züge wenden können, während die Busse den Tunnel auf der schon vorher bestehenden Rampe verlassen. Der Stutzen wurde auch in Hinsicht auf eine nördliche Verlängerung, die jetzt im Bau ist, errichtet. Die Stadtbahn fährt seit dem 18. Juli 2009 durch den Tunnel.

Die Strecke südlich der Station International District/Chinatown verläuft ebenerdig mit ein paar Bahnübergängen und parallel zum SODO-Busway. Einige Abschnitte liegen unterhalb der Auffahrten zur Autobahn I-90, deren Korridor eines Tages von der Eastside Light Rail genutzt werden soll.

Nach zwei typischen ebenerdigen Stationen, Stadium und SODO, biegt die Stadtbahn Richtung Osten ab und erreicht eine 600 m lange Hochbahntrasse (mit dem Stadtbahnbetriebshof südlich davon), bevor sie in den 1,5 km langen Beacon Hill-Tunnel einfährt, der eine 49 m tiefe Station mit diesem Namen enthält. Der U-Bahn-mäßige Abschnitt führt vom Ostportal weiter auf einem Viadukt bis zum Hochbahnhof Mount Baker. Die folgende Strecke durch Columbia City und Rainier Beach hat eine stadtbahnmäßige Trassierung auf dem Mittelstreifen des Martin Luther King Jr Way South mit mehreren Bahnübergängen. Rainier Beach ist die letzte Station auf dem Stadtgebiet von Seattle, etwas südlich gibt es zwischen den beiden Streckengleisen ein Kehrgleis. Die Bahn fährt rund 1,2 km weiter ebenerdig, bevor sie dann eine Hochbahnstrecke erklimmt, die fast bis zum Flughafen reicht. Zunächst verläuft die Strecke durch Industriegebiete und dann entlang der I-5 und I-405. In der Stadt Tukwila gibt es nur eine Zwischenstation, Tukwila International Boulevard, ein wichtiger Knoten mit zahlreichen Busverbindungen und einem großen Parkplatz. Erste Pläne beinhalteten jedoch eine Umsteigestation zwischen Stadtbahn und Sounder-Pendlerzug an der Boeing Access Road, die jedoch vorerst nicht realisiert wurde. Die heutige Endstation SeaTac/Airport liegt direkt auf dem Flughafengelände, aber die Fahrgäste müssen durch ein Parkdeck gehen, um das Terminalgebäude zu erreichen.

nally laid proved to be inadequate by modern standards and had to be replaced. At the same time, the roadway in the stations was lowered to create low-level platforms, both for the trains and the new buses. Trolleybus operation was not resumed when the tunnel re-opened on 24 September 2007, but instead, new articulated hybrid New Flyer buses with a roof-mounted battery pack now serve the routes through the tunnel, supposedly because the rather small tube profile (5.50 m) prevented the installation of two parallel overhead lines. The hybrid Allison system means that at lower speed the bus is largely electrically driven, and therefore no exhaust fumes are released into the tunnel.

The tunnel upgrading project also included the construction of a tunnel stub under Pine Street for trains to reverse, while the buses leave the tunnel on the already existing ramp. The stub was also built in provision for a northern extension now under construction. Light rail trains started running through the tunnel on 18 July 2009.

The route south of International District/Chinatown station runs at grade with a few level crossings, and parallel to the SODO Busway. Some sections lie below the access viaducts for I-90, a corridor planned to also be used by the Eastside Light Rail.

After serving two typical surface stations, Stadium and SODO, light rail trains turn east and climb onto a 600 m elevated structure (with the light rail's maintenance yard located to the south), before entering the 1.5 km Beacon Hill tube tunnel, which contains the 49 m deep station of that name. The metro-like section continues as trains leave the tunnel on the eastern side on a viaduct to serve the elevated Mount Baker station. The following route through Columbia City and Rainier Beach has a more light rail-style alignment, lying on a reserved lane in the median of Martin Luther King Jr Way South and with several level crossings. Rainier Beach is the last stop within the City of Seattle; just south of it, there is a turnback siding between the two running tracks. Trains continue at grade for some 1.2 km before changing to an elevated metro-like structure which continues almost all the way to the airport. It first runs through industrial areas and then alongside I-5 and I-405, with just a single intermediate station in the City of Tukwila, Tukwila International Boulevard, a major hub with many bus connections and a large car park. Initial plans, however, included a light rail/commuter rail interchange at Boeing Access Road, which was later deferred. Although the present terminus at SeaTac/Airport is located within the airport complex, rail passengers have to walk through a car park deck to reach the terminal building.

Beacon Hill – einer der tiefsten U-Bahnhöfe Nordamerikas
– *one of North America's deepest underground stations*

Die Zukunft der Stadtbahn

Sound Transit verfolgt ehrgeizige Pläne zur Erweiterung des Stadtbahnnetzes, insbesondere durch eine Nordverlängerung auf einer weitgehend U-Bahn-mäßigen Trasse in mehreren Stufen bis nach Lynnwood. Der seit März 2009 im Bau befindliche Abschnitt soll im Jahr 2016 eröffnet werden. Dabei handelt es sich um eine 5 km lange, in großer Tiefenlage verlaufende Strecke unter dem Capitol Hill bis zur University of Washington nördlich der Wasserstraße, die den Lake Washington mit dem Puget Sound verbindet. In der nächsten Stufe werden die Züge etwa 2021 Northgate auf einer 6,9 km langen, größtenteils unterirdischen Strecke erreichen. Der Baubeginn ist für 2013 vorgesehen. In einer späteren Phase wird die Stadtbahn 13,6 km weiter nach Norden im Mittelstreifen der I-5 oder neben ihr weiterfahren, auch wenn die genaue Trassenführung und Lage der Bahnhöfe noch nicht entschieden ist.

Am südlichen Ende soll eine 2,5 km lange Hochbahn bis zu einem neuen Endpunkt an der South 200th Street/Ecke 28th Avenue South in der Stadt SeaTac errichtet werden. Die Central Link wird somit zu einer 55 km langen Nord-Süd-Linie, die später eventuell weiter nach Süden bis Redondo/Star Lake (7,5 km) und sogar bis Tacoma verlängert werden könnte.

Gleichzeitig schreitet das East Link-Projekt voran, um die Stadtbahn auch in die Städte östlich des Lake Washington, wie Bellevue und Redmond (Heimat von Microsoft), zu bringen. Die Bahnen werden den See auf der bestehenden I-90-Pontonbrücke überqueren, indem sie die bestehenden mittleren HOV-Fahrspuren übernehmen. Die Trasse östlich von Mercer Island wird eine Mischung aus aufgeständerten und ebenerdigen Abschnitten sowie einem kurzen Tunnel im Stadtzentrum von Bellevue sein. Bei einem Baubeginn im Jahr 2015 ist die Eröffnung des 22,4 km langen East Link 2023 vorgesehen.

Stadtbahn-Fahrzeuge

Bis 2014 wird die Stadtbahn-Flotte auf 62 Fahrzeuge anwachsen, die von Kinkisharyo-Mitsui in Japan hergestellt und in einem Boeing-Hangar in Everett nördlich von Seattle montiert werden. Die 70% niederflurigen Zweirichtungsfahrzeuge sind 29,0 m lang und 2,65 m breit. Die Bodenhöhe an den Türen beträgt 355 mm. Neben den motorisierten Drehgestellen unter die erhöhten Endabschnitten haben die Doppelgelenkwagen ein drittes, nicht motorisiertes Fahrwerk unter dem kurzen Mittelteil. Die Wagen sind mit Fahrradhaken ausgestattet. In der Regel werden derzeit 2-Wagen-Züge eingesetzt, auch wenn die Bahnsteige lang genug für 4-Wagen-Züge wären. Die Höchstgeschwindigkeit ist 105 km/h. Die Stromversorgung erfolgt über eine Oberleitung mit 1500 V Gleichstrom. Der Tunnel und die Hochbahnabschnitte sind mit einem automatischen Zugsicherungssystem von Ansaldo STS ausgerüstet.

Kinkisharyo

Columbia City – Kunst findet man auch an oberirdischen Stationen.
– *surface stations have also been enhanced with works of art.*

Light Rail Future

Sound Transit has ambitious plans to expand the present single-line system, notably by extending it north in various stages all the way to Lynnwood on a metro-like alignment. The section under construction since March 2009, and scheduled to open in 2016, is a 5 km deep-level underground route under Capitol Hill to the University of Washington which is located just north of the waterway that links Lake Washington to Puget Sound. In the next stage, trains will reach Northgate in around 2021 on a 6.9 km route lying mostly underground. Construction is planned to start in 2013. In a future stage, trains will continue 13.6 km north alongside or in the median of I-5, although the exact alignment and the station locations have not yet been finalised.

At the southern end, a 2.5 km elevated extension is planned to reach a new terminus at South 200th Street & 28th Avenue South in the City of SeaTac. Seattle's Central Link will thus become a 55 km north-south trunk line, which could later be extended south to Redondo/Star Lake (7.5 km), and eventually to Tacoma.

At the same time, the East Link project is progressing, too. This will bring light rail service to the Eastside, i.e. the cities east of Lake Washington like Bellevue and Redmond (home to Microsoft). Trains will cross the lake on the existing I-90 floating bridge by taking over the existing central HOV lanes. The alignment east of Mercer Island will be a mix of elevated and at-grade sections, with a short tunnel planned in downtown Bellevue. With construction starting in 2015, the opening of the 22.4 km East Link is envisaged for 2023.

Light Rail Rolling Stock

By 2014, the light rail fleet will consist of 62 vehicles manufactured by Kinkisharyo-Mitsui in Japan and assembled in a Boeing hangar in Everett, north of Seattle. Each of the double-ended, 70% low-floor vehicles is 29.0 m long and 2.65 m wide. The floor height at the doors is 355 mm. Besides the motorised bogies under the raised end sections, the bi-articulated vehicles have a third, unpowered set of wheels under the short centre module. The cars are equipped with bicycle racks. Two-car trains are normally used now, but platforms were built long enough for four-car trains. The maximum speed of the light rail vehicles is 105 km/h. Power is supplied via a 1500 V dc overhead catenary. The underground and elevated sections are operated under the Ansaldo STS automatic train protection system.

Lake Union Park

Pacific Place (Westlake Hub)

🚊 SEATTLE STREETCAR

Zwei Jahre vor der Eröffnung der Central Link Light Rail kehrte bereits die konventionelle Straßenbahn nach Seattle zurück. Die eingleisige Endstelle der kurzen Linie in der Innenstadt liegt am Verkehrsknoten Westlake unweit der Stationen der Monorail sowie der unterirdischen Stadtbahn. Von hier aus fährt die Tram straßenbündig nach Norden entlang der Westlake Avenue bis South Lake Union, einem europäisch anmutenden Sanierungsgebiet, wo unter anderem der weltweit bekannte Online-Händler Amazon.com beheimatet ist. Die Linie wird daher auch als „**South Lake Union Streetcar Line**" bezeichnet. Richtung Norden biegt die Straßenbahn rechts in die Thomas Street und dann links in die Terry Avenue, während sie Richtung Süden durchgehend auf der Westlake Avenue verkehrt. Beide Gleise treffen am Lake Union Park wieder aufeinander, bevor sie 300 m weiter nordöstlich enden; die Trams wenden auf einem abmarkierten Stumpfgleis in der Mitte der Fairview Avenue. Ein kleines Depot befindet sich zwei Blocks östlich der Terry Avenue an der Harrison Street.

Der *Seattle Streetcar* gehört der Stadt Seattle und wird in deren Auftrag von *King County Metro* betrieben. Eine einfache Fahrt kostet immerhin 2,50 $. Gefahren wird alle 15 Minuten mit zwei von drei 20 m langen und 2,46 m breiten 12-Trio-Fahrzeugen von Inekon, von denen jedes eine unterschiedliche Farbgebung hat. Sie sind den Fahrzeugen in Portland ähnlich, mit Drehgestellen unter den erhöhten Endabschnitten und einem schwebenden Niederflur-Mittelteil. Im Gegensatz zur Central Link werden die Straßenbahnen mit konventionellem 750 V Gleichstrom versorgt.

Eine zweite Straßenbahnstrecke, die „**First Hill Streetcar Line**", ist derzeit im Bau. Sie wird im Bereich der Stationen International District/Chinatown und King Street beginnen und an der zukünftigen unterirdischen Stadtbahn-Station Capitol Hill enden. Die Strecke führt über die Jackson Street, die 14th Avenue, den Yesler Way und den Broadway und stellt die erste von mehreren vorgeschlagenen Routen dar.

Seattle hatte einst ein großes elektrisches Straßenbahnnetz und aufgrund seiner hügeligen Topographie auch Cable Cars wie in San Francisco. Lange Überlandstraßenbahnstrecken führten bis Everett und Tacoma.

Two years before the opening of Central Link Light Rail, urban rail returned to Seattle in the form of a short conventional streetcar line. Its downtown single-track terminus is at the Westlake Hub, close to that of the monorail and the underground light rail station. From here, trams run on-street north along Westlake Avenue to South Lake Union, a European-style redeveloped area in which, among other companies, the headquarters of global online retailer Amazon.com are located. The line is therefore also known as the **South Lake Union Streetcar Line**. *Northbound trams turn right into Thomas Street and then left into Terry Avenue, while southbound trams stay on Westlake Avenue. Both tracks rejoin at the Lake Union Park and continue northeast for some 300 m; the vehicles reverse beyond the final stop on a single-track stub on a marked-off lane in the middle of Fairview Avenue. A small depot and workshop is located two blocks east of Terry Avenue just off Harrison Street.*

The Seattle Streetcar is owned by the City of Seattle and operated by King County Metro on their behalf. A single ride costs no less than $2.50. Service is provided every 15 minutes by two of the three avilable 20 m Inekon 12-Trio vehicles, each of which carries a different livery and is 2.46 m wide. They are similar to those in operation in Portland, with bogies under the raised end sections and a floating low-floor middle section. Unlike Central Link, the streetcars draw power from a conventional 750 V dc overhead line.

A second streetcar route, the **First Hill Streetcar Line**, *is currently under construction. It will run from the transport hub at International District/Chinatown and King Street stations to the future underground light rail station at Capitol Hill, via Jackson Street, 14th Avenue, Yesler Way and Broadway. This is the first of several proposed routes.*

Seattle once had a large network of electric streetcars, and due to its hilly topography, San Francisco-style cable cars, too. Long interurban lines reached places like Everett and Tacoma.

SEATTLE Streetcar

2.1 km (+ 4.2 km im Bau | *under construction*)
7 Haltestellen | *stops* (+ 10 im Bau | *under construction*)

12 Dec 2007: Westlake Center – Fairview & Campus Drive
2014: Jackson & 1st Ave – Capitol Hill (Broadway & Denny)

Fairview & Campus Drive – nördliche Straßenbahnendstelle | *northern streetcar terminus*

Vom 29. Mai 1982 bis 18. November 2005 fuhr der **Waterfront Streetcar** regelmäßig zwischen Broad Street (Pier 90) und Main Street (ab 1993 bis South Jackson Street). Die Linie wurde mit W2-Straßenbahnen aus Melbourne betrieben. Die Strecke könnte nach Abriss der Hochstraße Alaskan Way wieder aufgebaut werden.

*From 29 May 1982 to 18 November 2005, the **Waterfront Streetcar** ran regularly between Broad Street (Pier 90) and Main Street (from 1993 to South Jackson Street). It was operated with ex Melbourne W2 trams. It may be reinstated once the elevated Alaskan Way has been demolished.*

Occidental Park (Main St & Occidental Ave)

Mark Kavanagh

13

Seattle Center – Space Needle + Experience Music Project

⊤ SEATTLE MONORAIL

Die Seattle Alweg Monorail verbindet den Knoten Westlake mit dem Seattle Center, dem Gebiet der Weltausstellung von 1962 mit dem Wahrzeichen Space Needle. Mit mehreren Museen und Veranstaltungsorten lockt das Expo-Gelände weiterhin viele Besucher an und sorgt auch nach 50 Jahren für eine gute Auslastung der Monorail. Die Züge fahren alle 10 Minuten von 7:30 bis 23:00 Uhr. Eine einzelne Fahrt kostet 2,25 $, ORCA-Karten werden nicht akzeptiert.

Die 1,6 km lange Einschienenbahn wurde am 24. März 1962 eröffnet. Sie wird mit zwei von Linke-Hofmann-Busch in Deutschland gebauten Zügen, einem roten und einem blauen, betrieben. Sie fahren jeweils auf einem eigenen Betonfahrweg bis zu 9 m über dem Straßenniveau. Das ALWEG-System wurde in Deutschland vom schwedischen Ingenieur A̲xel L̲ennart W̲enner-G̲ren entwickelt. Er errichtete die Bahn in Seattle als Demonstrationsanlage mit der Absicht, diese Technologie an andere Städte in Europa und Nordamerika zu verkaufen. Jeder 4-teilige Zug ist 36 m lang und hat 64 Reifen, wovon 16 den Zug tragen und 48 als Führungsräder dienen. Die Stromversorgung erfolgt über eine Stromschiene mit 700 V Gleichstrom.

Während die Station am Seattle Center einen typischen metromäßigen Mittelbahnsteig aufweist, ist der Seitenbahnsteig am Westlake Center vom 2. Obergeschoss des Einkaufszentrums zugänglich: Wenn der rote Zug auf dem östlichen Balken in Betrieb ist, wird der westliche Fahrbalken des blauen Zugs durch ausfahrbare Bahnsteigplatten überbrückt, um das Aus- und Einsteigen zu ermöglichen! Die ursprüngliche südliche Endstation überspannte die Pine Street, bis sie 1988 verlegt wurde.

More a tourist attraction than a form of public transport, the Seattle Alweg Monorail links the Westlake hub to the Seattle Center, the area of the 1962 World's Fair with Seattle's best-known landmark, the Space Needle. With several museums and venues, the Expo area still attracts many visitors, and after 50 years, the Monorail is as popular as ever. Trains run every 10 minutes from 07:30 to 23:00. A single fare is $2.25 and ORCA cards are not accepted.

The 1.6 km Monorail was opened on 24 March 1962. It is operated with two trains, one red and one blue, built by Linke-Hofmann-Busch in Germany. Each runs on a dedicated fixed guideway made of concrete beams, some of which are 9 m above street level. The ALWEG system was designed in Germany by Swedish engineer A̲xel L̲ennart W̲enner-G̲ren, whose intention was to build a demonstration line to sell the technology to other cities in Europe and North America. Each 4-section train is 36 m long and has 64 tyres, with 16 carrying the train and 48 guiding it. Power is supplied via a 700 V dc contact rail.

While the Seattle Center station features a typical metro-style island platform, the Westlake Center side platform is accessible from the second floor of the shopping mall — when the red train is in operation on the eastern beam, the blue train's western beam is bridged with retractable platform extensions to allow alighting and boarding! The original southern terminus spanned across Pine Street, but was relocated in 1988.

Blue Train @ Stewart Street

Red Train @ Seattle Center

SOUNDER

Neben der Central Link Light Rail und der Straßenbahn in Tacoma gehört zum Netz von *Sound Transit* auch eine „Sounder" genannte Pendlerbahn. Sie wird im Auftrag von *Sound Transit* von der Eisenbahngesellschaft BNSF auf deren eigenen Gleisen betrieben.

Der Sounder-Betrieb begann am 18. September 2000 mit typischen Bombardier-Doppelstockwagen, die von Diesellokomotiven gezogen bzw. geschoben werden. Morgens gibt es sieben Züge Richtung Norden von Tacoma nach Seattle (64 km) und nachmittags zwei. In der entgegengesetzten Richtung gilt ein umgekehrter Fahrplan. Seit dem 8. Oktober 2012 werden in der Hauptlastrichtung fünf Züge bis Lakewood, 13 km südlich von Tacoma, durchgebunden.

Die Nordlinie nach Everett (56 km) wurde am 21. Dezember 2003 eingerichtet und bietet vier Züge nur in der Pendler-Hauptlastrichtung (außerdem können hier zwei Amtrak-Züge von Pendlern genutzt werden).

Seattle King Street

Tacoma Dome

Besides the Central Link Light Rail and the streetcar in Tacoma, Sound Transit also provides a commuter rail service. Called the **Sounder**, it is operated by BNSF on their own tracks and on behalf of Sound Transit.

Launched on 18 September 2000, typical Bombardier double-deck carriages pulled or pushed by diesel locomotives provide 7 northbound trips from Tacoma to Seattle (64 km) in the morning and two in the afternoon, with an inverted schedule in the opposite direction. Since 8 October 2012, five peak-direction trains have originated at or continued to Lakewood, 13 km south of Tacoma.

The northern line to Everett (56 km) was introduced on 21 December 2003 and has four trains, which only run in the main commuting direction (plus two Amtrak services available for commuters).

Union Station > Convention Center – Tw. 1002 Richtung Süden auf dem Abschnitt, wo die Strecke von der Commerce Street in die Pacific Avenue schwenkt. – *southbound car no. 1002 on the section where the route switches from Commerce Street to Pacific Avenue*

TACOMA, WA

Tacoma liegt etwa 50 km südlich von Seattle. Die beiden Städte sind durch häufige Express-Busse von *Sound Transit*, den Sounder-Pendlerzug sowie ein paar Amtrak-Fernzüge miteinander verbunden. Wie Seattle ist auch Tacoma eine wichtige Hafenstadt am Puget Sound. Die Stadt hat rund 200.000 Einwohner (129,7 km²) und ist Teil der Metropolregion von Seattle.

🚊 Tacoma Link

Trotz des offiziellen Namens in Anlehnung an die Central Link Light Rail in Seattle handelt es sich in Tacoma um eine herkömmliche Straßenbahn, vergleichbar mit dem Seattle Streetcar, sie wird aber wie Central Link von *Sound Transit* betrieben. Mit einer Gesamtlänge von nur 2,6 km gehört sie zu den kleinsten Straßenbahnen der Welt. Sie stellt eine Verbindung von der Verkehrsdrehscheibe am Tacoma Dome (Sounder-Bahnhof, große Park & Ride-Anlage und Amtraks Tacoma-Bahnhof in der Nähe) in die Innenstadt her, die in den letzten Jahren einem Sanierungsprogramm unterzogen wurde. Die Fahrt mit der Straßenbahn ist kostenlos. Der Betrieb wird mit zwei tschechischen 10T-Niederflur-Gelenkfahrzeugen von Škoda abgewickelt, wie sie auch in Portland eingesetzt werden. Die Tram fährt alle 12 Minuten auf einer Strecke, die zwischen Union Station (bis 1984 der Hauptbahnhof der Stadt) und der südlichen Endstation eingleisig ist. Ein kleines Depot befindet sich am südlichen Ende der Linie. Zunächst gab es fünf Haltestellen, bis im Jahr 2011 eine zusätzliche Haltestelle an der Commerce Street/S 11th Street eingerichtet wurde.

Tacoma is located some 50 km south of Seattle, to where it is linked by frequent Sound Transit express buses, the Sounder commuter rail and a few Amtrak long-distance trains. Like Seattle, Tacoma is an important seaport on Puget Sound. The city has some 200,000 inhabitants (129.7 km2) and is part of the larger Seattle metropolitan region.

🚊 Tacoma Link

Despite its official name, which is in line with Seattle's Central Link Light Rail, Tacoma's urban rail system is a conventional streetcar line similar to that in Seattle, but like Central Link, it is operated by Sound Transit. With a total route length of only 2.6 km, it is one of the smallest tram systems in the world. The main purpose of its construction was to provide a link from the transportation hub at Tacoma Dome (Sounder commuter rail, large park & ride facility and Amtrak's Tacoma station nearby) to the city centre, which has been undergoing a revitalisation programme. Riding the streetcars is free. Normal service is provided by two Czech-built low-floor articulated Škoda 10 T vehicles, like those in Portland. They run every 12 minutes on a route which is

TACOMA Streetcar

2.6 km
6 Haltestellen | *stops*

22 Aug 2003: Tacoma Dome – Theater District

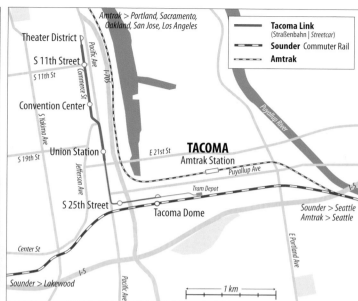

Škoda: niederfluriges Mittelteil | *low-floor centre section*

Wie die meisten amerikanischen Städte hatte Tacoma einst ein großes Straßenbahnnetz und sogar eine Cabel Car-Linie, aber alle städtischen Schienenverkehrsmittel verschwanden bis 1938.

single-track between Union Station (the city's main railway station until 1984) and the southern terminus. A small depot is located at the southern end of the line. Initially boasting five stops, an additional stop was added at Commerce Street & S 11th Street in 2011.

Like most American cities, Tacoma once had a large streetcar network and even a cable-car route, but all urban rail systems had disappeared by 1938.

Theater District – Tw. 1001 an der eingleisigen nördlichen Endstation – *car no. 1001 at the single-track northern terminus*

SW 5th Avenue & Mill Street – einziger Abschnitt, wo Stadtbahn und Straßenbahn derzeit parallel fahren.
– *the only section where light rail trains and streetcars run next to each other.*

PORTLAND, OR

Neben dem rund 230 km weiter nördlich gelegenen Seattle ist Portland die einzige größere Stadt im Nordwesten der USA. Sie erstreckt sich auf beiden Seiten des Willamette-Flusses, der nur 18 km flussabwärts in den mächtigen Columbia-Fluss mündet. Letzterer bildet nicht nur die nördliche Stadtgrenze, sondern auch die Grenze zwischen den US-Bundesstaaten Oregon und Washington. Trotz einer Entfernung von rund 100 km (130 km auf dem Wasserweg) vom Pazifischen Ozean ist Portland ein wichtiger Seehafen dank des schiffbaren Columbia-Flusses. Während sich die östlichen Vororte auf eher flachem Gebiet ausdehnen, ist die Innenstadt von den westlichen Vororten durch eine Hügelkette, die Tualatin Mountains, getrennt. Die eigentliche Stadt (347,9 km²) hat knapp 600.000 Einwohner. Im Großraum, der das Multnomah, Clackamas und Washington County in Oregon sowie Vancouver (WA) jenseits des Columbia-Flusses umfasst, leben etwa 2 Mio. Menschen.

Wie Seattle ist Portland an den Rest des Landes einmal täglich durch den Amtrak-Zug „Empire Builder" angebunden, der aus Chicago über Minneapolis/St. Paul kommt und in Spokane geteilt wird, angebunden. Außerdem kommt hier der „Coast Starlight" auf dem Weg von Seattle über Sacramento, Oakland und San Jose nach Los Angeles vorbei. Seattle erreicht man auch mehrmals täglich mit einem „Cascades"-Zug.

Der öffentliche Nahverkehr wird in den drei Counties in Oregon größtenteils von TriMet (*Tri-County Metropolitan Transportation District of Oregon*) durchgeführt und umfasst Busse, Stadtbahn sowie eine Vorortbahn. Dazu kommen die

Besides Seattle, some 230 km further north, Portland is the only major city in the Northwest of the U.S.A. The city extends on both sides of the Willamette River, which joins the mighty Columbia River only 18 km downstream. The latter forms not only the northern city boundary, but also the border between the U.S. states of Oregon and Washington. Although located some 100 km (130 km by waterways) from the Pacific Ocean, Portland is an important seaport thanks to the navigable Columbia River. While the eastern suburbs extend on rather flat lands, the downtown area is separated from the western suburbs by a ridge of hills, the Tualatin Mountains. The city proper (347.9 km2) has a population of just under 600,000, with some 2 million in the metropolitan area, which includes Multnomah, Clackamas and Washington Counties in Oregon, plus Vancouver, WA, across the Columbia River.

Like Seattle, Portland is linked to the rest of the country once a day by Amtrak's "Empire Builder" to Chicago via Minneapolis/St. Paul (the train splits at Spokane), and the "Coast Starlight", which runs south to Los Angeles via Sacramento, Oakland and San Jose, and north to Seattle. This city can also be reached by taking one of several daily "Cascades" trains.

Public transport in the three Oregon counties is mostly organised by TriMet (*Tri-County Metropolitan Transportation District of Oregon*), and includes buses, light rail and a commuter rail line. There is also the city-owned streetcar

SW Harrison Street – Tw. 004 von Škoda auf dem Weg Richtung South Waterfront | *Škoda car no. 004 bound for South Waterfront*

städtische Straßenbahn und sogar eine privat betriebene Seilbahn. Letztere ist allerdings nicht in das ansonsten sehr gute einheitliche Tarifsystem integriert, das mit Abschaffung des ehemaligen 3-Zonen-Tarifs im September 2012 sogar noch vereinfacht wurde (gleichzeitig fiel auch die Freifahrtzone für Bahnen in der Innenstadt weg). Eine einfache Fahrt kostet 2,50 $ (1,00 $ nur für die Straßenbahn) und eine Tageskarte nur $ 5,00. Ein TriMet-Kundencenter ist im Touristenbüro am Pioneer Courthouse Square untergebracht.

system and a privately operated aerial cable car. Except the latter, all modes are perfectly integrated into a single fare system, which was simplified even more in September 2012 when the former 3-zone system was abolished (along with the 'free rail zone', though). A single ride costs $2.50 ($1.00 for streetcar only), and a day pass is available at just $5.00. A TriMet information counter is located inside the Tourist Office at Pioneer Courthouse Square.

SW 1st Avenue & Oak Street
– Bombardier-Hochflurwagen 119 in neuem Anstrich auf der Blue Line
– *Bombardier high-floor car no. 119 in new livery on the Blue Line*

NE Holladay Street & MLK Jr Blvd (Convention Center)
– Siemens-Niederflurwagen 414 vom Typ 4 stadtauswärts auf der Green Line
– *Siemens type 4 low-floor car no. 414, outbound on the Green Line*

Expo Center

N Vancouver Ave

NE Knott St

Albina/Mississippi

NE 15th Ave

Fremont Bridge

Hwy 30

I-405

I-5

NE Martin Luther King Jr Blvd

Willamette River

NW Naito Parkway

NE Broadway & 2nd

NE Broadway

NW 3rd Ave

NE Grand & Broadway

NE Weidler & 6th

NE Weidler

N Broadway & Wheeler

NW Northrup & 12th

NW 10th & Northrup

Broadway Bridge

NE Weidler & 2nd

NE 7th & Clackamas

NW 22nd   NW 21st   NW 18th

NW 14th

Interstate/Rose Quarter

NE Grand Ave

NE Wasco

NE Multnomah St

NW Northrup St

Streetcar Depot

Convention Center

NW 23rd & Marshall

NS

NW 21st   NW Lovejoy St

NW 13th

NW Lovejoy & 9th

PORTLAND Union Station

Steel Bridge

Rose Quarter TC

NE Holladay

NE 7th

NE Holladay St

Lloyd Center/ NE 11th

Airport

NW Lovejoy & 22nd

NW 18th

NW Johnson

NW Johnson

N Interstate Ave

Gresham

NW Glisan St

NW Glisan

NW Glisan

NW Hoyt

NW Glisan

Old Town/Chinatown

NE Holladay

NE Oregon & Grand

NE Martin Luther King Jr & Hoyt

NE Hoyt

I-84

Clackamas

NW Everett St

NW Everett

NW Everett

NW 11th Ave

NW 10th Ave

NW Broadway

NW 6th Ave

NW 5th Ave

NW Couch

NW Davis

NW Couch

Skidmore Fountain

Burnside Bridge

E Burnside St

E Burnside St

NW Couch

SW Pine

SW Stark

SW Oak

Oak/SW 1st

SE Oak

W Burnside St

JELD-WEN Field

SW Alder

SW Morrison St

Galleria/ SW 10th

1)

Mall/ SW 5th

SW 3rd

SE Washington

SE MLK Jr Blvd

SE Oak

Kings Hill/SW Salmon

SW Yamhill St

SW Morrison St

SW Taylor

2)

3)

Morrison Bridge

SE Belmont

SE Morrison

SE Morrison St

SE Belmont St

SW Yamhill

Library/SW 9th

Pioneer Sq South

Mall/ SW 4th

Yamhill District

SE Salmon

SE Taylor

Goose Hollow/SW Jefferson

SW Jefferson

SW Madison

SW Madison

City Hall/SW Jefferson

SE Hawthorne

SE Madison

SE Hawthorne Blvd

Hwy 26

SW 11th & Clay

CL

SW 10th & Clay

SW 5th Ave

SW 6th Ave

NW Naito Parkway

SE 11th Ave

SE 12th Ave

Beaverton

Hillsboro

SW Market & Park

SW Market & 5th

SW Mill & Park

SW Mill & 6th

SW Mill

Hawthorne Bridge

SE MLK Jr Blvd & Stephens

SE Grand & Mill

SW Montgomery

SW Broadway

SW Harrison & 3rd

SW Harrison & 1st

Marquam Bridge

SE Powell Blvd

PSU South/SW College

PSU South/ SW Jackson

SW Harrison

SW River Parkway & Moody

OMSI

CL

Green Line   PSU

Yellow Line

(SW Lincoln)

(OMSI/SE Water Ave)

(SE Clinton/12th)

SW Moody & Meade

(South Waterfront/SW Moody)

Ross Island Bridge

SE 17th & Rhine

Marquam Hill

Portland Aerial Tram

SW Moody & Gibbs

South Waterfront

OHSU Commons (A)

SW Terwilliger Blvd

SW Barbur Blvd

SW Moody & Gaines

SW Bond & Lane

SE McLoughlin Blvd

NS

SW Lowell & Bond

2015

SE 17th & Holgate)

1 km

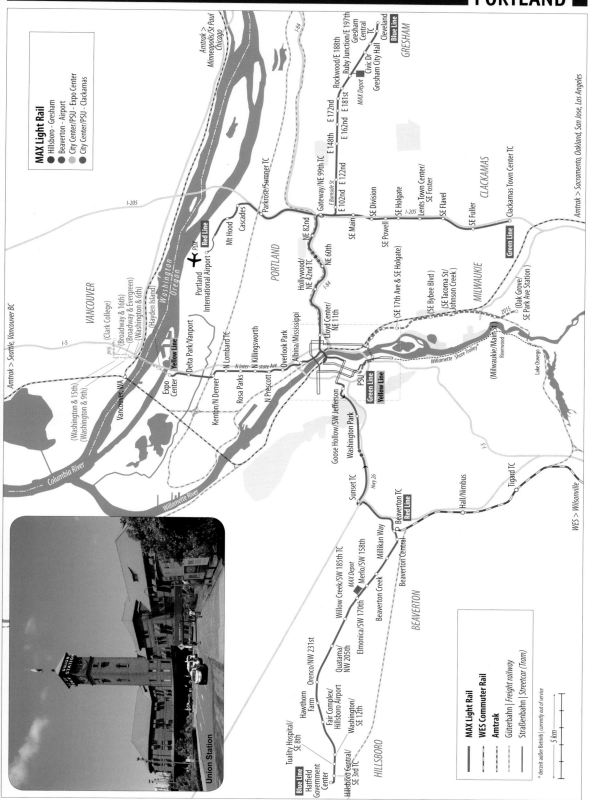

MAX Light Rail
- Hillsboro - Gresham
- Beaverton - Airport
- City Center/PSU - Expo Center
- City Center/PSU - Clackamas

Amtrak > Minneapolis/St Paul Chicago

I-84

Blue Line

Cleveland
Gresham Central TC
Gresham City Hall
Civic Dr
MAX Depot
Ruby Junction/E 197th
Rockwood/E 188th
E 181st
E 172nd
E 162nd
E 148th
E 122nd
E 102nd
E Burnside St
Gateway/NE 99th TC

GRESHAM

CLACKAMAS

Clackamas Town Center TC
SE Fuller
SE Flavel
SE Foster
Lents Town Center/ SE Holgate
SE Holgate
SE Division
SE Powell
SE Main
I-205

Green Line

Amtrak > Sacramento, Oakland, San Jose, Los Angeles

Parkrose/Sumner TC
Cascades
Mt Hood
NE 82nd
NE 60th
Hollywood/ NE 42nd TC
I-84
Lloyd Center/ NE 11th

PDX
Red Line
Portland International Airport

PORTLAND
Washington Oregon

(Hayden Island)

VANCOUVER

(Clark College)
(Broadway & 16th)
(Broadway & Evergreen)
(Washington & 6th)
Vancouver, WA
(Washington & 15th)
(Washington & 9th)

I-5

I-205

Amtrak > Seattle, Vancouver BC

Columbia River

Willamette River

Delta Park/Vanport
Yellow Line
N Lombard TC
Kenton/N Denver
Expo Center
Rosa Parks
N Killingsworth
N Prescott
N Denver
N Inter-state Ave.
Overlook Park
Albina/Mississippi

(SE 17th Ave & SE Holgate)
(SE Bybee Blvd)
(SE Tacoma St/ Johnson Creek)
(Oak Grove/ SE Park Ave Station)

MILWAUKIE

(Milwaukie/Main St)
Riverwood
Willamette Shore Trolley
Lake Oswego

2015

I-5

Green Line
Yellow Line

PSU
Washington Park
Goose Hollow/SW Jefferson

Sunset TC

Hwy 26

Beaverton TC
Red Line
Millikan Way
Beaverton Central
Hall/Nimbus
Tigard TC

WES > Wilsonville

BEAVERTON

Willow Creek/SW 185th TC
MAX Depot
Merlo/SW 158th
Elmonica/SW 170th
Beaverton Creek
Quatama/ NW 205th
Washington/ SE 12th
Fair Complex/ Hillsboro Airport
Hawthorn Farm
Orenco/NW 231st

HILLSBORO

Blue Line
Hatfield Government Center
Tuality Hospital/ SE 8th
Hillsboro Central/ SE 3rd TC

MAX Light Rail
WES Commuter Rail
Amtrak
Güterbahn | *Freight railway*
Straßenbahn | *Streetcar (Tram)*

5 km

* *derzeit außer Betrieb | currently out of service*

Rockwood/E 188th – 2010/11 neu gestaltete Haltestelle auf der Blue Line in Gresham, zuvor lagen die Bahnsteige versetzt zueinander.
– *Blue Line station in Gresham redesigned in 2010/11, prior to that the platforms were located on either side of the intersection.*

◉ MAX LIGHT RAIL

Die im Jahr 1986 eröffnete Stadtbahn von Portland gehört zur ersten Generation der modernen Stadtbahnen in den USA, solche, die zunächst mit Hochflurfahrzeugen mit Halt an Niedrigbahnsteigen in Betrieb genommen wurden. Das Netz besteht derzeit aus vier Farben gekennzeichnete Linien, darunter die 53 km lange Ost-West-Hauptstrecke (Blue Line), an die sich drei Nord-Süd-Äste anschließen (ein vierter ist derzeit im Bau). Wie bei den meisten modernen Stadtbahnen in den USA durchfahren die Züge die Innenstadt auf Straßenebene, jedoch meist auf eigener Trasse. Äußere Abschnitte sind jedoch durchweg auf einem eigenen Bahnkörper entweder völlig unabhängig trassiert oder mit einigen Bahnübergängen. Bis auf sechs sind alle Stationen typische Stadtbahnhaltestellen, an denen die Fahrgäste die Gleise überqueren.

MAX (*Metropolitan Area Express*) wird von TriMet betrieben. Die Bahnen verkehren von etwa 4:00 bis etwa Mitternacht, tagsüber alle 15 Minuten, mit einigen zusätzlichen HVZ-Zügen auf der Blue Line, samstags und sonntags alle 17½ Minuten.

● **Blue Line** (53 km, 47 Haltestellen)
Portlands erste Stadtbahnlinie verband das Stadtzentrum mit der östlichen Nachbarstadt Gresham (24 km). Die Bahnen fuhren damals an der noch bestehenden Schleife an der 11th Avenue ab. Richtung Osten verkehrt die Blue Line heute wie auch die Red Line entlang der Yamhill Street (Richtung Westen auf der Morrison Street). Dann biegt sie nach Norden in die 1st Avenue ab und verlässt die Innenstadt auf dem Oberdeck der denkmalgeschützten Steel Bridge, einer Doppelstock-Hubbrücke über den Willamette-Fluss aus dem Jahre 1912, auf der Amtrak- und Güterzüge auf der unteren Ebene rollen.

Opened in 1986, Portland's light rail system belongs to the first generation of modern light rail systems in the U.S., those which were initially operated with high-floor vehicles stopping at low-level platforms. The system currently consists of four colour-coded lines, a 53 km east-west route served by the Blue Line, and three north-south branches which were subsequently added. Another branch is now under construction. Like most modern light rail systems in the U.S., trains cross the city centre at street level, although mostly on dedicated transit lanes. The outer sections, however, are on a separate right-of-way either fully grade-separated or with some level crossings. All but six of the stations are typical light rail stops, with passengers crossing the tracks.

MAX (which stands for Metropolitan Area Express) is operated by TriMet, with trains running from around 04:00 to around midnight, every 15 minutes during daytime hours (with some extra peak-hour trains on the Blue Line). On Saturdays and Sundays, there is a train every 17½ minutes!

● *Blue Line* (53 km, 47 stations)
Portland's original light rail line connected the city centre to the eastern neighbouring city of Gresham (24 km). Trains used to depart from a loop that still exists at 11th Avenue to run east along Yamhill Street (westbound on Morrison Street). Now shared by the Red Line, trains turn north into 1st Avenue before leaving the downtown area on the upper deck of the listed Steel Bridge, a double-deck lift bridge across the Willamette River from 1912 which carries Amtrak and freight trains on its lower level. They continue on the

NE 60th Avenue
– Autobahn, Stadtbahn und Güterbahn im selben Korridor nebeneinander
– freeway, light rail and freight railway sharing the same corridor

Die Stadtbahn fährt nun knapp über 1 km auf dem abgetrennten Mittelstreifen der Holladay Street durch den Lloyd District, bevor sie schließlich die 7,5 km lange, völlig kreuzungsfrei trassierte Strecke zwischen einem Gütergleis der *Union Pacific* an der Nordseite und dem 6-spurigen Banfield Freeway (I-84/US-30) an der Südseite erreicht. Auf diesem Abschnitt gibt es drei Stationen, die über Treppen und Aufzüge von Straßenbrücken aus zugänglich sind. Die Blue Line erreicht schließlich Gateway, das sich zu einem wichtigen Umsteigeknoten entwickelt hat, seit die Red und Green Line hinzugekommen sind. Von Gateway folgt die Blue Line einer ehemaligen Überlandbahntrasse (Mount Hood Railway – stillgelegt 1927 – und *Portland Traction*-Linie nach Bull Run, auf der es seit 1958 keinen Personenverkehr mehr gab) im Mittelstreifen der East Burnside Street bis zur Endstation in Gresham. Der Abschnitt östlich von Ruby Junction wurde zunächst eingleisig errichtet, jedoch bis 1996 durchgehend zweigleisig ausgebaut.

Nach dem großen Erfolg der Eastside Line begann man im Jahr 1993 mit dem Bau der Westside Line, eine schwierigere Aufgabe, da es den 4,7 km langen, doppelröhrigen Robertson Tunnel unter den westlichen Hügeln von Portland zu errichten galt, einschließlich des U-Bahnhofs Washington Park, der mit 79 m unter der Straßenoberfläche tiefsten unterirdischen Station in Nordamerika. Die Tunnel wurden vom westlichen Ende in bergmännischer Bauweise und vom östlichen mit einer Tunnelbohrmaschine aufgefahren. Vom westlichen Portal bis zum Sunset Transit Center (2,2 km) folgt die Stadtbahnstrecke der Autobahn 26 (Sunset Highway) auf deren Nordseite. Nach Sunset drehen die Züge um 180 Grad in einem kurzen Tunnel (180 m) und dann 90 Grad nach Süden, um parallel zum Highway 217 weiterzufahren; hier gibt es noch einen 100 m langen Tunnel unter der Wilshire Street. Nach Sunset ist die Strecke für weitere 2,6 km völlig kreuzungsfrei, danach handelt es sich um eine typische Stadtbahntrassierung fast den ganzen Weg bis Hillsboro. Der Großteil der Strecke Beaverton – Hillsboro liegt auf einem Korridor der ehemaligen Forest Grove-Linie der *Oregon Electric Railway* (bis 1994 von Güterzügen der *Burlington Northern* genutzt). Beaverton Transit Center, die Endstation der Red Line, ist der verkehrsreichste Knotenpunkt in den westlichen Vororten, mit Übergang zu zahlreichen Buslinien und der WES-Vorortbahn auf die Stadtbahn. Die Hillsboro-Linie ist gut in die verschiedenen Stadtteile, von denen viele erst rund um die Stationen entstanden sind, eingebunden. Westlich der Station Washington/SE 12th fahren die Bahnen das letzte 1,7 km lange Stück bis zur Endstelle in Hillsboro straßenbündig, wobei die Gleise leicht erhöht und eingepflastert sind, so dass die Trasse von Einsatzfahrzeugen mitgenutzt werden kann.

Eine Fahrt auf der gesamten 53 km langen Blue Line dauert etwa 100 Minuten.

reserved median of Holladay Street through the Lloyd District for just over 1 km before entering a 7.5 km completely grade-separated section flanked by a Union Pacific freight track on the northern, and the 6-lane Banfield Freeway (I-84/US-30) on the southern side. The three stations on this segment are accessible from road bridges via stairs and lifts. The Blue Line then reaches Gateway, which has become a major hub since the Red and Green Lines were added to the system. From Gateway, the Blue Line follows old interurban rights-of-way (Mount Hood Railway, closed in 1927, and Portland Traction line to Bull Run, without passenger service since 1958) in the median of East Burnside Street all the way to its terminus in Gresham. The section east of Ruby Junction was initially built single-track, but became fully double-track in 1996.

With the Eastside line having proved highly successful, in 1993 Portland started to build the **Westside MAX**, a more difficult task as it included the 4.7 km twin-tube Robertson Tunnel under the west hills of Portland, with Washington Park station at 79 m below the surface being the deepest transit station in North America. The tunnels were built by drilling and blasting from the western end, and using a tunnel boring machine from the eastern. From the western portal to Sunset Transit Center (2.2 km), the route follows Highway 26 (Sunset Hwy) on its northern side. After Sunset, trains turn 180 degrees in a short tunnel (180 m) and then 90 degrees south to get aligned with Highway 217; there is another 100 m tunnel where the route passes under Wilshire Street. After Sunset, the route remains completely grade-separated for another 2.6 km, with a conventional light rail alignment following almost all the way to Hillsboro. Most of the Beaverton – Hillsboro route runs on a corridor formerly occupied by the Forest Grove line of the Oregon Electric Railway (until 1994 used by Burlington Northern freight trains). Beaverton Transit Center, the terminus of the Red Line, is the busiest hub in the western suburbs, with many buses and the WES commuter railway offering a connection to MAX. The Hillsboro line is well-integrated into the different neighbourhoods, many of which have been built around the stations. After stopping at Washington/SE 12th, trains enter Hillsboro on a 1.7 km street alignment, but with a slightly raised, paved trackbed, which can be used by emergency vehicles.

PORTLAND MAX (Light Rail)

83.2 km (4.9 km unterirdisch | *underground*)
75 Haltestellen | *stations* (1 unterird. | *underground*)

05 Sept 1986: Downtown Portland (11th Ave) – Gresham (Cleveland Ave)
     Mar 1990: + Mall/SW 4th & Mall/SW 5th
     Sept 1990: + Convention Center
31 Aug 1997: Downtown Portland (11th Ave) – Kings Hill/SW Salmon
12 Sept 1998: Kings Hill/SW Salmon – Hillsboro (Hatfield Gov. Center)
10 Sept 2001: Gateway/NE 99th TC – Portland International Airport
01 May 2004: Interstate/Rose Quarter – Expo Center
12 Sept 2009: Gateway/NE 99th TC – Clackamas Town Center TC
               Rose Quarter – PSU (Portland Transit Mall on 5th & 6th Aves)
02 Sept 2012: + PSU South (5th & Jackson + 6th & College)
     2015: PSU – Milwaukie (Park Ave)

Washington Park – einziger U-Bahnhof in Portland, dafür mit 79 m der tiefste in Nordamerika. Vom nahen Zoo aus verkehrt eine Parkeisenbahn.
– *the only underground station in Portland, but at 79 m the deepest in North America. The adjacent zoo is the departure point for a children's railway.*

● **Red Line** (41 km, 25 Haltestellen)
Bis auf den 9 km langen Abzweig zum Flughafen fährt die Red Line auf ihrer 41 km langen Strecke auf denselben Gleisen wie die Blue Line (von Beaverton bis Gateway). Südlich der 3-gleisigen Station Gateway drehen sich die Züge mehr als 180 Grad nach Norden auf einem eingleisigen Viadukt, um an die Ostseite der Autobahn I-205 zu kommen und die MAX-Strecke zur bzw. von der Innenstadt zu unterqueren; die Strecke wird etwa 450 m weiter nördlich wieder zweigleisig. Kurz darauf taucht die Red Line unter den nach Norden verlaufenden Spuren der Autobahn I-205 hindurch, um in deren Mittelstreifen für die nächsten 3 km zu verbleiben. Auf diesem Abschnitt liegt die Station Parkrose/Sumner, wo die Fahrgäste trotz der Lage auf der Autobahn das Gleis nach Norden überqueren müssen, um die Station zu verlassen. Weiter nördlich schwenken die Züge mithilfe einer Überführung aus dem Autobahnmittelstreifen aus und erreichen die Stationen Cascades und Mount Hood in einem neuen Gewerbegebiet. Die Zufahrt zum Flughafen ist auf den letzten 1,2 km eingleisig. Die Endstelle selbst hat zwei Stumpfgleise, der Zugang erfolgt über das nördliche Bahnsteigende; die Check-in-Schalter sind nur ein paar Schritte entfernt.

● **Yellow Line** (12,5 km, 17 Haltestellen)
Anders als bei den Verlängerungen für die Red und Green Line wurde für die Yellow Line, die im Jahr 2004 eröffnet wurde, eine städtischere Trassierung auf einem besonderen Gleiskörper im Mittelstreifen der North Interstate Avenue gewählt.

A ride on the 53 km Blue Line from end to end takes about 100 minutes.

● *Red Line (41 km, 25 stations)*
Except for the 9 km Airport branch, the Red Line shares its 41 km route with the Blue Line (from Beaverton to Gateway). Just south of the 3-track Gateway station, it turns more than 180 degrees north on a single-track viaduct, gets aligned at grade along the eastern side of I-205, then passes below the main MAX route to/from downtown before becoming double-track some 450 m further north. Shortly after, the Red Line trains dive under the northbound freeway lanes to continue in the I-205 median for the next 3 km. This section includes Parkrose/Sumner station, where, despite its freeway location, passengers have to cross the northbound track to exit the station. Continuing north, trains leave the freeway median on a flyover and serve Cascades and Mount Hood stations in a new office and retail development. On its approach to the airport, the line becomes single-track for the last 1.2 km. The terminus has two stub tracks, with platform access from the northern end; the check-in counters are only a few steps away.

● *Yellow Line (12.5 km, 17 stations)*
Unlike the Red and Green Line extensions, the Yellow Line, which opened in 2004, follows a more urban alignment on a reserved right-of-way in the median of North Interstate Avenue. It diverges from the east-west trunk route right

Beaverton Transit Center – Siemens Types 2 + 3
– Endstation der Red Line und von WES | *Red Line and WES terminus*

Hatfield Government Center (Hillsboro) – Siemens Type 4
– Endstation der Blue Line | *Blue Line terminus*

Alle Stadtbahnlinien überqueren den Willamette-Fluss auf der *Steel Bridge*, einer Hubbrücke von 1912, auf deren unteren Ebene die Eisenbahn verkehrt. – *All light rail lines cross the Willamette River on the Steel Bridge, a lift bridge from 1912, with the lower level being used by mainline railways.*

Die Yellow Line zweigt von der Ost-West-Stammstrecke direkt nach der Überquerung des Willamette-Flusses ab und erschließt die Stadtteile von North Portland entlang der Interstate Avenue. An mehreren Haltestellen entlang dieser Strecke gibt es versetzt angeordnete Seitenbahnsteige, wobei die Stadtbahn jeweils nach der Kreuzung hält. Nördlich der Haltestelle Kenton/N Denver überquert sie auf einem 1,2 km langen Viadukt mehrere Straßen, ein Gewerbegebiet und den Columbia Slough, bevor sie schließlich die Haltestelle Delta Park/Vanport erreicht, die wie die 3-gleisige Endstation Expo Center eine große Anzahl an Parkplätzen bietet. Im Stadtzentrum nutzte die Yellow Line zunächst die ursprüngliche Innenstadtstrecke entlang der Yamhill bzw. Morrison Street und endete an der 11th Avenue-Schleife. Während der nur von der Yellow Line befahrene Abzweig 9,3 km lang ist, hat die gesamte Linie eine Länge von 12,5 km, wovon 3,2 km gemeinsam mit der Green Line befahren werden.

Ab Expo Center war von Anfang an eine Nordverlängerung über den Columbia-Fluss bis Vancouver im Bundesstaat Washington geplant, dieses Projekt ist jedoch mit dem Neubau der I-5-Autobahnbrücke (derzeit eine Hubbrücke!) verknüpft, was im Laufe des nächsten Jahrzehnts geplant ist. Dadurch wird das Stadtbahnnetz um 4,7 km wachsen, wovon 3,5 km im Bundesstaat Washington liegen werden.

● **Green Line** (23 km, 23 Haltestellen)
Das Projekt „Green Line" umfasste sowohl den neuen Ast nach Clackamas als auch die Schaffung einer zweiten Innenstadtstrecke, um die ursprüngliche zu entlasten.

Die zweite Innenstadtstrecke beginnt an der westlichen Auffahrt zur Steel Bridge. Auf einer kurvenreichen Strecke gelangen die Züge in die Nähe der Union Station, wo keine Vorortzüge, aber zahlreiche Fernzüge halten. Das Gleis Richtung Süden folgt dann der 5th Avenue, Richtung Norden hingegen

after crossing the Willamette River. Several stops along Interstate Avenue in the North Portland neighbourhoods have staggered side platforms, with trains stopping after passing the respective road intersections. The trains then leave the street alignment at Kenton/N Denver station and climb onto a 1.2 km viaduct, which takes the Yellow Line over several roads, an industrial park and Columbia Slough before arriving at Delta Park/Vanport station, which like the 3-track terminus at Expo Center, offers a large number of parking spaces. In the city centre, the Yellow Line initially used the original cross-downtown route along Yamhill and Morrison Streets and terminated at the 11th Avenue loop. While the exclusive Yellow Line branch is 9.3 km long, the entire line is 12.5 km, 3.2 km of which is shared with the Green Line.

From Expo Center, a northern extension across the Columbia River to Vancouver in Washington State has been planned from the beginning, but this project is linked to the reconstruction of the I-5 freeway bridge (currently a lift bridge!), which is planned to be carried out over the next decade. This will add 4.7 km to the light rail network, 3.5 km of which will be in Washington State.

● *Green Line* (23 km, 23 stations)
The Green Line project included both a new branch to Clackamas and the creation of a second cross-downtown route to relieve the original corridor.

The second downtown route begins on the western approaches to the Steel Bridge. On a winding route, trains get close to Union Station, which has no commuter rail service, but several long-distance trains. The southbound track follows 5th Avenue, whereas the northbound runs on 6th Avenue; trains therefore cross the track in the opposite direction near Union Station. Portland's Greyhound Bus Terminal is located between the Hoyt and Glisan stops. The

Cascades – Zwei NF-Wagen vom Typ 2 stadteinwärts auf der Red Line – *two type 2 low-floor cars inbound on the Red Line*

N Killingsworth Street (N Interstate Ave) – Yellow Line Station

der 6th Avenue, weshalb sich die beiden Gleise in der Nähe der Union Station kreuzen. Portlands Greyhound-Busstation befindet sich zwischen den Haltestellen Hoyt und Glisan. Die *Portland Transit Mall* entlang der 5th und 6th Avenue war bereits 1977 als Bustrasse eingerichtet worden, sie wurde nun für die Aufnahme der Stadtbahn umgebaut. Bahnen und Busse halten abwechselnd, weshalb die Gleise wiederholt von Randlage in Mittellage und umgekehrt schwenken. Die Züge zeigen als Ziel „City Center/PSU" und wenden in einer Schleife von der 5th zur 6th Avenue am südlichen Rand der Portland State University.

Die 10,2 km lange Verlängerung nach Clackamas zweigt von der Blue Line etwa 500 m südlich der Station Gateway ab. Sie verläuft bis Clackamas Town Center neben der I-205, die ersten 1,8 km auf der Ostseite, bevor sie dann in einem Tunnel unter der Autobahn auf die westliche Seite schwenkt. Es gibt nur einen kleinen Bahnübergang für den motorisierten Verkehr in der Nähe der Haltestelle SE Main als Zufahrt zu einem Parkplatz sowie einen weiteren nördlich der Station SE Flavel. Trotz der schnellbahnartigen Trassierung haben alle Stationen Bahnübergänge als Zugang zu den Mittelbahnsteigen.

Mit Fertigstellung der Green Line im Jahr 2009 wurde auch die Yellow Line auf die neue Transit Mall in der Innenstadt gelegt. Die jeweils südlichste Station entlang der Transit Mall wurde erst 2012 in Betrieb genommen, nachdem der Bau eines Studentenwohnheims auf dem Gelände zwischen 5th & 6th Avenue und College & Jackson Street abgeschlossen worden war.

● Die Zukunft von MAX

Offiziell als „Portland - Milwaukie Light Rail Transit Project" bezeichnet ist seit Juli 2011 eine südliche Verlängerung der Transit Mall-Strecke im Bau, wodurch das Netz um weitere 11,7 km wachsen wird. Die manchmal auch als Orange Line präsentierte Strecke (mit einer nördlichen Endstation an der Union Station), könnte ab 2015 auch gemeinsam mit der Yellow Line betrieben werden. Die neue Strecke zweigt von der bestehenden PSU-Schleife ab und verläuft in einem städtischen Umfeld entlang der Lincoln Street, überquert dann die Straßenbahntrasse entlang der Harrison Street und Moody Avenue sowie den Harbor Drive auf einem Viadukt, bevor sie dann unterhalb des Autobahndreiecks I-5/I-405 die Moody Avenue erreicht. Sie biegt schließlich nach Osten ab und überquert den Willamette-Fluss auf einer neuen, für Stadtbahn, Fußgänger und Radfahrer reservierten Brücke, wobei die Gleise

Portland Transit Mall along 5th and 6th Avenues had existed as a bus-only corridor since 1977, and was now rebuilt to accommodate light rail trains, too. Trains and buses have alternating stops, so the tracks continuously switch from side to centre lanes and back. The trains' destination is shown as 'City Center/PSU', and trains loop from 5th to 6th Avenue at the southern end of the Portland State University campus.

The 10.2 km Clackamas extension diverges from the Blue Line some 500 m south of Gateway station. It runs alongside I-205 all the way to Clackamas Town Center, for the first 1.8 km on its eastern side before switching to the western side in a tunnel under the freeway. There are only two minor level crossings for vehicular traffic, one near SE Main station to access a car park and another one just north of SE Flavel station. Despite the high-speed alignment, all stations have level crossings for passengers to access their island plat-forms.

Upon completion of the Green Line in 2009, the Yellow Line was also rerouted onto the new Transit Mall in the downtown area. The first/last stop along the Transit Mall was only brought into service in 2012 after the construction of a student residence on the terrain bordered by 5th & 6th Avenues and College & Jackson Streets had been completed.

● MAX Future

Officially titled the "Portland - Milwaukie Light Rail Transit Project", a southern extension to the Transit Mall route has been under construction since July 2011. This will add an-other 11.7 km to the present system. Sometimes referred to as the Orange Line (with a northern terminus at Union Sta-tion), it might also be operated jointly with the Yellow Line when the extension opens in 2015. The new route diverges from the PSU loop and runs through an urban area along Lincoln Street, then crosses the streetcar route on Harrison Street and Moody Avenue as well as Harbor Drive on a viaduct before getting aligned alongside Moody Avenue on its way below the I-5/I-405 freeway interchange. It then turns east to cross the Willamette River on a new dedicated light rail, pedestrian and cyclist bridge, where tracks will be shared with streetcars. Beyond Oregon Museum of Science and Industry (OMSI) station, the MAX trains will mostly follow the Union Pacific line (which carries the "Coast Starlight"), except for a detour along SE 17th Avenue. The last kilometre of track before the terminus at SE McLoughlin Boulevard &

Type 1

von der Straßenbahn mitgenutzt werden. Hinter dem Oregon Museum of Science and Industry (OMSI) folgen die MAX-Züge meist der Union Pacific-Strecke, auf der der „Coast Starlight" fährt, jedoch mit einem Umweg entlang der SE 17th Avenue. Den letzten Kilometer vor der Endstation SE McLoughlin Blvd & Park Avenue in Oak Grove wird die Stadtbahn auf der alten Trasse der Portland Traction verkehren, die Teil der ersten Interurban-Linie in den USA war, die von 1893 bis 1958 Portland mit Oregon City verband.

● MAX-Fahrzeuge

Derzeit stehen vier verschiedene Fahrzeuge zur Verfügung, die offiziell als „Typ 1-4" bezeichnet werden:

Die 26 Gelenkwagen vom **Typ 1** wurden von Bombardier als Hochflurwagen für die erste Linie 1986 in Betrieb genommen. Um mobilitätseingeschränkten Fahrgästen das Einsteigen zu ermöglichen, waren alle Stationen mit Rollstuhlliften ausgestattet. Der Typ 1 verkehrt heute immer paarweise mit Wagen des Typs 2 oder 3, damit jeder Zug auch ohne die externen Aufzüge behindertengerecht zugänglich ist.

Für die Eröffnung der Weststrecke 1997/98 produzierte Siemens in Sacramento 52 Wagen vom **Typ 2** (SD660), die ersten teilweise niederflurigen Fahrzeuge in Nordamerika. Die Bodenhöhe an den Türen beträgt 350 mm, trotzdem gibt es ausfahrbare Rampen, um die kleine Lücke zwischen Zug und Bahnsteig für Rollstuhlfahrer zu überbrücken. Anders als der Typ 1 hat der Typ 2 zwei Gelenke, das kurze Mittelteil wird von einem dritten, nicht angetriebenen Fahrwerk getragen.

Die Eröffnung der Yellow Line im Jahr 2004 brachte 27 Wagen des **Typs 3**, der außer einer neuen Farbgebung weitgehend identisch mit dem Typ 2 ist.

Die 22 Siemens S70-Fahrzeuge des **Typs 4** folgten zur Eröffnung der Green Line im Jahr 2009. Sie haben ein deutlich moderneres Äußeres und einen niedrigeren Energieverbrauch aufgrund der leichteren Bauweise. Bei 29,4 m Länge über Kupplung sind sie etwa 1 m länger als die älteren Typen, wobei alle vier Typen 2,65 m breit sind. Sie sind 70% niederflurig mit Hochflurbereichen über den Enddrehgestellen und weitgehend identisch mit den S70-Wagen in San Diego und anderen US-Städten, haben aber nur eine Fahrerkabine und laufen daher immer paarweise. Im Mai 2012 wurden 18 zusätzliche S70-Wagen zur Auslieferung ab August 2014 bestellt.

Alle Typen sind auf allen Linien zu sehen. Aufgrund der kurzen Häuserblöcke (61 m) in der Innenstadt, wo die Bahnsteige meist in den Bürgersteig integriert sind, ist die Zuglänge auf nur zwei Wagen begrenzt, daher hat auch der U-Bahnhof Washington Park nur 60 m lange Bahnsteige. Alle Züge sind klimatisiert und laufen unter Oberleitung mit 750 V Gleichstrom. Es gibt zwei Betriebshöfe, in Gresham (Ruby Junction) und in Beaverton (Elmonica).

Park Avenue in Oak Grove climbs up the old Portland Traction right-of-way, part of the first interurban line in the United States, which between 1893 and 1958 linked Portland to Oregon City.

● MAX Rolling Stock

The light rail system is currently served by four different types of train, officially classified as 'types 1-4':

*The 26 articulated vehicles of **type 1** were manufactured by Bombardier as high-floor cars for the original line brought into service in 1986. To allow boarding for mobility-impaired passengers, all stations were equipped with wheelchair lifts. The type 1 cars now always run in pairs with type 2 or 3 cars, and thus each train grants full accessibility without external lifts.*

*For the opening of the Westside MAX in 1997/98, Siemens produced 52 cars of **type 2** (SD660) in Sacramento, the first partly low-floor vehicles in North America. The floor height at the doors is 350 mm; despite allowing stepfree entry, they are equipped with small retractable boards to bridge the small gap between train and platform for wheelchair access. Unlike type 1, they have two articulations, with a short centre module between them which is carried by the third, unpowered bogie.*

*The opening of the Yellow Line in 2004 brought **type 3**, although except for a new livery, the 27 cars are largely identical to those of type 2.*

*The 22 Siemens S70 vehicles, classified as **type 4**, were acquired for the opening of the Green Line in 2009. They appear more modern and have a lower energy consumption due to their lighter design. At 29.4 m over couplers, they are about 1 m longer than the older types, all four types being 2.65 m wide. They are 70% low-floor, with raised sections above the end bogies. They are basically identical to the S70 cars in service in San Diego and other U.S. cities, but have only one driver's cab, and are therefore always run in pairs. In May 2012, 18 additional S70 cars were ordered for delivery from August 2014.*

Every train type runs on every line. Due to the short blocks (61 m) in the downtown area, where platforms are mostly integrated into the sidewalks, train compositions are limited to just two cars; hence even the underground station under Washington Park only has 60 m platforms. All trains are air-conditioned and run under a 750 V dc overhead catenary. There are two depots, one in Gresham (Ruby Junction) and one in Beaverton (Elmonica).

Type 4

◉ PORTLAND STREETCAR

Portland war nicht nur eine der ersten US-Städte, die eine moderne Stadtbahn bauten, sondern es war auch die erste, die im Jahr 2001 die klassische Straßenbahn zurückholte. Mehrere andere Städte wie Memphis oder Tucson hatten dieses Verkehrsmittel zwar in den Innenstädten bereits wiedereingeführt, jedoch mit historischen Fahrzeugen. Portlands ursprüngliche Straßenbahnen, die ein weitreichendes Netz bedient hatten, waren bis 1950 verschwunden.

Die erste neue Straßenbahnlinie verband die Portland State University und die Innenstadt mit den beliebten Vierteln Pearl District und Nob Hill im Nordwesten. Sie wurde später nach Südwesten erweitert, um das Sanierungsgebiet an der South Waterfront anzuschließen, womit eine Gesamtlänge von 6,5 km erreicht wurde (parallele Abschnitte werden nur einmal gezählt). Nachdem der Abschnitt auf der Moody Avenue zwischen River Parkway und Gibbs Street im Jahr 2011 zweigleisig ausgebaut wurde, gibt es jetzt nur noch einen sehr kurzen eingleisigen Abschnitt zwischen der 4th und 5th Avenue, der in beiden Richtungen befahren wird.

Im Jahr 2012 hat sich die Größe des Straßenbahnnetzes mit Inbetriebnahme eines Großteils der zukünftigen Ringlinie am Ostufer nahezu verdoppelt. Die Mitnutzung der Stadtbahngleise auf der neuen Südbrücke über den Willamette-Fluss wird einen vollen Ringbetrieb ermöglichen. Die nördliche Flussquerung erfolgt auf der historischen Broadway Bridge.

Während die ursprüngliche Linie jetzt als Nord-Süd-Linie (NS) bezeichnet wird, wird die neue Strecke durch die Central Loop Line (CL) befahren, der Abschnitt auf der 10th bzw. 11th Avenue wird von beiden Linien bedient. Beide Linien verkehren derzeit alle 14-18 Minuten.

Obwohl er der Stadt Portland gehört, ist der *Portland Streetcar* tariflich in das TriMet-Netz integriert. Es werden aber auch Fahrscheine nur für die Straßenbahn angeboten (1,00 $).

Der Betrieb wird mit drei weitgehend identischen Typen abgewickelt: 1) Inekon 12-Trio, 2) Škoda 10T und 3) United Streetcar 100, wobei letztere Wagen dem tschechischen Ori-

Portland was not only one of the first U.S. cities to introduce modern light rail, but in 2001 it also became the first to bring back conventional streetcars. Several other cities, like Memphis and Tucson, had revived this form of transport in downtown areas, but using vintage or heritage tram vehicles. Portland's original streetcars, which used to serve a large network, had disappeared by 1950.

The first line linked Portland State University and the downtown area to the popular neighbourhoods of Pearl District and Nob Hill in the northwest. It was later extended southwest to serve the South Waterfront redevelopment area, bringing the total length to 6.5 km (counting parallel sections only once). The section on Moody Avenue between River Parkway and Gibbs Street was doubled in 2011, and now only a very short single-track section is used in both directions between 4th and 5th Avenues.

In 2012, the streetcar system was almost doubled in length when the major part of the Loop project on the Eastside was brought into service. By sharing tracks on a new southern bridge across the Willamette River, streetcars will be able to operate on a circular route. In the north, the river is crossed on the historic Broadway Bridge.

While the original line is now operated as the North-South Line (NS), the new route is served by the Central Loop Line (CL), with both lines sharing the downtown portions along 10th & 11th Avenues. Headways on both lines are currently every 14-18 minutes.

Although owned by the City of Portland, the Portland Streetcar is fully integrated with the TriMet fare system. There are also exclusive streetcar tickets at $1.00.

Service is provided by three, largely identical types of vehicles: 1) Inekon 12-Trio, 2) Škoda 10T and 3) United Streetcar 100, with the latter being manufactured locally, following the original Czech design, by United Streetcar, a subsidiary of Oregon Iron Works Inc. in Clackamas, as a fully 'Buy America' compliant product. All trams are

Škoda 10T # 005

Mark Kavanagh

United Streetcar Prototype # 015 (Broadway Bridge)

PORTLAND Streetcar

11.8 km
41 Haltestellen | *stops*

20 July 2001: NW 23rd & Marshall – PSU (Mill & 5th)
11 Mar 2005: PSU – SW River Parkway
20 Oct 2006: SW River Parkway – SW Moody & Gibbs
17 Aug 2007: SW Moody & Gibbs – SW Lowell & Bond (loop)
22 Sept 2012: NW 10th Ave & Lovejoy – OMSI

SW 11th Avenue & Yamhill Street – Inekon Tram # 009
– links die ursprüngliche Stadtbahnschleife (siehe Foto links unten) | *on the left, the original light rail loop (see photo bottom left)*

ginaldesign folgend vor Ort von United Streetcar, einer Tochter von Oregon Iron Works Inc., in Clackamas hergestellt werden. Alle Straßenbahnen sind 20 m lang und 2,46 m breit, mit Drehgestellen unter den erhöhten Endabschnitten und einem schwebenden Niederflur-Mittelteil. Sie haben keine Kupplungen und können daher nur als Einzelwagen verkehren. Die Oberleitung führt 750 V Gleichstrom. Das Depot befindet sich zwischen Northrup und Lovejoy Street, Ecke NW 15th/16th Avenue, versteckt unter der aufgeständerten Autobahn I-405.

20 m long and 2.46 m wide, with bogies under the raised end sections and a floating low-floor middle section. They have no couplers and can only operate as single units. The streetcars take power from a 750 V dc overhead line. Their depot is located between Northrup and Lovejoy Streets at NW 15th/16th Avenue, hidden under the elevated I-405 freeway.

Heute verkehren Museumsfahrzeuge (wie Nachbau Nr. 511) entlang der Transit Mall zwischen Union Station und PSU an ausgewählten Sonntagen, meist vor Weihnachten.

Vintage trolleys (like replica car no. 511) now run along the Transit Mall between Union Station and PSU on select Sundays, mostly in the period before Christmas.

Maurits van den Toorn

Chris McDowell

Blick nach Osten über das Willamette-Tal: Über der Kabine der Seilbahn ist die Baustelle der Stadtbahn/Straßenbahn-Brücke zu erkennen.
– *view towards the east over the Willamette Valley: the construction site for the light rail/streetcar bridge is visible just above the cable car cabin.*

◉ PORTLAND AERIAL TRAM

Ausgehend von der South Waterfront und somit an die Innenstadt durch die Straßenbahn angebunden, legt die Luftseilbahn 1000 m zurück, um den Oregon Health & Science University (OHSU) Campus auf dem Marquam Hill zu erreichen. Auf der 3-minütigen Fahrt überwinden die Kabinen einen Höhenunterschied von 150 m. Auch wenn die Bahn in erster Linie errichtet wurde, um die verschiedenen Bereiche des Krankenhauses zu verbinden, hat sie sich zu einer wichtigen Touristenattraktion (4,00 $ für die Berg- und Talfahrt) entwickelt, da sie einen spektakulären Blick auf den Willamette-Fluss, die südlichen Teile der Innenstadt sowie die östlichen Ebenen, an klaren Tagen mit dem Mount Hood im Hintergrund, bietet.

Die Seilbahn wurde von der US-Tochter der österreichisch-schweizerischen Firma Doppelmayr gebaut und am 15. Dezember 2006 eröffnet. Die beiden Kabinen haben jeweils eine Kapazität von 78 Passagieren. Es gibt eine einzige 60 m hohe Stütze kurz oberhalb der Talstation.

Starting from the South Waterfront and thus linked to downtown by Portland's streetcar, the aerial cable car travels 1000 m to reach the Oregon Health & Science University (OHSU) campus on Marquam Hill. On its 3-minute journey, the cabins negotiate a difference in altitude of 150 m. Although primarily designed to link the various areas of the hospital, it has become an important tourist attraction ($4.00 for a round trip) as it provides spectacular views of the Willamette River, the southern parts of downtown, as well as the eastern plains, with Mount Hood visible in the background on a clear day.

The cable car was built by the U.S. subsidiary of the Austrian-Swiss company Doppelmayr and opened on 15 December 2006. Each of the two cabins has a passenger capacity of 78 per car. There is a single 60 m tower a short distance from the lower terminus.

Talstation im Entwicklungsgebiet mit Übergang zur Straßenbahn
– *The lower station lies in a redevelopment area and provides interchange to the streetcar.*

Beaverton TC – zweiteiliger Dieseltriebwagen von Colorado Railcar als nachmittäglicher Pendlerzug abfahrbereit Richtung Wilsonville
– two-car Colorado Railcar DMU, ready to depart for Wilsonville on an afternoon commuter service

ⓢ WES (Westside Express Service)

Auf dem Stadtbahnplan von Portland ist auch eine Vorortbahn eingezeichnet, die aber im Gegensatz zu anderen Städten in der Hauptverkehrszeit nicht die Innenstadt mit den Vorstädten verbindet, sondern als Zubringer zur Stadtbahn fungiert.

Die 23,7 km lange WES beginnt gegenüber der Stadtbahnstation in Beaverton, verläuft dann nach Süden etwa 500 m entlang der SW Lombard Avenue auf einem eigens errichteten Gleis, bevor sie die modernisierte Güterbahnstrecke nach Wilsonville erreicht, die von der *Portland & Western Railroad* (P&W) betrieben wird. Die Trasse von Beaverton bis Tigard gehörte einst zur *Red Electric* (jetzt *Southern Pacific*), weiter südlich dann zur *Oregon Electric* (OE). Der Überlandpersonenverkehr von Portland nach Salem und Eugene endete bereits 1933.

WES wurde am 2. Februar 2009 in Betrieb genommen und bietet Montag bis Freitag morgens und nachmittags je acht Fahrten in beiden Richtungen im regelmäßigen 30-Minuten-Takt. Dank mehrerer Unternehmen entlang der Strecke sind die Züge in beiden Richtungen gut ausgelastet. Der Betrieb wird mit drei Colorado Railcar-Dieseltriebwagen und einem Steuerwagen durchgeführt. Im Jahr 2011 erweiterte TriMet die Flotte mit zwei von der *Alaska Railroad* erworbenen Budd Company Rail Diesel Cars.

Die fünf Stationen haben Hochbahnsteige und erlauben daher einen behindertengerechten Einstieg. Da die Strecke weiterhin von Güterzügen mit breiteren Wagen befahren wird, wurde an den Zwischenstationen Hall-Nimbus, Tigard und Tualatin wie in Kassel eine Art Gleisverschlingung eingebaut.

The Portland urban rail map also includes a commuter rail line, but unlike in other cities, it is not a rush-hour shuttle between downtown and outlying suburbs, but a feeder line for the light rail system.

The 23.7 km WES starts opposite the light rail station at Beaverton and runs south for some 500 m along SW Lombard Avenue on a purpose-built track. It then joins the upgraded freight line operated by the Portland & Western Railroad (P&W) south to Wilsonville on what was once an old Red Electric right-of-way from Beaverton to Tigard, now owned by the Southern Pacific, and then on part of the Oregon Electric network (OE). Interurban passenger service from Portland to Salem and Eugene had ceased by as early as 1933.

WES was introduced on 2 February 2009 and from Monday to Friday provides eight morning and eight afternoon round trips at regular 30-minute intervals. Thanks to several companies located along the route, trains are busy with commuters in both directions. It is served by three Colorado Railcar DMUs (diesel multiple units) and one control trailer, all specially built for this service. In 2011, TriMet added two Budd Company Rail Diesel Cars (RDCs) purchased from the Alaska Railroad to the fleet.

The five stations are equipped with high platforms to allow level access; as the line is still used by freight trains with wider carriages, a sort of gauntlet track was installed at the intermediate Hall-Nimbus, Tigard and Tualatin stations.

Sunrise – Gold Line-Zug mit einem CAF-Wagen vorne unterwegs ins Stadtzentrum | *Gold Line train with a leading CAF car on its way to the city centre*

SACRAMENTO, CA

Sacramento ist die Hauptstadt des Bundesstaats Kalifornien und befindet sich etwa 140 km nordöstlich von San Francisco. Die eigentliche Stadt (254 km²) hat knapp 475.000 Einwohner, sie ist jedoch das Zentrum einer Metropolregion mit rund 1,4 Mio. Menschen (einschließlich Folsom, Rancho Cordova, Elk Grove und Roseville).

In Sacramento halten die täglich verkehrenden Amtrak-Züge „Coast Starlight" von Seattle nach Los Angeles und „California Zephyr" von Chicago nach Emeryville. Ab Sacramento fahren wochentags außerdem 15 „Capitol Corridor"-Züge nach Oakland, davon sieben weiter bis San José (an Wochenenden weniger häufig). Einmal täglich kommt man mit einem „Capitol Corridor"-Zug auch ins weiter nördlich gelegene Auburn. Zweimal täglich gibt es außerdem eine Direktverbindung nach Bakersfield über Stockton („San Joaquin"). Sacramento ist auch Standort des amerikanischen Siemens-Werks, wo Hunderte von Stadtbahnwagen für den nordamerikanischen Markt hergestellt worden sind.

Für den öffentlichen Nahverkehr im Großraum von Sacramento (670 km²) ist *Sacramento Regional Transit District* (RT) zuständig. Nachdem die alte Straßenbahn bis 1947 verschwunden war, ist heute die moderne Stadtbahn das einzige Schienenverkehrsmittel. Sie ist voll ins RT-Tarifsystem integriert. Einzelfahrten ohne Umsteigen kosten 2,50 $ und Tageskarten 6,00 $ (letztere sind auch auf einigen anderen Lokalbussen gültig).

Located some 140 km northeast of San Francisco, Sacramento is the state capital of California. Although the city proper (254 km2) has a population of just 475,000, it is the centre of a metropolitan area with some 1.4 million inhabitants (including Folsom, Rancho Cordova, Elk Grove and Roseville).

Sacramento is a stop on Amtrak's daily "Coast Starlight" from Seattle to Los Angeles and "California Zephyr" from Chicago to Emeryville. It is also the departure point for 15 weekday "Capitol Corridor" trains to Oakland, with 7 of them continuing to San Jose; this route is also served on weekends, though less frequently. One daily train runs further north to Auburn, and two "San Joaquin" trains a day provide a direct link to Bakersfield via Stockton. Sacramento is also the site of Siemens' US manufacturing plant, where hundreds of light rail cars have been produced for the North American market.

Public transport in the Sacramento metropolitan area (670 km2) is provided by the Sacramento Regional Transit District (RT). With the first-generation streetcars having disappeared by 1947, the urban rail system today only features light rail.

The light rail lines are well-integrated into the RT fare system, with single fares costing $2.50 (no transfer!), and a day pass available at $6.00 (also valid on some other local buses).

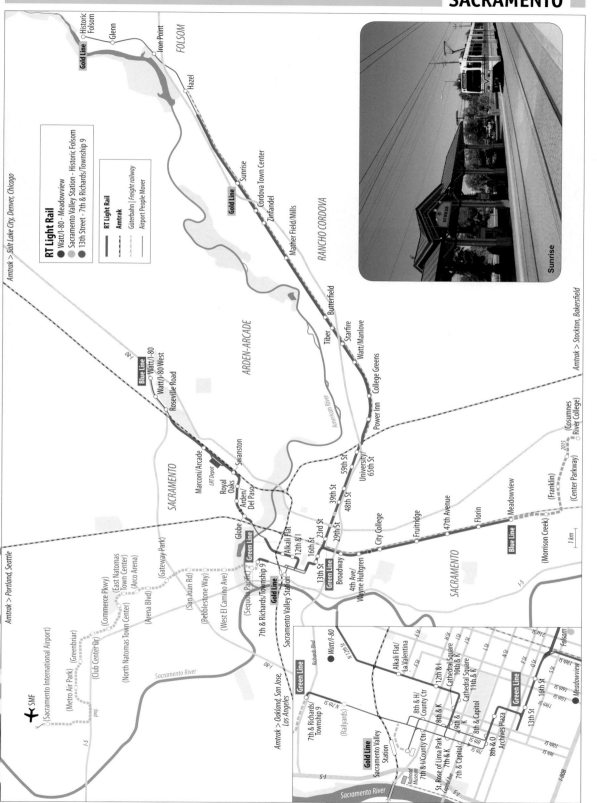

RT Light Rail
- Watt/I-80 – Meadowview
- Sacramento Valley Station – Historic Folsom
- 13th Street – 7th & Richards/Township 9

Legend:
- RT Light Rail
- Amtrak
- Güterbahn | *Freight railway*
- Airport People Mover

Gold Line — Historic Folsom, Glenn, Iron Point, *FOLSOM*, Hazel

Amtrak > Salt Lake City, Denver, Chicago

Gold Line — Sunrise, Cordova Town Center, Zinfandel, Mather Field/Mills, *RANCHO CORDOVA*

Butterfield, Tiber, Starfire, Watt/Manlove, College Greens, Power Inn

ARDEN-ARCADE

American River

Amtrak > Stockton, Bakersfield

Blue Line — Watt/I-80, Watt/I-80 West, Roseville Road

SACRAMENTO

Marconi/Arcade, Swanston, Royal Oaks, Arden/Del Paso, LRT Depot

Globe, Green Line

59th St, University/65th St, 48th St, 39th St, 29th St, 23rd St, 16th St, 12th & I, Alkali Flat, 13th St

City College, Broadway, 4th Ave/Wayne Hultgren

Fruitridge, 47th Avenue, Florin, Meadowview

(Franklin), (Center Parkway), (Cosumnes River College), 2015

(Morrison Creek)

Blue Line — Meadowview

SACRAMENTO

1 km

✈ SMF

(Metro Air Park)
(Sacramento International Airport)
(Greenbriar)
(Club Center Dr)
(Commerce Pkwy)
(East Natomas Town Center)
(Arco Arena)
(Gateway Park)
(San Juan Rd)
(Arena Blvd)
(North Natomas Town Center)
(Pebblestone Way)
(West El Camino Ave)

Amtrak > Portland, Seattle

Sacramento River

I-80

Amtrak > Oakland, San Jose, Los Angeles

(Rallyards)

Gold Line — Sacramento Valley Station

Sequoia Pacific
7th & Richards/Township 9
Sacramento Valley Station

Green Line — 7th & Richards/Township 9

Inset map

Sacramento River

(Railroad Museum)

Gold Line — Sacramento Valley Station

St. Rose of Lima Park, 7th & K, 7th & Capitol, 7th & I/County Ctr

Green Line — 7th & Richards/Township 9

Richards Blvd, Watt/I-80, N 7th St

Alkali Flat/La Valentina, 12th & I, 8th & H/County Ctr, 8th & K, 9th & K, 8th & O, 8th & Capitol, Cathedral Square 10th & K, Cathedral Square 11th & K, Archives Plaza

Green Line — 13th St, 16th St, 19th St, Folsom, Meadowview

Sunrise

8th & Capitol – gemischter Zug aus Siemens- (links) und CAF-Wagen (rechts) vor dem kalifornischen Parlamentsgebäude
– *mixed train made up of Siemens (left) and CAF cars (right) in front of the Californian State Capitol*

RT Light Rail

Die Stadtbahn von Sacramento gehört zur ersten Generation von modernen Stadtbahnen in den USA, die in den 1980er Jahren mit Hochflurwagen, welche an Niedrigbahnsteigen halten, in Betrieb genommen wurden und in der Innenstadt wie herkömmliche Straßenbahnen verkehren, während sie auf Außenstrecken oft Eisenbahn- oder Autobahn-Korridore nutzen. Anfangs gab es in Sacramento mehrere eingleisige Abschnitte, von denen einige später zweigleisig ausgebaut wurden. Aber noch heute wird der Betrieb durch lange eingleisige Abschnitte eingeschränkt, was jedoch teilweise während der Hauptverkehrszeiten durch den Einsatz von 100 m langen 4-Wagen-Zügen kompensiert wird.

Seit Eröffnung des kurzen Abschnitts zum Township 9 Mitte 2012 besteht das Netz aus drei durch Farben unterschiedene Linien: die Blue, Gold und Green Line. Die Linienfarben wurden im Jahr 2005 eingeführt.

Die Stadtbahn verkehrt von ca. 4:30 Uhr bis etwa Mitternacht, wobei der Abschnitt zwischen Sunrise und Folsom nach 19:00 Uhr nicht bedient wird! Tagsüber herrscht auf der Blue und Gold Line ein 15-Minuten-Takt, aber nach 18:00 Uhr und am Wochenende nur ein 30-Minuten-Takt. Die Green Line wird nur alle 30 Minuten bedient, am Wochenende gar nicht.

● **Blue Line** (25,7 km, 24 Haltestellen)
Sacramentos Nord-Süd-Linie verläuft fast ausschließlich innerhalb der Stadtgrenzen. Der nördliche Ast ist Teil der ursprünglichen Strecke von 1987. Es gab frühe Pläne für eine 11 km lange nordöstliche Verlängerung bzw. einen Abzweig in Richtung Antelope Road, die aber bislang nicht verwirklicht wurden. Die heutige Linie beginnt eingleisig im Mittelstreifen der I-80, wobei die ersten drei Stationen vor allem als Park &

Sacramento's urban rail system is a typical example of the first modern light rail systems introduced in the U.S. in the 1980s, with high-floor cars stopping at low platforms and running on-street like conventional trams in the city centre, while often using railway and freeway corridors on the outer sections. Initially, there were several single-track portions, some of which were later doubled, but the system's capacity today is still limited by lengthy single-track sections, although this is partly compensated for by operating 100 m long 4-car trains during peak hours.

With a short segment to Township 9 having opened in mid-2012, the system now consists of three colour-coded lines: the Blue, Gold and Green Lines. Line colours were introduced in 2005.

Light rail trains operate from about 04:30 to around midnight; the section between Sunrise and Folsom is not served after 19:00! Light rail trains run every 15 minutes on the Blue and Gold Lines during daytime hours, but only every 30 minutes after 18:00 and on weekends. The Green Line is served every 30 minutes, with no trains on weekends.

● ***Blue Line*** *(25.7 km, 24 stations)*
Sacramento's north-south line runs almost entirely within the city borders. The northern leg is part of the original route opened in 1987. Early plans to build an 11 km north-eastern extension or a branch towards Antelope Road have not come to fruition yet. The existing line starts single-track in the median of I-80, with the first three stations primarily used for park & ride. The right-of-way of the outer section as well as the bridge over the railway were once meant to be part of a freeway project, but this was later abandoned

Ride-Anlagen dienen. Die Trasse dieses äußeren Abschnitts sowie die Brücke über die Eisenbahn waren einst für eine geplante Autobahn errichtet worden, die dafür vorgesehenen Budgetmittel kamen dann dem Stadtbahnbau zugute. Die Strecke wird kurz vor Erreichen der Bahnstrecke der ehemaligen *Southern Pacific* (jetzt *Union Pacific*) zweigleisig. Die Stadtbahn verkehrt auf den nächsten 3,3 km an der Westseite der Eisenbahn. Südlich der Station Swanston biegt sie nach Westen auf einen neuen, im Jahr 2009 eröffneten Abschnitt ein, der die ursprüngliche, eingleisige Trasse über die Evergreen Street ersetzte. Nach Royal Oaks wird die Strecke städtischer, mit einem teilweise abmarkierten, straßenbündigen Abschnitt entlang des Del Paso Boulevard zwischen den Haltestellen Arden/Del Paso und Globe. Während die meisten anderen Abschnitte auf dem nördlichen Ast in den frühen 1990er Jahren zweigleisig ausgebaut wurden, ist die Brücke über den American River bis heute eingleisig. Die Stadtbahn fährt weiter in Richtung Innenstadt straßenbündig auf der 12th Street, wobei nur das stadtauswärtige Gleis abmarkiert ist. Schließlich biegt sie nach Westen in die autofreie K Street, wo die am stärksten frequentierten Innenstadthaltestellen liegen. Die Nord-Süd-Route durch die Innenstadt wird auch von den beiden anderen Linien befahren und verläuft erst durch parallele Straßen, nach Norden auf der 8th und nach Süden auf der 7th Street, bevor die beiden Gleise auf der O Street wieder zusammenlaufen. Ab hier verkehrt die Stadtbahn vom Autoverkehr weitgehend ungestört, auch wenn auf der 12th Street Anwohner die Gleise befahren müssen. Westlich der Station 13th Street, wo jetzt die Green Line endet, können Züge abgestellt werden.

Nach der Station 16th Street verlässt die Blue Line die ursprüngliche Strecke von 1987 und verläuft Richtung Süden auf einer typischen zweigleisigen Stadtbahntrasse entlang der Westseite einer Güterbahn, völlig ebenerdig und mit zahlreichen, durch Schranken gesicherten Bahnübergängen. Lediglich an der Florin Road wurde für die Stadtbahn eine Überführung errichtet. Die aktuelle Endstation Meadowview ist ein wichtiger Umsteigepunkt zum Busverkehr. Nach ihrer Inbetriebnahme im September 2003 wurde die ‚South Line' als eigene Linie betrieben, seit der Netzreform im Juni 2005 ist sie Teil der Blue Line.

Die Blue Line wird bis 2015 um 6,9 km nach Süden bis Cosumnes River College (CRC) verlängert. Die Strecke verlässt die UP-Bahnstrecke südlich der Station Morrison Creek und verläuft dann in östlicher Richtung entlang des Cosumnes River Boulevard, bis sie schließlich nach Süden in die Bruceville Road einbiegt. Die Verlängerung umfasst zwei Brücken, eine über den Morrison Creek und die Güterbahn und die andere über das östliche Ende des Cosumnes River Boulevard. Die Blue Line könnte später nach Süden bis Elk Grove verlängert werden.

● **Gold Line** (36,2 km, 28 Haltestellen)
Die Ost-West-Linie beginnt am Amtrak-Bahnhof, wo sie das dem alten Bahnhofsgebäude am nächsten liegende Gleis

13th Street – Siemens-Wagen in neuem Anstrich | *Siemens car in new livery*

SACRAMENTO Light Rail

62 km (+ 6.9 km im Bau | *under construction*)
47 Haltestellen | *stations* (+ 4 im Bau | *under construction*)

12 Mar 1987: Watt/I-80 – 8th & O
05 Sept 1987: 8th & O – Butterfield
14 July 1994: + 39th Street & 48th Street stops
06 Sept 1998: Butterfield – Mather Field/Mills
26 Sept 2003: 16th Street – Meadowview
11 June 2004: Mather Field/Mills – Sunrise
15 Oct 2005: Sunrise – Historic Folsom
08 Dec 2006: Downtown Loop – Sacramento Valley Station
09 Jan 2012: + 8th & H/County Center stop
15 June 2012: H Street – 7th & Richards/Township 9
2015: Meadowview – Cosumnes River College

and the assigned funds were diverted to the light rail project instead. The route becomes double-track just before it crosses the former Southern Pacific (now Union Pacific) railway route, to which the light rail line gets aligned on the western side for the next 3.3 km. Just south of Swanston station, the trains turn west on a new section, which replaced a former single-track detour via Evergreen Street in 2009. Leaving Royal Oaks, the route becomes more urban, with a partly marked-off on-street section along Del Paso Boulevard between Arden/Del Paso and Globe stations. While most other sections on the northern leg were doubled in the early 1990s, the bridge over the American River remains single-track. Trains continue into downtown on 12th Street, with only the outbound track being marked off. Trains finally turn west into car-free K Street to serve the busiest downtown stops. The north-south route through the city centre is shared with the other two lines, the tracks running first on parallel streets, north on 8th Street and south on 7th Street, before rejoining on O Street. From there they are separated from road traffic, although local traffic may interfere on 12th Street. Trains can be parked on sidings to the west of 13th Street station, now the terminus of Green Line trains.

Beyond 16th Street station, as the trains leave the original 1987 light rail route, they run south on a typical double-track light rail right-of-way, which is aligned on the western side of a freight line, lies completely at grade and has numerous level crossings protected by barriers. There is a flyover for light rail trains to avoid an intersection at Florin Road, though. The current terminus at Meadowview is a major transfer point for connecting buses. Opened in September 2003, the South Line was operated as a separate line until the reconfiguration of the network in June 2005, when it became part of the Blue Line.

The Blue Line is currently being extended 6.9 km further south to Cosumnes River College (CRC), with the work scheduled for completion in 2015. The route diverges from the UP corridor south of Morrison Creek station, following an easterly direction along Cosumnes River Boulevard before turning south into Bruceville Road. The extension includes two bridges, one over Morrison Creek and the freight railway, and the other over the eastern end of Cosumnes River Boulevard. The Blue Line could later be extended south to Elk Grove.

● *Gold Line* (36.2 km, 28 stations)
Sacramento's east-west light rail line starts at the city's Amtrak station, where it occupies the track closest to the old station building. The mainline platforms, previously

Archives Plaza – Siemens-Wagen in altem Anstrich | *Siemens car in old livery*

Sacramento Valley Station – Hochbahnsteig an der vorderen Tür – *high-level platform at the front door*

übernahm. Die Fernbahnsteige lagen früher direkt parallel nördlich der Stadtbahn, sie wurden jedoch im Jahr 2012 nach Norden verschoben und verlängert. Der Stadtbahnast zum Bahnhof wurde im Jahr 2006 in Betrieb genommen. Vom Bahnhof ausgehend ist die Strecke zwei Häuserblocks lang eingleisig, dann biegt das Gleis Richtung Süden in die 7th Street ein und trifft nach drei Blocks auf die Blue Line, während das Gleis Richtung Norden parallel in der 8th Street liegt (die Haltestelle H Street /County Center wurde erst im Jahr 2012 in Vorbereitung auf die Green Line eingefügt).

Die Gold Line zweigt von der Blue Line direkt nach der Station 16th Street ab und folgt der ursprünglichen Strecke von 1987 Richtung Folsom. Der Abzweig ist niveaufrei, indem die Gold Line auf einen 580 m langen Viadukt fährt, der eine UP-Güterbahn und die 19th bis 21st Street überspannt. Der Viadukt war zunächst eingleisig, wurde aber in Verbindung mit dem South Line-Projekt zweigleisig ausgebaut. Wieder auf Straßenebene folgt die Gold Line einer alten Eisenbahntrasse. Gleich nach der Station University/65th Street gibt es eine weitere, 450 m lange Hochbahnstrecke, die erst unter dem Lincoln Highway und dann über die Bahnstrecke nach Stockton sowie ein Gütergleis führt, das der Stadtbahn dann bis zur Hazel Avenue folgt. Wie viele andere Abschnitte auf der ursprünglichen Route war auch dieser Viadukt zunächst eingleisig, wurde aber nur wenige Jahre später zweigleisig ausgebaut. Während das parallele Gütergleis durchgehend ebenerdig liegt, wurden für die Stadtbahn an zwei verkehrsreichen Kreuzungen Überführungen gebaut, an der Watt Avenue (erst 2009) und am Sunrise Boulevard. Ab kurz vor College Greens bis zur Endstation in Folsom verläuft die Stadtbahnstrecke entlang des Folsom Boulevard. 4 km hinter Sunrise, wo wochentags jeder zweite Zug endet, wird die Strecke eingleisig, auf den restlichen 7,8 km gibt es dann keine Begegnungsmöglichkeit mehr.

● **Green Line** (3,5 km, 7 Haltestellen)
Die heutige Green Line ist nur der erste Abschnitt einer 20,5 km langen Strecke zum Sacramento International Airport. Die Linie zweigt von der gemeinsamen Innenstadtstrecke in der Nähe des Bahnhofs ab und verläuft dann ca. 1 km eingleisig nach Norden bis zur B Street, die restlichen 600 m sind zweigleisig. Die Endstation befindet sich in einem Entwicklungsgebiet, dem River District. Von hier aus soll die Strecke nach Norden durch South und North Natomas entlang der Truxel Road und des East Commerce Way verlaufen und dann über den Meister Way zum Flughafen erreichen. Sie wird meist ebenerdig ausgeführt, aufgeständert aber über den American River, die I-80, die El Centro Road (Hwy 99) und auf dem letzten Teilstück vor dem Flughafen.

located parallel and directly north of the light rail track, were moved further north in 2012 to allow for their extension. The railway station branch was added to the light rail network in 2006. Starting from the railway station, the line is single-track for the length of two blocks before the southbound track turns south into 7th Street and joins the Blue Line after three blocks, while the northbound route runs parallel on 8th Street (a stop was only added at H Street/County Center in 2012 in preparation for the Green Line).

The Gold Line diverges from the Blue Line right after the 16th Street stop to follow the original 1987 alignment towards Folsom. The junction is grade-separated as the Gold Line trains climb a 580 m long viaduct which spans over a UP freight line and 19th to 21st Streets. This viaduct was initially single-track, but was doubled in conjunction with the South Line project. Back on street level, the line follows an old railway corridor. Right after University/65th Street station, there is another 450 m flyover that first takes the line below Lincoln Highway and then over the main line to Stockton, as well as a freight track which follows the light rail route all the way to Hazel Avenue. Like many other sections on the original route, this viaduct was initially built single-track, but it was doubled after just a few years. While the freight track remains at grade, two overpasses were built for light rail trains to avoid two busy intersections, one at Watt Avenue (added in 2009) and the other at Sunrise Boulevard. From a point shortly before College Greens station and all the way to the terminus at Historic Folsom, the light rail route runs alongside Folsom Boulevard. The line becomes single-track 4 km after Sunrise station, on weekdays the terminus of every other train, and no passing loops are available for the remaining 7.8 km.

● ***Green Line*** *(3.5 km, 7 stations)*
Today's Green Line is actually the first step of a 20.5 km extension to Sacramento International Airport. The line diverges from the shared downtown route near the railway station, running about 1 km on a single track north to B Street before becoming double-track for the remaining 600 m. The terminus is located in an area currently under development known as the River District. From here, the line will head north through South and North Natomas along Truxel Road and East Commerce Way, approaching the Airport via Meister Way. It will be mostly at grade, although aerial structures will be built over the American River, I-80, El Centro Road (Hwy 99) and on the final approach to the airport terminal.

● Stadtbahnfahrzeuge

Bei der Stadtbahn von Sacramento sind zwei Arten von Gelenkfahrzeugen im Einsatz, ältere von Siemens/Duewag und neuere von CAF. Da alle Wagen hochflurig sind, aber nur an niedrigen Bahnsteigen gehalten wird, sind alle Stationen mit einem kurzen Hochbahnsteig ausgestattet, um einen behindertengerechten Einstieg an der vordersten Tür des Zuges zu ermöglichen, wo außerdem der Fahrer manuell eine Spaltüberbrückung ausklappt. Nur die stadteinwärtige Haltestelle 12th & I Streets ist nicht behindertenfreundlich. Wie in Denver gibt es also auch in Sacramento bislang keine Niederflur-Fahrzeuge.

1) 36 U2a-Fahrzeuge von **Siemens/Duewag** (Serie 100) kamen in zwei Serien nach Sacramento, 26 in den Jahren 1986/87 und 10 im Jahr 1991. Sie sind den SD100 und SD160 ähnlich, die in mehreren in diesem Buch behandelten Städten eingesetzt werden. Sie sind 24,2 m lang und 2,65 m breit.

2) 40 ähnliche Fahrzeuge (Serie 200) wurden von der spanischen Firma **CAF** in den Jahren 2002/03 gebaut. Sie sind mit 25,6 m etwas länger und können an ihrer runderen Front und an ihren blauen Schwenktüren erkannt werden.

Beide Typen können in einem Zugverband laufen, der aus bis zu vier Fahrzeugen bestehen kann. 4-Wagen-Züge werden in der Tat während der Hauptverkehrszeiten eingesetzt, während zu anderen Zeiten 2-Wagen-Züge üblich sind. Die Fahrzeuge sind für eine Höchstgeschwindigkeit von 88 km/h ausgelegt.

3) Im Jahr 2003 erwarb RT 21 Hochflur-Fahrzeuge von Santa Clara VTA (San Jose, siehe S. 74), aber nahm sie nie in Betrieb. Im Juni 2012 wurde schließlich ein Vertrag mit Siemens unterzeichnet, wonach die von **UTDC** gebauten Fahrzeuge generalüberholt und schließlich zum aktiven Wagenpark hinzugefügt werden sollen. Sie werden für die Einführung von Express-Fahrten auf der Gold Line ab 2014 sowie für die Verlängerung der Blue Line bis Cosumnes River College im Jahr 2015 benötigt.

Die Stadtbahnstrecken auf eigenem Gleiskörper sind mit einer automatischen Zugsicherungsanlage ausgerüstet, während auf den straßenbündigen Strecken in der Innenstadt auf Sicht gefahren wird. Die meisten Bahnübergänge sind mit herkömmlichen Bahnschranken gesichert.

Der Stadtbahnbetriebshof befindet sich auf der Nordstrecke zwischen den Stationen Swanston und Marconi/Arcade.

● *Light Rail Rolling Stock*

The Sacramento light rail system is operated with two types of articulated vehicles, older Siemens/Duewag and newer CAF cars. As they are all high-floor but stop at low platforms, stepfree access is reserved for people with reduced mobility. This is achieved via a short high-level platform located at the front end of the train, plus a board manually folded out by the driver. Only the inbound stop at 12th & I Streets does not allow wheelchair boarding. Like Denver, Sacramento has thus not introduced any modern low-floor trains.

*1) 36 **Siemens/Duewag** U2a vehicles (100-series), similar to the SD100 and SD160 in use in several cities covered in this book, were delivered to Sacramento in two batches, 26 in 1986/87 and 10 in 1991. They are 24.2 m long and 2.65 m wide.*

*2) 40 similar cars were built by **CAF** of Spain in 2002/03 (200-series); at 25.6 m, they are slightly longer and can be distinguished by a more rounded front and blue sliding doors.*

The two types can operate in one trainset, which is formed of up to four cars. 4-car trains are indeed used during peak hours, while 2-car trains are common at other times. They are designed for a maximum speed of 88 km/h.

*3) In 2003, RT purchased 21 high-floor vehicles from Santa Clara VTA (San Jose, see p. 74), but they were never put into service; in June 2012, a contract was signed with Siemens to refurbish the cars built by **UTDC** so they could finally be added to the active fleet. They are required for the introduction of limited-stop express trains on the Gold Line in 2014, and for the Blue Line extension to Cosumnes River College in 2015.*

The segregated light rail routes are equipped with three-aspect (red, yellow, green) automatic block signalling, while 'line of sight' operation is used on city streets. Most intersections are protected by standard railroad crossing gates.

The workshops for light rail vehicles are located on the northern route between Swanston and Marconi/Arcade stations.

Innenansicht eines Siemens-Wagens | *Inside a Siemens car*

Ausklappbare Spaltüberbrückung an der ersten Tür – *Unfoldable bridge plate at the first door*

SAN FRANCISCO BAY AREA, CA

In der San Francisco Bay Area leben rund 7 Mio. Menschen. Das Gebiet umfasst San Francisco und das San Mateo County auf der Halbinsel, das Santa Clara County mit San Jose im Süden (s. S. 74), das Alameda und Contra Costa County in der East Bay-Region, außerdem die weniger dicht besiedelten Counties Marin, Napa, Solano und Sonoma im Norden (außerhalb der Karte rechts). Die größten Städte in der Bay Area sind San Jose (970.000 Einw.; 457 km²), San Francisco (805.000; 600 km²), Oakland (391.000; 144 km²) und Fremont (214.000; 200 km²).

Für Eisenbahnfreunde bietet die Bay Area eine Vielfalt an Bahnen, wie man sie sonst nirgendwo in Nordamerika findet. Städtische Schienenverkehrsmittel reichen von den historischen Cable Cars und Museumsstraßenbahnen in San Francisco über die Muni Metro, eine Mischung aus klassischer Straßenbahn und moderner Stadtbahn, bis hin zur Stadtbahn von San Jose oder BART, einem der modernsten Schnellbahnsysteme in den USA. Dazu kommen die typischen Doppelstockwagen auf der Caltrain-Regionalbahn und der automatische Peoplemover am Flughafen von San Francisco (ein weiterer ist am Flughafen Oakland im Bau). San Francisco verfügt außerdem über eines der größten Obusnetze der Welt.

Amtrak-Züge erreichen die Stadt San Francisco nicht direkt, sie bedienen jedoch mehrere Bahnhöfe entlang der East Bay: Der „Coast Starlight" von Seattle nach Los Angeles hält in Martinez, Richmond, Emeryville, Oakland (Jack London Square) und San Jose und der „California Zephyr" von Chicago endet in Emeryville. Der „San Joaquin" fährt vier Mal täglich von Oakland durch das Central Valley nach Bakersfield. Als Regionalbahn bietet der „Capitol Corridor" wochentags 15 Züge zwischen Sacramento und Oakland, davon fahren 7 weiter bis San Jose. Diese Strecke wird auch an Wochenenden bedient, wenn auch weniger häufig. In Zukunft sollen Hochgeschwindigkeitszüge von Los Angeles auf den Caltrain-Gleisen über San Jose das Zentrum von San Francisco erreichen.

Als Folge der Vielzahl verschiedener Verkehrsunternehmen in der Bay Area existiert kein integriertes Tarifsystem. Mit „Clipper", einer 2010 nach mehreren Jahren Erprobung eingeführten Smartcard, kann man die meisten Verkehrsmittel in der Region, einschließlich Fähren, nutzen. Für San Francisco gibt es verschiedene Touristentickets (siehe S. 54).

Home to some 7 million people, the San Francisco Bay Area comprises San Francisco and San Mateo County on the peninsula, Santa Clara County with San Jose in the south (see p. 74), Alameda and Contra Costa Counties in the East Bay region, plus the less densely populated Marin, Napa, Solano and Sonoma Counties in the north (just off the map on the right). The largest cities in this area are San Jose (970,000 inh.; 457 km2), San Francisco (805,000; 600 km2), Oakland (391,000; 144 km2) and Fremont (214,000; 200 km2).

For the railway enthusiast, the Bay Area offers a variety of trains found nowhere else in North America. Urban rail systems include the historic cable cars and heritage streetcars in San Francisco; Muni Metro's mix of classic tram and state-of-the-art light rail; BART, one of the most advanced rapid transit systems in the U.S.; the modern light rail system in San Jose; the typical double-deck carriages on Caltrain's regional line; plus an automatic people mover at San Francisco International Airport (with one also under construction at Oakland International Airport). San Francisco also boasts one of the largest trolleybus systems in the world.

Amtrak's trains do not serve San Francisco directly, but instead they make several stops along the East Bay, with the "Coast Starlight" from Seattle to Los Angeles calling at Martinez, Richmond, Emeryville, Oakland (Jack London Square) and San Jose, and the "California Zephyr" from Chicago terminating at Emeryville. The "San Joaquin" runs four times a day from Oakland through the Central Valley to Bakersfield. Like a commuter railway, the "Capitol Corridor" has 15 trains on weekdays between Sacramento and Oakland, with 7 continuing to San Jose; this route is also served on weekends, though less frequently. In the future, California High-Speed Rail trains from Los Angeles will share the Caltrain corridor from San Jose to San Francisco.

As a result of the multitude of different transit operators in the Bay Area an integrated fare system does not exist. The 'Clipper', a smartcard introduced in 2010 after several years of testing, can be used on all major transport systems in the region, including ferries. For special San Francisco tourist options see p. 54.

SAN FRANCISCO BAY AREA

BART (Mo-Fr tagsüber | Mon-Fri daytime hours)
- Pittsburg/Bay Point – San Francisco Int'l Airport
- Richmond – Fremont
- Daly City – Dublin/Pleasanton
- Richmond – Millbrae
- Daly City – Fremont

━━━	**BART**
D	Betriebswerkstatt | Maintenance facility
- - -	eBART (im Bau | under construction)
– – –	Oakland Airport Peoplemover (i.B. | u/c)
━╫━	**Commuter Rail**
━╫━	**Amtrak**
═╪═	Güterbahn | Freight railway
───	VTA Light Rail
*	Halt nur am Wochenende | weekends-only station

San Pablo Bay

Solano County

Amtrak > Sacramento, Salt Lake City, Denver, Chicago Portland, Seattle

Antioch-Pittsburg

Amtrak > Stockton, Bakersfield

(Hercules)

Martinez

Contra Costa County

North Concord/Martinez

Pittsburg/Bay Point

(Pittsburg/Railroad Ave)

2016

(Antioch/Hillcrest Ave)

Concord

(San Rafael)

SMART

(Larkspur Landing)

Richmond

El Cerrito del Norte

El Cerrito Plaza

North Berkeley

Berkeley

Downtown Berkeley

Ashby

Emeryville

Rockridge

MacArthur

19th St/Oakland

12th St/Oakland City Center

Lake Merritt

Pleasant Hill/Contra Costa Centre

Walnut Creek

Lafayette

Orinda

Marin Co.

Pacific Ocean

Embarcadero

Civic Center/UN Plaza

16th St Mission

24th St Mission

Glen Park

Balboa Park

Daly City

Colma

South San Francisco

San Bruno

San Bruno

Millbrae

San Francisco

22nd Street

West Oakland

Oakland Jack London Sq

Fruitvale

Coliseum/Oakland Airport

Oakland Coliseum

OAK

Oakland International Airport

San Leandro

Alameda County

Bay Fair

West Dublin/Pleasanton

(Livermore)

Dublin/Pleasanton

Livermore

ACE > Stockton

Castro Valley

Hayward

Hayward

Pleasanton

South Hayward

55

Glen Park

Bayshore

San Francisco Bay

South San Francisco

San Bruno

San Bruno

SFO

San Francisco International Airport

Millbrae

Broadway*

Burlingame

San Mateo

Hayward Park

Hillsdale

Belmont

San Carlos

Redwood City

San Mateo County

Union City

Fremont Centerville

Fremont

(Irvington)

2015

Warm Springs/South Fremont

ACE

Atherton*

Menlo Park

Palo Alto

California Avenue

Caltrain

San Antonio

Mountain View

Sunnyvale

Lawrence

Great America

(Milpitas)

(Berryessa)

2018

(Alum Rock)

SJC

Santa Clara

College Park

San Jose Diridon

(Downtown San Jose)

Tamien

Capitol

Santa Clara County

Blossom Hill

Caltrain > Gilroy
Amtrak > Los Angeles

75

5 km

Mo-Fr bis 20:00
Mon-Fri before 20:00

Mo-Fr nach 20:00; Sa & So
Mon-Fri after 20:00; Sat & Sun

BART

Caltrain

San Bruno

Rental Car Center

West Field Road

San Francisco International Airport

AirTrain

International Terminal G

Garage G & BART

Garage A

International Terminal A

Domestic Terminal 3

Domestic Terminal 2

Domestic Terminal 1

SFO

Millbrae

Richmond – A-Wagen Nr. 1226 | A-car no. 1226

bɑ̃ BART *(Bay Area Rapid Transit)*

Auch 40 Jahre nach Eröffnung ihres ersten Abschnitts gehört BART noch zu den modernsten Schnellbahnen Nordamerikas. Sie ist technisch gesehen eine richtige *Metro* (völlig kreuzungsfrei und automatisch betrieben), auch wenn sie teilweise eher den Charakter einer S-Bahn aufweist. Während die Stationen im städtischen Bereich oft nur etwa 550 m voneinander entfernt liegen, beträgt der Bahnhofsabstand auf Außenstrecken typischerweise 4-6 km, der längste liegt zwischen Castro Valley und West Dublin/Pleasanton mit 13,5 km! Einzigartig ist BART in den USA bezüglich der (indischen) Breitspur von 1676 mm, während sonst überall die Normalspur von 1435 mm üblich ist.

Das heutige BART-Netz besteht aus fünf Linien, die auf mehreren Abschnitten parallel verkehren. Auch wenn sie auf dem Netzplan farblich dargestellt sind, werden sie in der Regel nach ihren Endpunkten bezeichnet. Alle Äste werden von etwa 4:00 Uhr bis Mitternacht befahren, an Wochentagen tagsüber mindestens alle 15 Minuten (20 Minuten am Wochenende), d.h. durch die Transbay Tube und San Francisco rollt alle 3-4 Minuten ein Zug. Die rote und grüne Linie verkehren nur montags bis samstags bis ca. 19:00 Uhr. Wenn die rote Linie nicht in Betrieb ist oder samstags in Daly City endet, wird die gelbe Linie durch Kopfmachen am Flughafen nach Millbrae durchgebunden. Die drei Sonntagslinien fahren erst ab etwa 8:00 Uhr.

Seit ihrer Eröffnung im Jahr 1972 verwendet BART ein automatisches Zahlungssystem. Die Fahrpreise richten sich nach der Entfernung und gehen von 1,75 $ bis 11,05 $. Fahrten unter der Bucht hindurch sowie zum Flughafen schließen einen Zuschlag ein. Der Fahrpreis kann mit der Clipper-Smartcard oder mit einer exklusiven BART-Wertkarte entrichtet werden.

40 years after its first segment was opened, BART is still one of North America's most advanced rapid transit systems. It works like a state-of-the-art metro (completely grade-separated and automatically driven), although it also functions as a high-speed suburban or regional rail system. While on urban sections, stations are often only some 550 m apart, distances between stations on outer stretches are typically 4-6 km, with the longest stretch between Castro Valley and West Dublin/Pleasanton measuring 13.5 km! BART is unique in the U.S., having a 1676 mm (Indian) broad gauge instead of the otherwise typical 1435 mm standard gauge.

The five lines which comprise BART today, share the same route along some sections. Although colour-coded on system maps, they are generally referred to by their end points. All branches are served from roughly 04:00 until midnight, with a train at least every 15 minutes during daytime hours on weekdays (20 minutes weekends), resulting in a BART train every 3-4 minutes rolling through the Transbay Tube and San Francisco. The red and green lines only operate Mondays to Saturdays until approximately 19:00. When the red line is not running or terminates at Daly City on Saturdays, the yellow line is extended to Millbrae by reversing at the Airport. The three Sunday lines only start service at around 08:00.

From its opening in 1972, BART has used automatic fare collection, with fares calculated by distance travelled, ranging from $1.75 to $11.05. Trips through the Transbay Tube and those terminating at the airport carry a surcharge. Fares can be paid with the Clipper smartcard or with a BART-only stored value ticket.

 Entwicklung von BART

Zu einer Zeit, als andere Städte in den USA gerade ihre letzten städtischen und Überland-Straßenbahnlinien aufgegeben hatten und der Autobahnbau boomte, erkannte die Bay Area schon sehr früh, dass der Bau neuer Straßen aufgrund der geographischen Besonderheiten der Region nicht die Verkehrsprobleme lösen würde. So wurde im Jahr 1957 der fünf Counties umfassende *Bay Area Rapid Transit District* gegründet und im Jahr 1962 von den Wählern in den Counties von San Francisco, Alameda und Contra Costa ein ehrgeiziges Schnellbahnprojekt genehmigt, nachdem das Marin und San Mateo County ausgestiegen waren. Der Rückzug des Marin County bedeutete, dass ein zweiter westlicher Ast entlang der Geary Street in San Francisco und dann nach Norden auf dem geplanten Unterdeck der Golden Gate Bridge nicht mehr zur Debatte stand.

Das endgültige Projekt umfasste den Bau eines 115 km langen, völlig kreuzungsfreien regionalen Metronetzes, dessen Herzstück die 5,8 km lange Transbay Tube, der Tunnel unter der Bucht von San Francisco, sein sollte. Die restlichen Strecken sollten eine Mischung aus unterirdischen Abschnitten in den dicht bebauten Gebieten von San Francisco und Oakland und Berkeley, Hochbahnabschnitten durch Vorstädte und ebenerdigen Abschnitten in Mittelstreifen von Autobahnen aufweisen. Als Endpunkte der vier Äste wurden Daly City, Richmond, Concord und Fremont festgesetzt. In der Innenstadt von San Francisco enthielt das Projekt einen doppelstöckigen, viergleisigen Tunnel für BART und Muni Metro. Der Bau begann offiziell im Juni 1964 an einer 7 km langen Teststrecke zwischen Concord und Walnut Creek, wo neue Fahrzeugkonzepte sowie das Zugbeeinflussungssystem entwickelt werden sollten. Die Bauarbeiten an den unterirdischen Anlagen starteten in Oakland im Januar 1966 und die ersten Segmente der Transbay Tube wurden im November 1966 abgesenkt. Trotz einiger Verzögerungen und steigender Kosten wurde das gesamte Grundnetz, verglichen mit typischen Bauzeiten heutzutage, in Rekordzeit vollendet: Alle Abschnitte wurden zwischen September 1972 und September 1974 in Betrieb genommen.

Der Tunnelbau in San Francisco und auf der Nord-Süd-Strecke durch Oakland wurde im Schildvortrieb durchgeführt, während die offene Bauweise in Berkeley und am Ast durch Lake Merritt in Oakland zur Anwendung kam. Der Tunnel durch die Berkeley Hills zwischen Rockridge und Orinda wurde bergmännisch aufgefahren. Für die Transbay Tube hingegen wurden auf dem Festland 57 ca. 107 m lange Fertigteile aus Stahl und Stahlbeton gebaut, die dann eingeschwemmt und auf ein Sandbett abgesenkt wurden. Da San Francisco und die

 History of BART

At a time when other U.S. cities had just abandoned their last urban and interurban tram lines and freeway construction was booming, the Bay Area had already realised that building more roads would not solve their traffic problems, given the geographical peculiarities of the region. In 1957, the 5-county 'Bay Area Rapid Transit District' was established, and in 1962, an ambitious rapid transit project was approved by voters in San Francisco, Alameda and Contra Costa Counties, after Marin and San Mateo Counties had dropped out. The withdrawal of Marin County meant that a second western leg along Geary Street in San Francisco and then north via a lower deck of the Golden Gate Bridge was no longer considered.

The final project included the construction of a 115 km completely grade-separated regional metro system, the centrepiece of which would be the 5.8 km Transbay Tube. The remaining routes would be a mix of underground sections in the densely built-up areas of San Francisco, Oakland and Berkeley, elevated sections through the suburban areas, and at-grade sections in freeway medians. Daly City, Richmond, Concord and Fremont would become the initial termini of the four branches. For central San Francisco, the deal envisaged a bi-level 4-track tunnel shared by BART and Muni services. Construction was officially launched in June 1964, when a 7 km test track was built between Concord and Walnut Creek to develop new design concepts for the rolling stock and automatic train control system. Subway construction began in Oakland in January 1966, and the first segments of the Transbay Tube were lowered in November 1966. Despite some delays and rising costs, the entire basic network was still completed in record time compared to typical construction schedules nowadays, with all segments opening between September 1972 and September 1974.

The tunnelling through San Francisco and on the north-south route through Oakland was done with TBMs (tunnel boring machines), while cut-and-cover tunnels were realised through Berkeley and on the Lake Merritt branch in Oakland. The tunnel through the Berkeley Hills between Rockridge and Orinda was drilled using conventional mining techniques. The Transbay Tube, however, was built off-shore as 57 precast elements made of steel and reinforced concrete, each roughly 107 m long, which were then floated in and sunk into place on a sandbed. With San Francisco and its region lying along several fault lines, the tunnels all had to be made earthquake-proof. A magnitude 7.1 quake shook the area on 17 October 1989, and while the BART underwater

BART

162.6 km (+ 23.6 km im Bau | *under construction*)
44 Bahnhöfe | *stations* (+ 3 im Bau | *under construction*)

11 Sept 1972: MacArthur – Fremont (42 km)
29 Jan 1973: MacArthur – Richmond (16.8 km)
21 May 1973: MacArthur – Concord (30.5 km)
05 Nov 1973: Montgomery – Daly City (12.4 km)
16 Sept 1974: Montgomery – Oakland City Center / Lake Merritt (13 km)
27 May 1976: + Embarcadero
16 Dec 1995: Concord – North Concord/Martinez (3.6 km)
24 Feb 1996: Daly City – Colma (2.5 km)
07 Dec 1996: North Concord/Martinez – Pittsburg/Bay Point (8 km)
10 May 1997: Bay Fair – Dublin/Pleasanton (20 km)
22 June 2003: Colma – San Francisco Int'l Airport / Millbrae (13.8 km)
19 Feb 2011: + West Dublin/Pleasanton

2015: Fremont – Warm Springs/South Fremont (7.6 km)
2018: Warm Springs – Berryessa (16 km)

Walnut Creek – C-Wagen | *C-car*

19th St/Oakland – zweigleisige obere Ebene (Richtung Norden) | *double-track upper level (northbound)*

Key System

BART ist nicht die erste Bahn, die die San Francisco Bay quert: Ab Anfang des 20. Jahrhunderts existierte das so genannte *Key System*, ein Netz von Überlandstraßenbahnlinien in der gesamten East Bay-Region. Die meisten Linien gingen vom verkehrsreichen Fährhafen aus, der etwa 3,5 km westlich des Festlandes errichtet worden war und durch einen Damm und eine 2 km hölzerne Pfahlbrücke angebunden war. Nachdem die San Francisco - Oakland Bay Bridge im Jahr 1936 eröffnet worden war, begannen am 15. Januar 1939 spezielle Züge, die modernen Stadtbahnwagen ähnelten, auf dem Unterdeck der Brücke direkt von Oakland nach San Francisco zu verkehren. Die ersten Jahre wurde die ‚Bridge Railway' auch von Lokalbahnen der *Southern Pacific Interurban Electric* und der *Sacramento Northern* genutzt, die unter einer 1200-V-Oberleitung fuhren, während das Key System auf der Brücke und auf der Rampe zum San Francisco East Bay Terminal eine seitliche Stromschiene mit nur 600 V erhielt. Der Bahnbetrieb auf der Bay Bridge wurde am 20. April 1958 eingestellt, als die Vorplanungen für die Transbay Tube bereits liefen. Aus der Bahntrasse auf der Brücke wurden zusätzliche Fahrstreifen und aus der Endstelle in San Francisco wurde ein Busbahnhof, der später in Transbay Terminal umbenannt wurde. Dieser wurde schließlich im Jahr 2010 abgerissen, um den Bau einer neuen Verkehrsdrehscheibe mit einem unterirdischen Bahnhof für Caltrain und *California High Speed Rail* zu ermöglichen.

BART is not the first railway to cross the San Francisco Bay: from the early 20th century, the so-called Key System was an extensive network of interurban streetcar lines which used to radiate to the entire East Bay region from a busy ferry terminal built about 3.5 km west of the mainland, and connected to it by a causeway and a 2 km wooden trestle pier. With the San Francisco - Oakland Bay Bridge having been completed in 1936, specially designed trains, similar to high-floor light rail cars, started operating directly from Oakland to San Francisco on the lower deck of the bridge on 15 January 1939. For a few years, the 'Bridge Railway' was shared with suburban trains of Southern Pacific's Interurban Electric and the Sacramento Northern, which used a 1200 V overhead catenary, whereas the Key System only had 600 V and took power from a third rail on the bridge and loop access into San Francisco's East Bay Terminal. Rail operation across the Bay Bridge was discontinued on 20 April 1958, when planners were already designing the future Transbay Tube for BART. The trackbed on the bridge was converted into road lanes, and the San Francisco terminus became a bus station (later renamed Transbay Terminal) until it was demolished in 2010 to allow for the construction of a new transportation centre, which will include an underground station for Caltrain and California High Speed Rail.

gesamte Region entlang bekannter Bruchlinien liegen, mussten alle Tunnel erdbebensicher erstellt werden. Ein Beben der
Stärke 7,1 erschütterte die Region am 17. Oktober 1989, doch
der BART-Unterwassertunnel blieb intakt, während die parallele Bay Bridge schwer beschädigt wurde.

Alle U-Bahnhöfe wurden in offener Bauweise errichtet, so
dass durchweg geräumige Bahnsteighallen entstanden, außer
in der Innenstadt von San Francisco, wo die Decken eher
niedrig hängen, da auf der oberen Ebene der Bahnsteig der
Muni Metro unterzubringen war. Die beiden U-Bahnhöfe in der
Innenstadt von Oakland verfügen über drei Gleise, eins davon
auf der unteren Ebene für nach Süden verkehrende Züge. An
der Station 12th Street/Oakland City Center ist der Fahrplan
der einzelnen Linien Richtung Norden aufeinander abge-
stimmt, so dass man bequem umsteigen kann.

b◌ BART-Strecken

◉ Von Embarcadero bis Flughafen bzw. Millbrae
Nachdem die Züge durch die Transbay Tube San Francisco
erreichen, halten sie an vier Stationen entlang der zentralen
Market Street, eines der verkehrsreichsten ÖPNV-Korridore
der Welt, denn hier fahren elektrische Verkehrsmittel auf drei
Ebenen übereinander: BART auf Ebene -3, Muni Metro auf -2,
und über einem Zwischengeschoss schließlich Straßenbahnen
sowie Obusse an der Oberfläche. Embarcadero (spanisch
für Fähranleger) war ursprünglich als Station nur für die Muni
Metro geplant, wurde dann aber doch für beide Systeme
gebaut. Der durchschnittliche Abstand zwischen den vier innerstädtischen Stationen beträgt nur 600 m. Nach Civic Center
schwenkt die BART-Route nach Süden, während der Muni
Metro-Tunnel weiter nach Südwesten Richtung Castro führt.
BART folgt nun für etwa 3,5 km der Mission Street mit zwei U-
Bahnhöfen im Mission District, bevor sie Richtung Südwesten
unter den Fairmont Hills die Station Glen Park, den letzten voll-
ständig unterirdischen Bahnhof in San Francisco, erreicht. Die
Tunnelröhren enden auf halber Strecke zwischen Glen Park
und Balboa Park an der Ostseite der I-280. Die Station Balboa
Park liegt in einem offenen Einschnitt und ist ein wichtiger
Knotenpunkt in den südlichen Bezirken von San Francisco, wo
drei Muni Metro-Linien aus verschiedenen Richtungen enden.
Nach einem kurzen Tunnel südlich von Balboa Park endet die
ursprüngliche Strecke dann knapp hinter der Stadtgrenze in
Daly City im San Mateo County. 23 Jahre später wurde eine
Verlängerung meist neben der I-280 ohne Zwischenstation
bis Colma angefügt. Dies war die erste Stufe einer längeren
Erweiterung zum Flughafen SFO, die 2003 fertig gestellt
wurde. Obwohl diese Neubaustrecke weitgehend einer alten
Eisenbahntrasse folgt, wurde ein 8,6 km langer Tunnel in

tunnel remained intact, the parallel Bay Bridge was seriously
damaged.

All the underground stations were built by cut-and-cover,
resulting mostly in large spaces, except in downtown San
Francisco, where the ceilings were built lower to accommodate the Muni station on the upper level. The two stations in
downtown Oakland feature three tracks, with a single track
on the lower level for southbound trains. Northbound transfers are timed at 12th Street/Oakland City Center.

b◌ BART Routes

◉ Embarcadero to Airport & Millbrae
As trains enter San Francisco through the Transbay Tube,
they serve four stations along the central Market Street, one
of the busiest public transport corridors in the world. There
are three levels of electrified services — BART on level -3,
Muni Metro on -2, then a mezzanine, and finally heritage
streetcars as well as trolleybuses on the surface. Embarcadero (Spanish for ferry terminal) was initially planned to be
a Muni-only station, but was eventually fully built for both
systems. The average distance between the four downtown
stations is only 600 m. After Civic Center, the BART route
swings south, while the Muni tunnels continue southwest
towards the Castro. BART then follows Mission Street for
some 3.5 km, serving two underground stations in the Mission District before heading southwest under the Fairmont
Hills to Glen Park, the last fully underground station in San
Francisco. The tube tunnels end halfway between Glen Park
and Balboa Park stations on the east side of I-280. Balboa
Park station, lying in an open trench, is a major hub in the
southern districts of San Francisco, with three Muni Metro
lines converging from different directions. After a short
tunnel just south of Balboa Park, the original route ends just
across the city limit at Daly City in San Mateo County. 23
years later, a 1-station extension was added to Colma, running mostly alongside I-280. This was the first step towards
a longer extension to SFO Airport, which was completed in
2003. Although roughly following an old railway right-of-
way, an 8.6 km cut-and-cover tunnel was excavated under
the cities of South San Francisco and San Bruno, including
two underground stations. Some 500 m south of the tunnel
mouth, a large triangular junction was built for a branch to
the airport, while the main route continues south to Millbrae, where a station was laid out adjacent to the existing
Caltrain station. The distance from Embarcadero to the airport is 26 km and to Millbrae 27.4 km. The service patterns
have been changed several times since 2003, and Millbrae is
now directly served by red line trains from Richmond Mon-Fri

Embarcadero

Powell – neue, beleuchtete Beschilderung | *new illuminated signage*

18th St Mission – Zwischenebene | *mezzanine level*

offener Bauweise unter den Städten South San Francisco und San Bruno mit zwei U-Bahnhöfen errichtet. Etwa 500 m südlich des Tunnelmunds entstand ein großes Gleisdreieck für einen Abzweig zum Flughafen, während die Hauptstrecke weiter nach Süden bis Millbrae führt, wo eine Station neben dem bestehenden Caltrain-Bahnhof angelegt wurde. Die Entfernung von Embarcadero zum Flughafen beträgt 26 km und bis Millbrae 27,4 km. Nachdem das Betriebskonzept der beiden Äste seit 2003 mehrmals geändert wurde, wird Millbrae derzeit montags bis freitags bis 19:00 Uhr direkt von der roten Linie aus Richmond bedient, während sonst die gelbe Linie aus Pittsburg/Bay Point am Flughafen Kopf macht und nach Millbrae weiterfährt.

until 19:00, while at all other times, yellow line trains from Pittsburg/Bay Point reverse at the airport to continue to Millbrae.

● West Oakland to Richmond

At the eastern end of the Transbay Tube, trains reach the surface within the container port of Oakland. This area, as well as the north-south mainline railway and the adjacent I-880, is crossed on a viaduct that leads to the elevated West Oakland station. The line then descends before entering the Oakland tunnels, starting with a grade-separated triangular junction that features rather tight curves for what is otherwise a very generously laid-out system. The northern leg becomes bi-level, with two tracks leading north on the

Civic Center/UN Plaza

Civic Center/UN Plaza

South San Francisco

● Von West Oakland nach Richmond

Am östlichen Ende des Transbay-Tunnels erreichen die Züge das Tageslicht inmitten von Containern im Hafen von Oakland. Dieser Bereich sowie die Nord-Süd-Fernbahnstrecke und die parallel verlaufende I-880 werden auf einem Viadukt überquert, auf dem auch die Hochbahnstation West Oakland liegt. Die Strecke fällt dann langsam ab und verschwindet im Tunnel unter Oakland, wo sich gleich ein niveaufreies Gleisdreieck mit eher engen Radien für das sonst sehr großzügig trassierte System befindet. Der nördliche Ast wird doppelstöckig, mit zwei Gleisen Richtung Norden auf der oberen Ebene und einem nach Süden auf der unteren. Die beiden U-Bahnhöfe im Zentrum von Oakland, an der 12th und 19th Street unter dem Broadway, sind demnach ebenso doppelstöckig. Die

upper level, and one south on the lower. The two downtown Oakland stations, located at 12th and 19th Streets under Broadway, have the same bi-level configuration. The underground route then heads west, and, now widened to four tracks, reemerges to daylight as it enters the median of I-980. Located just north of the I-980 & I-580 interchange, MacArthur station provides southbound timed cross-platform rail transfers. The Richmond branch dives under the southbound road lanes, and continues through the northern parts of Oakland on an elevated structure in the middle of Martin Luther King Jr Way, but disappears underground as it enters Berkeley territory. The cut-and-cover tunnel lies under Adeline Street (with Ashby station) and Shattuck Avenue in downtown Berkeley, near the famous University. It then turns

19th St/Oakland

12th St/Oakland City Center

Downtown Berkeley

unterirdische Strecke schwenkt dann nach Westen und taucht schließlich viergleisig im Mittelstreifen der I-980 auf. Der Bahnhof MacArthur, gleich nördlich des Autobahnkreuzes I-980 & I-580, bietet planmäßiges Umsteigen am selben Bahnsteig in Fahrtrichtung Süden. Der Richmond-Ast taucht unter den westlichen Fahrspuren hindurch und verläuft dann als Hochbahn in der Mitte des Martin Luther King Jr Way durch die nördlichen Teile von Oakland, doch sobald das Stadtgebiet von Berkeley erreicht wird, verschwindet er im Untergrund. Der in offener Bauweise errichtete Tunnel liegt unter der Adeline Street (mit der Station Ashby) und der Shattuck Avenue im Zentrum von Berkeley, unweit der berühmten Universität. Die Trasse biegt dann stark nach Westen unter die Hearst Avenue Richtung North Berkeley ab, wo ein linearer Park, Teil des Ohlone Greenway, über dem BART-Tunnel angelegt wurde. Die Linie kommt nördlich der Hopkins Street wieder an die Oberfläche und folgt in etwa einer alten *Santa Fe*-Eisenbahntrasse, erst aufgeständert durch El Cerrito und dann teilweise ebenerdig bis Richmond (20,4 km ab der Verzweigung in Oakland), wo man zu den Amtrak-Zügen umsteigen kann.

● Von Oakland nach Pittsburg/Bay Point

Die Pittsburg-Linie fädelt nördlich von MacArthur aus und verläuft im Mittelstreifen der State Route 24. Nach 2,9 km und Halt in Rockridge verlässt sie die Autobahn und erreicht den 5,1 km langen Berkeley Hills Tunnel, der kurz vor Orinda wieder inmitten der Autobahn endet. Etwa 3,5 km östlich von Lafayette tauchen die Züge zur Umgehung eines Autobahndreiecks unter den nördlichen Fahrspuren hindurch, überqueren die I-680 auf einer Brücke und erreichen den Hochbahnhof Walnut Creek. Die Trasse verläuft dann weiter als Hochbahn oder auf einem Damm über Pleasant Hill/Contra Costa Centre bis zur ursprünglichen Endstation von 1973, dem Hochbahnhof Concord.

sharply west under Hearst Avenue towards North Berkeley station, where a linear park, part of the Ohlone Greenway, was laid out on top of the BART route. The line returns to the surface north of Hopkins Street and roughly follows an old Santa Fe railway alignment, running elevated through El Cerrito and then partly at grade into Richmond (20.4 km from the Oakland junction), where transfer is provided to Amtrak services.

● Oakland to Pittsburg/Bay Point

The Pittsburg line diverges just north of MacArthur station and runs in the median of State Route 24. After 2.9 km, having passed Rockridge, it leaves the centre of the freeway and enters the 5.1 km Berkeley Hills Tunnel, which ends just before arriving at Orinda station, again placed between the

Downtown Berkeley

West Oakland – Zug stadtauswärts mit C1-Wagen 369 an der Spitze | *outbound train with leading C1-car no. 369*

22 Jahre später wurde die Linie in zwei Stufen nach Nordosten verlängert. Der Abschnitt bis North Concord/Martinez umfasst nicht nur Viadukte, sondern auch Einschnitte unter dem Hickory Drive bzw. der 6th Street und der Olivera Road, wodurch die Schnellbahn weniger sichtbar wurde. Nördlich des ebenfalls im Einschnitt liegenden Bahnhofs North Concord/Martinez kommt BART auf den Mittelstreifen der State Route 4, wo sie bis zum heutigen Endpunkt Pittsburg/Bay Point bleibt, der 42,1 km von MacArthur entfernt liegt.

Eine 16 km lange Erweiterung befindet sich im Bau, jedoch in abgespeckter Form: Die als ‚eBART' (East Contra Costa BART Extension) bezeichnete Verlängerung umfasst zwei Stationen und soll mit Dieseltriebwagen betrieben werden. In Pittsburg/Bay Point kann man am selben Bahnsteig umsteigen. eBART entsteht zusammen mit dem Ausbau des Highway 4 und soll im Jahr 2016 eröffnet werden. Wenn die Fahrgastzahlen wachsen, kann die Strecke ausgebaut und vollständig an das BART-Netz angeschlossen werden.

● Von Oakland nach Fremont bzw. Dublin

Ausgehend vom Gleisdreieck in der Innenstadt von Oakland verläuft der Fremont-Ast nur ca. 1,5 km unterirdisch durch Lake Merritt (mit der BART-Leitstelle über dem U-Bahnhof), bevor er südlich der 5th Avenue an der Ostseite der Fernbahn auftaucht. An der 18th Avenue beginnt eine Hochbahnstrecke, die nach Süden bis Bay Fair reicht und etwa einen Block östlich der Eisenbahnlinie entlang der San Leandro Street und des San Leandro Boulevard verläuft. Die Station Coliseum befindet sich demnach auch einen Block östlich des gleichnamigen Amtrak-Bahnhofs. Ein derzeit im Bau befindlicher Peoplemover wird beide Stationen mit dem Flughafen von Oakland verbinden. Ab etwa halber Strecke zwischen Fruitvale und Coliseum verläuft ein Gütergleis neben der BART-Trasse,

freeway lanes. Some 3.5 km east of Lafayette station, the trains dive under the westbound road lanes to avoid the upcoming freeway junction, fly over I-680, and enter the elevated Walnut Creek station. They continue on an elevated structure or an embankment through Pleasant Hill/Contra Costa Centre to reach the original 1973 elevated terminus at Concord. 22 years later, the line was extended further northeast in two stages. The section to North Concord/Martinez includes not only viaducts, but also trenches to pass under Hickory Drive/6th St and Olivera Road, a type of grade-separation with less visual impact. Just north of North Concord/Martinez, a station also in a trench, the route enters the median of State Route 4 to continue to the present terminus at Pittsburg/Bay Point, 42.1 km from MacArthur.

A 16 km extension is now under construction, although built to reduced standards: dubbed 'eBART' (East Contra Costa BART Extension), the 2-station extension will be served by diesel multiple units. The shuttle will have cross-platform interchange at Pittsburg/Bay Point, with timed transfers. It is being built together with a Highway 4 widening project and is scheduled to open in 2016. If ridership grows, the eBart extension can be upgraded and fully integrated into the BART system.

● Oakland to Fremont & Dublin

Starting from the triangular junction in downtown Oakland, the Fremont branch only runs underground for about 1.5 km, going through Lake Merritt station (with the BART control centre above) before surfacing south of 5th Avenue on the east side of the mainline railway. At 18th Avenue, it climbs onto an elevated structure on which it remains all the way south to Bay Fair, running about one block east of the railway along San Leandro Street and San Leandro Boulevard. At

Fremont – bislang die südlichste Station | *so far the southernmost station*

Fruitvale – typische Hochbahnstrecke | *typical elevated route*

jedoch stets auf Straßenebene, und schließt die vielen Unternehmen in dieser Gegend an das Bahnnetz an. Es führt fast bis Fremont, da BART eigentlich einer Trasse der alten *Western Pacific Railroad* folgt. Nach der kreuzungsfreien Verzweigung südlich von Bay Fair geht die BART-Strecke Richtung Süden bis Hayward wieder in Hochlage, danach ist sie mit Ausnahme eines 1 km langen Viadukts nördlich von Union City zur Überquerung des Gütergleises entweder ebenerdig oder auf einem Damm bis zur Endstation in Fremont. Fremont liegt 38,1 km vom Abzweig in Oakland entfernt.

Der 20 km lange Abzweig nach Dublin wurde 1997 in Betrieb genommen. Er verläuft im Mittelstreifen der I-238, die wenig später in die I-580 mündet, welche durch die Hügel führt, die die East Bay vom Tri-Valley im östlichen Alameda County trennen. Ursprünglich fuhren die Züge 16,3 km nonstop von Castro Valley nach Dublin/Pleasanton, bis im Jahr 2011 eine Zwischenstation eingefügt wurde. Eine 8,5 km lange Verlängerung entlang des gleichen Korridors bis zur Isabel Avenue in Livermore ist geplant.

● BART-Verlängerung nach San Jose (Silicon Valley)
Der erste 7,5 km lange Abschnitt einer lange geplanten Erweiterung von Fremont aus ins Santa Clara County befindet sich seit dem Frühjahr 2010 im Bau. Es wird zunächst nur eine Station, Warm Springs/South Fremont, geben, später kann eine Zwischenstation in Irvington südlich des Washington Boulevard eingefügt werden. Von Fremont ausgehend wird die Linie für ca. 1,5 km unterirdisch durch den Fremont Central Park und durch den Lake Elizabeth verlaufen, von dem ein Teil vorübergehend trockengelegt wurde, um den Tunnel in offener Bauweise zu errichten. Unmittelbar östlich des Sees erreicht die Trasse die bestehende *Union Pacific*-Gütereisenbahn und folgt dieser ebenerdig an der Ostseite bis nach San Jose. Die Station Warm Springs/South Fremont am South Grimmer Boulevard wird voraussichtlich Ende 2015 eröffnet.

Der Bau der nächsten Etappe von Warm Springs bis Berryessa im Nordosten von San Jose begann im Frühjahr 2012 mit einem Fertigstellungstermin im Jahr 2018. Die Strecke durch Milpitas verläuft weiter entlang des UP-Bahnkorridors, wobei die BART-Trasse eine Mischung aus ebenerdigen, Einschnitt- und Viaduktabschnitten aufweisen wird. Die Zwischenstation Milpitas wird im Einschnitt liegen und ein Umsteigen zur Stadtbahn von San Jose (Station Montague) bieten, während der Endbahnhof Berryessa in Hochlage zwischen der Berryessa und der Mabury Road errichtet wird (siehe S. 75). Das als „BART Silicon Valley" bezeichnete Projekt soll die Schnellbahn später unterirdisch durch die Innenstadt von San Jose bis zum Caltrain/Amtrak-Bahnhof in Santa Clara bringen.

Coliseum, the Amtrak station of the same name is thus also one block west. A people mover is now under construction to link both stations to Oakland International Airport. From about halfway between Fruitvale and Coliseum, a freight track that serves many businesses in the area runs alongside the BART line, though it remains at street level. It almost reaches Fremont, as BART actually follows an old Western Pacific Railroad route. After the grade-separated junction south of Bay Fair, the line returns to an elevated structure as it heads south to Hayward, but then remains at ground level or on embankments down to the Fremont terminus, except for a 1 km viaduct just north of Union City station, where it crosses the aforementioned freight track. Fremont is 38.1 km from the Oakland junction.

The 20 km Dublin branch was added in 1997. It runs within the median strip of I-238, which soon merges with I-580 on its way through the hills which separate the East Bay from the Tri-Valley region in eastern Alameda County. Initially, a 16.3 km nonstop run from Castro Valley to Dublin/Pleasanton, an intermediate station was added in 2011. An 8.5 km extension along the same corridor to Isabel Avenue in Livermore is planned.

● BART Extension to San Jose (Silicon Valley)
The first 7.5 km section of a long-planned extension from Fremont into Santa Clara County has been under construction since spring 2010. There will initially be only one station, Warm Springs/South Fremont, but with an option for a future intermediate station at Irvington, south of Washington Boulevard. Leaving Fremont, the line will go underground through Fremont Central Park for about 1.5 km, cutting through Lake Elizabeth, a part of which was temporarily drained to allow open-pit construction. Just east of the lake, the route joins the existing UP rail corridor, which it follows at grade on its eastern side down into San Jose. Warm Springs/South Fremont station at South Grimmer Boulevard is scheduled to open in late 2015.

The construction of the next stage from Warm Springs to Berryessa in northeastern San Jose began in spring 2012 for completion in 2018. The route will continue through Milpitas along the UP rail corridor. The alignment is a mix of at-grade, open cut and aerial structures, with the intermediate Milpitas station in a trench providing interchange with San Jose's light rail system (Montague station), and the elevated Berryessa terminus being built between Berryessa and Mabury Roads (see p. 75). 'BART Silicon Valley' will ultimately run underground through downtown San Jose to terminate at Santa Clara Caltrain/Amtrak station.

West Dublin/Pleasanton – neuester BART-Bahnhof von 2011 | *newest BART station from 2011*

SFO AirTrain ist ein kostenloser, voll automatisierter People-mover am internationalen Flughafen von San Francisco. Er verkehrt 24 Stunden am Tag, wobei die Red Line als Ringlinie im Uhrzeigersinn in 9 Minuten die BART-Station, alle Terminals sowie die Terminal-Parkhäuser miteinander verbindet, während die Blue Line in entgegengesetzter Richtung fährt und zusätzlich noch das Mietwagen-Center anschließt (19 Minuten für einen Umlauf mit Halt an allen 9 Stationen).

Der AirTrain wurde von Bombardier gebaut und am 24. Februar 2003 eröffnet. Er wird mit 38 gummibereiften, durch eine mittlere Führungsschiene geleiteten Innovia APM 100-Wagen betrieben. Die Züge werden mit CITYFLO 650-Technologie gesteuert. Das 10 km lange System wird von Bombardier gewartet und betrieben.

SFO AirTrain is a free, fully automated people mover at the San Francisco International Airport. Operating 24 hours a day, the Red Line covers its clockwise circuit in 9 minutes, serving BART, all the terminals and the terminal parking garages, whereas the Blue Line loops in the opposite direction and in addition goes to the rental car center (thus requiring 19 minutes for the full circuit, stopping at all 9 stations).

AirTrain was built by Bombardier and opened on 24 February 2003. It uses 38 Innovia APM 100 cars, which are rubber-tyred and steered by a central guideway. The trains are controlled by CITYFLO 650 technology. The 10 km system is operated and maintained by Bombardier.

SFO AirTrain (*Photo © Bombardier*)

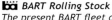

MacArthur – modernisierter A-Wagen links, C-Wagen rechts | *modernised A-car on the left, C-car on the right*

ぬ BART-Fahrzeuge

Die aktuelle BART-Flotte besteht aus 669 Fahrzeugen dreier verschiedener Typen, die im selben Zugverband verkehren können. BART verwendet eine Spurweite von 1676 mm (üblich in Indien, Pakistan, Argentinien und Chile) sowie eine seitliche Stromschiene mit 1000 V Gleichstrom und wurde von Anfang an ausschließlich im ATO-Modus (Automatic Train Operation) betrieben, wobei sich die Aufgaben des Fahrers auf die allgemeine Betriebsüberwachung und Abfertigung in den Bahnhöfen beschränken. Die Strecken sind nicht mit zusätzlichen Streckensignalen ausgestattet, weshalb die Züge im Normalbetrieb nicht manuell gefahren werden können. Die Züge verkehren in verschiedenen Zuglängen, von 3- bis 4-Wagen-Zügen während der Schwachlastzeiten bis hin zu 8- bis 10-Wagen-Zügen (max. 216 m) während der Hauptverkehrszeiten. Sie erreichen eine Höchstgeschwindigkeit von 128 km/h.

● Die erste Bestellung ging im Juli 1969 an Rohr Industries in San Diego und umfasste 137 **A-Wagen** (Serie 100 & 200) mit und 303 **B-Wagen** (Serie 500 bis 700) ohne Führerstand; nach 10 Prototypen wurden die Serienfahrzeuge zwischen 1971 und 1974 ausgeliefert. Mit 22,86 m sind die A-Wagen 1,5 m länger als die B-Wagen, da sie zusätzlich jene stromlinienförmige Glasfaser-Fahrerkabine besitzen, die BART ihr futuristisches Aussehen gab. Dieses aerodynamische Element stammt aus dem Flugzeugbau, bis dahin das Hauptaufgabengebiet von Rohr Industries. Alle Wagen sind 3,20 m breit. Die B-Wagen konnten nur zwischen A-Wagen positioniert werden, aber da die A-Wagen nur an ihren flachen Enden gekuppelt werden können, war eine Kürzung oder Verlängerung eines Zuges nur umständlich im Betriebshof möglich. Die breiten, freischweben-

ぬ BART Rolling Stock

The present BART fleet of 669 cars includes three different types, which can run within the same trainset. BART uses a track gauge of 1676 mm (common in India, Pakistan, Argentina and Chile), third-rail power supply with 1000 V dc, and has exclusively been operated in ATO (automatic train operation) mode from the beginning, with the driver's duties limited to general supervision and dispatching in stations. The lines are not equipped with additional wayside signals; therefore, the trains cannot be driven manually in normal service. Trains operate in different consists, from 3 to 4-car trains during off-peak to 8 to 10-car trains (max. 216 m) during rush hour. They reach a maximum speed of 128 km/h.

● *The initial fleet ordered from Rohr Industries in San Diego in July 1969 consisted of 137 A-cars (100 & 200 series) with driver's cabs and 303 B-cars (500 to 700-series) without driver's cabs; after testing 10 prototype cars, the serial-production cars were delivered between 1971 and 1974. At 22.86 m, the A-cars are 1.5 m longer than the B-cars, as they include the streamlined fibreglass driver's cab which gave BART its futuristic look. This aerodynamic feature was inspired by aircraft design, the field in which Rohr Industries had been active until then. All cars are 3.20 m wide. The B-cars can only be positioned between A-cars, but as the A-cars can only be coupled at their flat end, changing the length of a train was only possible in the yard and was rather cumbersome. The large, cantilevered and upholstered seats together with the carpeted floors gave them a living room-like feel. Between 1995 and 2000, many of the original cars were refurbished, rebuilt and given the prefix 1. There are*

Innenraum des Wagens 1821 | *Inside car no. 1821*

Neue Plastiksitzbezüge im Tw 1690 | *New vinyl seat covers in car no. 1690*

Pittsburg/Bay Point – kuppelbereiter C1-Wagen 312
– *C1-car no. 312 ready to be coupled*

Walnut Creek – B-Wagen können nur zwischen A- oder C-Wagen fahren.
– *B-cars can only run between A or C-cars.*

den und gepolsterten Sitze zusammen mit dem Teppichboden verliehen den Wagen eine gewisse Wohnzimmer-Atmosphäre. Zwischen 1995 und 2000 wurden viele der ursprünglichen Wagen renoviert und umgebaut, sie tragen jetzt die vorangestellte Ziffer 1. Heute sind 59 A-Wagen und 380 B-Wagen in Betrieb, nachdem einige A-Wagen in B-Wagen umgewandelt worden sind (Serie 1800/1900).

● Um den Fuhrpark zu vergrößern und eine flexiblere Zugbildung zu ermöglichen, wurden 150 **C-Wagen** von Alstom in Frankreich für die Lieferung zwischen 1988 und 1990 bestellt. Sie verfügen zwar über eine Fahrerkabine, aber ohne die stromlinienförmige Front. Stattdessen haben sie eine mittige Tür, die in einen Übergang verwandelt werden kann, wenn das Fahrzeug mit einem anderen gekuppelt wird. Die C-Wagen können somit in beliebiger Position innerhalb eines Zugverbands eingesetzt werden. Ansonsten sind sie den B-Wagen in den Ausmaßen ähnlich und von 300 bis 450 nummeriert.

Die nächste, 80 Fahrzeuge umfassende Bestellung ging 1992 an das amerikanische Unternehmen Morrison-Knudson: Die C2-Wagen (Serie 2500) sind weitgehend identisch mit dem Vorgängertyp, der jetzt als C1 klassifiziert wird.

● Um die mittlerweile bis zu 40 Jahre alten Wagen zu ersetzen, erhielt Bombardier im Mai 2012 den Auftrag zum Bau von insgesamt 410 Wagen zur Auslieferung ab 2017. Die Gesamtzahl könnte sich auf 775 Neuwagen erhöhen. Sie sind für eine einfache Zugteilung zwecks Flügelung außerhalb der Spitzenzeiten konzipiert. Sie haben auf jeder Seite drei Türen anstelle von bisher zwei und zeigen neben dem Fahrtziel auch die Linienfarbe an. Sie werden einen blau-weißen Innenraum mit typischerer Schnellbahnbestuhlung aufweisen.

Für die BART-Züge gibt es vier Betriebshöfe: nördlich von Richmond, südlich von Concord, zwischen South Hayward und Union City sowie an der Station Colma.

now 59 A-cars and 380 B-cars in service, after some A-cars were converted to B-cars (1800/1900 series)

● To increase the fleet and achieve a more flexible train formation, 150 **C-cars** were ordered from Alstom of France for delivery between 1988 and 1990. They feature a driver's cab but without the streamlined front, and instead have a centre door which can be converted into a gangway when the car is coupled to another vehicle. The C-cars can thus be placed in any position within a given trainset. Otherwise, they are similar to the B-cars in size and are numbered 300 to 450.

Another order was placed with the American company Morrison-Knudson in 1992 for 80 vehicles referred to as C2-cars (2500-series), as they are largely identical to the previous class, now known as type C1.

● To replace the now 40-year old cars, an order for a total of 410 cars was signed with Bombardier in May 2012 for delivery starting in 2017. The total number could be increased to 775 new cars. They will be designed for easy splitting to allow each section of a train to continue in a different direction during off-peak hours. They will have three doors on each side instead of two on the present cars, and will also indicate the line colour next to the destination. They will feature a blue-and-white interior with more typical rapid transit-like seating.

For the BART rolling stock there are four maintenance facilities: north of Richmond; south of Concord; between South Hayward and Union City; and next to Colma station.

Vorschlag für die Innenraumgestaltung sowie das äußere Erscheinungsbild der neuen Bombardier-Züge nach Stand 03/2012
– *Proposal for the interior design and the outside appearance of the new Bombardier cars, as of 03/2012.*

BART

Caltrain-Endbahnhof in San Francisco aus dem Jahr 1976, als die SP-Strecke von der Ecke 3rd & Townsend zurückgezogen wurde.
San Francisco's Caltrain Depot from 1976, when the SP line was pulled back from 3rd & Townsend.

CALTRAIN

Caltrain verbindet San Francisco mit dem Silicon Valley und erschließt Redwood City in San Mateo County sowie Palo Alto (Heimat der renommierten Stanford University), Mountain View und San Jose im Santa Clara County. Da die Züge in San Francisco mindestens stündlich von 5:00 Uhr bis Mitternacht abfahren (bis zu fünf Züge pro Stunde während der Hauptverkehrszeiten), kann man Caltrain im Gegensatz zu typischen „Commuter Railways" auch als Vorortbahn bezeichnen. Außerhalb der Hauptverkehrszeiten halten die Züge an allen Stationen (*Local*), aber während der Spitzenzeiten verkehren sie als Semi-Express (*Limited*) oder Express (*Baby Bullet*) mit Halt jeweils nur an bestimmten Stationen. Von 46 Zügen täglich fahren 20 von San Jose Diridon weiter bis Tamien und drei bis Gilroy (nur Hauptlastrichtung). Selbst an Wochenenden herrscht ein Stundentakt. Eine Fahrt von San Francisco bis San Jose Diridon (76 km) dauert mit einem *Local* 90 Minuten, mit einem Express-Zug hingegen nur 60 Minuten.

Bislang wird Caltrain mit Doppelstock-Wendezügen auf einer nicht elektrifizierten zweigleisigen Strecke betrieben, aber eine Streckenmodernisierung und Elektrifizierung in Verbindung mit dem *California High Speed Rail*-Projekt ist bereits beschlossen. Caltrain untersteht dem *Peninsula Corridor Joint Powers Board* (PCJPB), einer gemeinsamen Behörde der drei Counties, durch die die Strecke führt, die im Jahr 1863 von der *Southern Pacific* (SP) gebaut wurde. SP stellte den Personenverkehr auf dieser Strecke zwar nie ein, aber als sie dazu entschlossen war, besorgte *Caltrans* (Kaliforniens Verkehrsministerium) neues Rollmaterial und führte im Jahr 1985 die heutige Marke ‚Caltrain' ein. Nach der Bildung des PCJPB 1987 erwarb dieses 1991 die Bahntrasse und beauftragte Amtrak mit dem Betrieb, den jedoch im Mai 2012 *TransitAmerica Services Inc.* übernahm. Seit 2003 besteht in Millbrae eine Umsteigemöglichkeit zwischen Caltrain und BART. In Zukunft werden zwischen den beiden Systemen in San Jose und Santa Clara weitere Knotenpunkte entstehen.

Im Zuge des Hochgeschwindigkeitsprojekts wird Caltrain unterirdisch von der heutigen Endstation in San Francisco zum zukünftigen Transbay Transit Center verlängert werden.

Caltrain links San Francisco to Silicon Valley, serving Redwood City in San Mateo County, and Palo Alto (home to the renowned Stanford University), Mountain View and San Jose in Santa Clara County. With trains departing from San Francisco's Caltrain Depot at least hourly from 05:00 to midnight (with up to five trains an hour during rush hour), Caltrain is more a suburban than a commuter railway. During off-peak hours, trains stop at all stations (Local), but during rush hour, they run semi-express (Limited) or express (Baby Bullet), calling only at selected stations. Of the 46 daily trains, 20 continue from San Jose Diridon to Tamien, and three to Gilroy (peak direction only). On weekends, there is an hourly service, too. A trip from San Francisco to San Jose Diridon (76 km) on a local train takes 90 minutes, and on an express only 60 minutes.

At present, Caltrain operates push-pull trains with double-deck carriages on a non-electrified double-track line, but it has been decided to upgrade and electrify the route in conjunction with the California High Speed Rail project. Caltrain is governed by the Peninsula Corridor Joint Powers Board (PCJPB), which depends on the three counties the line, built by the Southern Pacific (SP) in 1863, runs through. SP never stopped running passenger trains on the line, but when it intended to, Caltrans (California's transport department) purchased new rolling stock and introduced the 'Caltrain' brand in 1985. Founded in 1987, the PCJPB purchased the right-of-way in 1991 and contracted Amtrak to be the day-to-day operator, but since May 2012, TransitAmerica Services, Inc. has operated the service. Since 2003, interchange between Caltrain and BART has been available at Millbrae. In the future, other interchanges between the two systems will be created in San Jose and Santa Clara.

In San Francisco, Caltrain will be extended underground from its present terminus to the future Transbay Transit Center, sharing tracks with California's high speed trains.

Mit der Bezeichnung **SMART** für *Sonoma-Marin Area Rail Transit* ist in den Counties nördlich von San Francisco eine *Sprinter*-ähnliche Lokalbahn von Larkspur Landing (Fährverbindung nach San Francisco) nach Cloverdale geplant. Die erste Phase (61 km von Santa Rosa bis San Rafael – 9 Stationen) soll 2016 eröffnet werden.

*Dubbed **SMART** for Sonoma-Marin Area Rail Transit, a Sprinter-like regional rail line is planned in the counties north of San Francisco from Larkspur Landing (ferry connection to San Francisco) to Cloverdale, with an initial 61 km segment between Santa Rosa and downtown San Rafael (9 stations) scheduled to open by 2016.*

Millbrae – Gemeinschaftsbahnhof mit BART | *Interchange with BART*

Mountain View

Caltrain – Nippon Sharyo *'Gallery Car'*

San Francisco Caltrain Depot

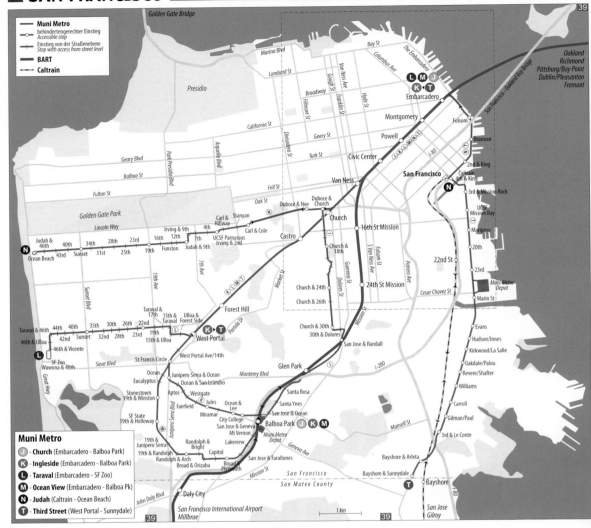

Muni Metro
behindertengerechter Einstieg
Accessible stop
Einstieg von der Straßenebene
Stop with access from street level
BART
Caltrain

Muni Metro
- **J** - **Church** (Embarcadero - Balboa Park)
- **K** - **Ingleside** (Embarcadero - Balboa Park)
- **L** - **Taraval** (Embarcadero - SF Zoo)
- **M** - **Ocean View** (Embarcadero - Balboa Pk)
- **N** - **Judah** (Caltrain - Ocean Beach)
- **T** - **Third Street** (West Portal - Sunnydale)

SAN FRANCISCO, CA

Die eigentliche Stadt San Francisco umfasst den Großteil des Gebiets, das auf der Karte oben abgebildet ist. Sie hat eine Fläche von nur 121,4 km² und 805.000 Einwohner. Die Stadt ist bekannt für ihre hügelige Topographie, wobei der höchste Punkt in der Gegend der Twin Peaks 283 m über dem Meeresspiegel liegt. Sie ist daher nicht nur der ideale Ort für die beliebten Cable Cars, sondern auch für Obusse, Straßenbahnen und Stadtbahnen, die die regionalen Schienenverkehrsmittel BART und Caltrain ergänzen. Innerhalb von San Francisco fungiert BART wie eine U-Bahn-Linie mit Zügen alle paar Minuten und kurzen Stationsabständen. Außer BART und Caltrain wird der gesamte städtische Nahverkehr durch Muni, die *San Francisco Municipal Transportation Agency* (SFMTA), abgewickelt. Einzelfahrten mit Umsteigemöglichkeit kosten 2,00 $, auch zahlbar mit Clipper-Smartcards. Eine einzelne Fahrt mit dem Cable Cars kostet jedoch 6,00 $! Für Besucher sind im Tourist Office neben der Station Powell praktische ‚MUNI Visitor Passports' für 1, 3 oder 7 Tage erhältlich, die 14 $, 21 $ bzw. 27 $ (einschließlich Cable Cars!) kosten.

The City of San Francisco proper comprises most of what is shown on the map above, a land area of just 121.4 km2 with a population of 805,000. The city is well known for its hilly topography, with a maximum elevation of 283 m in the Twin Peaks area, making it the ideal location not only for the popular cable cars, but also for trolleybuses, streetcars and light rail, which complement the regional rail services like BART and Caltrain. Within San Francisco, BART operates like a metro line with trains every few minutes and relatively closely spaced stations. Except for BART and Caltrain, all urban transport is provided by Muni, the 'San Francisco Municipal Transportation Agency' (SFMTA). Cash fares (including transfers) are $2.00, also payable with Clipper smartcards. A single ride on a cable car, however, costs $6.00! For tourists, easy-to-use MUNI Visitor Passports are available at the Tourist Office next to Powell station, priced at $14, $21 and $27 for 1, 3 or 7 days respectively (including cable cars!).

San Francisco Bay

Jefferson & Taylor
Jefferson & Powell
Jefferson & The Embarcadero
Jones & Beach
Beach & Mason
Hyde & Beach
Beach & Stockton
North Point St
The Embarcadero & Bay
Bay St
Taylor & Bay
Chestnut
Chestnut St
Lombard St
Greenwich St
Greenwich
Filbert St
Green
Union St
Green St
Broadway
Vallejo St
Broadway
Pacific Ave
Jackson St
The Embarcadero & Washington
Washington St
Clay St
(Chinatown)
Ferry Terminal/Market
Sacramento St
California & Drumm
Ferry Plaza (Don Chee Way & Steuart)
California St
Pine St
Main & Drumm
Embarcadero
Bush St
1st & Battery
Folsom
Sutter St
2nd & Montgomery
Temporary
Transbay Terminal
Post St
3rd &
Kearny/Geary
Montgomery
Geary St
4th & Stockton
(Transbay Transit Center)
(Union Sq./
Market St.)
Ellis
5th & Powell
Brannan
Powell
(Yerba Buena/
Moscone)
Eddy St
2nd & King
Turk St
Golden Gate Ave
McAllister St
(4th & Brannan)
Civic Center
San Francisco
Caltrain
4th & King
Van Ness
Mission Rock
UCSF
Mission Bay
Duboce & Church
Duboce & Noe
14th & Church
Church
Mariposa
15th & Sanchez
16th & Noe
16th St Mission
20th St
Castro
17th & Castro
22nd St
23rd St

Balboa Park
S.F. Zoo
Balboa Park

24th St Mission

Marin St

Streetcar (Straßenbahn)
Cable Car
Trolleybus (Obus)
Muni Metro
behindertengerechter Einstieg
Accessible stop
Einstieg von der Straßenebene
Stop with access from street level
BART
Caltrain
① Cable Car Depot & Museum
② Streetcar Museum

Muni Metro
Depot

Sunnydale

Balboa Park

1 km

Ⓝ Ⓣ **Brannan & The Embarcadero** + San Francisco - Oakland Bay Bridge

ᨏᨏᨏᨏ MUNI METRO

Das Muni Metro-Netz besteht aus sechs Linien, die mit einem Buchstaben und einer Straße bzw. einem Stadtteil, durch den sie verlaufen, bezeichnet werden. Das Herzstück des Netzes ist ein Tunnel entlang der Market Street, der von allen Linien genutzt wird. Die Linien K und T werden gemeinsam als eine durchgehende Linie betrieben.

Die Muni Metro kann als ‚Premetro' klassifiziert werden. Sie weist eine große Vielfalt an Trassierungen auf:
1) U-Bahn mit richtigen Metro-Stationen (mit 100 m langen und 85 cm hohen Bahnsteigen) und automatischem Zugbetrieb;
2) Stadtbahntrassen wie in Los Angeles auf der Linie T nach Sunnydale: meist auf eigenem Gleiskörper, aber mit zahlreichen Bahnübergängen, und mit behindertengerechten Hochbahnsteigen an allen Stationen;
3) kurze abgetrennte Trassen auf den Westästen, aber ohne richtige Stationen, mit Ausnahme von zweien auf der Linie M;
4) konventionelle straßenbündige Abschnitte im Mischbetrieb mit dem Autoverkehr und Einstieg von der Straße an zahlreichen, kaum als solche erkennbaren Haltestellen.

Wegen der vielen Haltestellen mit Einstieg von der Straße bzw. von Niedrigbahnsteigen sind die Hochflurbahnen mit absenkbaren Stufen ausgestattet. Einige Stationen haben für einen behindertengerechten Einstieg kurze Hochbahnsteige, die sich manchmal in einiger Entfernung befinden, so dass bei Bedarf ein zusätzlicher Halt erforderlich ist.

Die Muni Metro verkehrt von 5:00 bis 1:00 Uhr, an Wochentagen meist alle 10 Minuten (mit einigen zusätzlichen HVZ-Zügen) und am Wochenende je nach Linie alle 10-15 Minuten, so dass theoretisch alle 2 Minuten ein Zug auf dem gemeinsamen unterirdischen Abschnitt rollt.

The Muni Metro system consists of six lines, each identified by a letter and a street or neighbourhood they run through. The centrepiece of the network is a tunnel along Market Street which is shared by all the lines. The K and T lines are operated jointly as a single line.

Muni Metro can be classified as a 'premetro' and features a variety of alignments:
1) Subway with full-scale metro stations (100 m long and 85 cm high platforms) and automatic train operation;
2) L.A.-style light rail alignment on the T line to Sunnydale: mostly on a reserved right-of-way but with several level crossings, and fully accessible high platforms at all stations;
3) Short dedicated lanes on the western branches, without proper stations, except for two on the M line;
4) Conventional on-street running mixed with road traffic and boarding from street level, with numerous barely identifiable stops.

Due to the many street-level or low-platform stops, the high-floor trains are equipped with movable steps, which are lowered on the western branches. Some stops have mini-high platforms (sometimes located some distance from the regular stop and requiring an additional halt) to allow boarding for people with restricted mobility.

Muni Metro trains run from 05:00 to 01:00, generally every 10 minutes on weekdays (with some extra peak-hour trains) and every 10-15 minutes on weekends, depending on the line, and thus, in theory, there is a train every 2 minutes on the shared underground section.

ⅿⓤⓝⓘ Entwicklung der Municipal Railway

San Francisco gehört zu den wenigen Städten in den USA, die die alte Straßenbahn nicht vollständig aufgegeben hatten (die anderen sind Philadelphia, Cleveland, Newark, Pittsburgh, Boston und New Orleans), sondern diese zu einer Art Stadtbahn weiterentwickelt haben.

Zu Beginn des 20. Jahrhunderts war die Innenstadt von San Francisco die Domäne der privat betriebenen Kabelstraßenbahnen (siehe S. 70), von denen die meisten allmählich in den *United Railroads* (URR) aufgingen. Eine Elektrifizierung mit Oberleitungen wurde aus ästhetischen Gründen vor allem entlang der Market Street abgelehnt, stattdessen wurde ein Unterleitungssystem für die nicht so steilen Strecken wie jene entlang der Geary Street vorgeschlagen. Die Sachlage änderte sich am 18. April 1906, als ein verheerendes Erdbeben und ein anschließender Großbrand viele Strecken und Fahrzeuge zerstörte und eine gründliche Rekonstruktion ohnehin erforderlich wurde. Daraufhin wurden viele Kabelbahnen auf Oberleitungsbetrieb umgestellt. Die Stadtregierung hatte erfolglos versucht, die Straßenbahnen in öffentliches Eigentum zu überführen, bis sie schließlich am 28. Dezember 1912 die ersten eigenen Linien der *Municipal Railway* auf der Geary Street von Kearney & Market Street bis zur 33rd Avenue (Linie B) und einen Abzweig auf der 10th Avenue zum Golden Gate Park (Linie A) in Betrieb nahm. Die Strecke hatte eine maximale Steigung von 9,2%. Sechs Monate später wurde der Betrieb an beiden Enden verlängert und so eine durchgehende Linie vom Fährhafen bis zum Pazifikstrand geschaffen. Auf der unteren Market Street ersetzte die städtische Straßenbahn die letzten Pferdebahnen und teilte sich anfangs die Gleise mit den *United Railroads* auf der viergleisigen Strecke hinunter zu den Fähren.

Anlässlich der für 1915 geplanten ‚Panama-Pacific Exposition‘ wuchs das Netz der städtischen Straßenbahn in den folgenden Jahren sehr rasant, entweder durch den Kauf und die Modernisierung privater Strecken oder durch den Ausbau des eigenen Netzes. Die meisten Linien verliefen radial, mit Ausnahme der Linie H auf der Van Ness und Potrero Avenue, der einzigen Tangentiallinie. Eine der neuen Routen, die das Ausstellungsgelände erschließen sollten, war die Linie F,

Nur die gelb gestrichene Fläche markiert die Stadtbahnhaltestelle.
Only the area painted yellow marks the light rail stop.

ⅿⓤⓝⓘ History of the Municipal Railway

San Francisco was one of the few cities in the U.S. that did not completely abandon its first-generation streetcar system (the others being Philadelphia, Cleveland, Newark, Pittsburgh, Boston and New Orleans), but eventually upgraded it into something like a light railway.

At the beginning of the 20th century, San Francisco's central area was the domain of cable-hauled, privately operated streetcars (see p. 70), most of which gradually merged as the 'United Railroads'. Electrification with overhead wires was opposed for aesthetic reasons, especially along Market Street, and an underground electrical conduit system was instead proposed for the less steep routes like that along Geary Street. Things changed on 18 April 1906, when a devastating earthquake and subsequent fire destroyed many routes and vehicles. As a thorough reconstruction was then required anyway, many lines were converted from cable to overhead catenary operation. The city government had taken steps towards bringing the streetcars into public ownership, but these efforts remained unsuccessful. Eventually, on 28 December 1912, the first streetcars of the 'Municipal Railway' began running on Geary Street from Kearney & Market Streets to 33rd Avenue (line B), with a branch on 10th Avenue down to Golden Gate Park (line A). It had a maximum gradient of 9.2%. Six months later, service was extended at both ends, creating a through line from the Ferry Building to the Pacific Ocean. On lower Market Street, the Municipal Railway replaced the last horse-drawn cars and initially shared tracks with United Railroads on their 4-track route down to the ferries.

In anticipation of the Panama-Pacific Exposition planned for 1915, the Municipal Railway expanded rapidly over the following years, either by purchasing and upgrading private lines or by building completely new routes, most of them radial. The exception was the H line, Muni's only crosstown line, which ran along Van Ness and Potrero Avenues. One of the new routes to serve the Exposition area, the F line, required the construction of the 278 m Stockton Street Tunnel, which opened on 28 December 1914 and is used today by trolleybuses (the Central Subway is currently being built beneath it).

After the 1915 Expo, Muni's intention was to build new lines to undeveloped areas in the western part of the Mission District and on the west side of the Twin Peaks. The first of the still existing routes to be built was the J line from Van Ness Avenue southwest on Market Street and then south on Church Street to 30th Street. Due to the steep gradients in the area of Mission Dolores Park, the route was laid out on a dedicated right-of-way to the east of Church Street between 18th and 22nd Streets, avoiding the 21st Street summit.

Opening up new areas for urban expansion in the southwestern part of the city was only possible by digging a tunnel through the Twin Peaks hills. A 3.65 km tube was excavated in two and a half years and completed in July 1917. It included a shallow station called Eureka Valley close to the eastern portal at Market & Castro Streets, and a deep-level station at Laguna Honda (later Forest Hill). The area around the then impressive West Portal was just starting to see some development when the K line began running through the tunnel on 3 February 1918. Meanwhile, four tracks had been laid on Market Street all the way from Van Ness Avenue to the Ferry Building, with the inner tracks

---

Muni Metro

~ 47.5 km (+ 2.5 km im Bau | under construction)
~ 10.4 km unterirdisch | underground
~ 119 Bahnhöfe bzw. Haltestellen | stations or stops (+ 4 i. B. | u/c)

11 Aug 1917:	Ⓙ (Ferry Bldg –) Market & Van Ness – Church & 30th
03 Feb 1918:	Ⓚ Market & Church – St Francis Circle (Twin Peaks Tunnel)
21 Feb 1919:	Ⓚ St Francis Circle – Brighton Ave*
12 Apr 1919:	Ⓛ West Portal – Taraval & 33rd Ave**
06 Oct 1925:	Ⓜ St Francis Circle – Broad & Plymouth
21 Oct 1928:	Ⓝ Market & Duboce – Ocean Beach (Sunset Tunnel)
15 Sept 1937:	Ⓛ Taraval & 33rd Ave – SF Zoo
23 Apr 1979:	Ⓚ Harold Ave – Balboa Park
18 Feb 1980:	Ⓝ Duboce & Church – Embarcadero
1980:	Ⓜ Broad & Plymouth – Balboa Park
11 June 1980:	ⓀⓁⓂ Van Ness – Castro
19 June 1993:	Ⓙ Church & 30th – Balboa Park
10 Jan 1998:	Ⓝ Embarcadero – 4th & King
07 Apr 2007:	Ⓣ 4th & King – Sunnydale
2019:	4th & King – Chinatown

* auf bestehenden URR-Gleisen | over existing URR track
** teilweise gemeinsam mit URR | partly shared with URR

Ⓚ Ⓛ Ⓜ **Forest Hill** – ältester U-Bahnhof in San Francisco von 1918 | *oldest underground station in San Francisco from 1918*

welche den Bau des 278 m langen Stockton Street Tunnel erforderte. Dieser wurde am 28. Dezember 1914 eröffnet und wird heute von Obussen durchfahren (die Central Subway wird derzeit darunter gebaut).

Nach der Ausstellung von 1915 hatte Muni die Absicht, neue Strecken in bislang unbebaute Gebiete im westlichen Teil des Mission District und auf der Westseite der Twin Peaks zu bauen. So entstand mit der Linie J die erste der heute noch bestehenden Strecken von der Van Ness Avenue nach Südwesten auf der Market Street und dann nach Süden entlang der Church Street bis zur 30th Street. Aufgrund der Steigungen im Bereich des Mission Dolores Park wurde die Strecke zwischen 18th und 22nd Street auf einer eigenen Trasse östlich der Church Street angelegt, um die höchste Stelle an der 21st Street zu umgehen.

Die Erschließung neuer Stadterweiterungsflächen im Südwesten der Stadt war nur durch den Bau eines Tunnels unter den Twin Peaks möglich. Das 3,65 km lange Bauwerk wurde nach zweieinhalb Jahren Bauzeit im Juli 1917 vollendet. Es umfasste eine flachliegende Station namens Eureka Valley nahe dem östlichen Portal an der Market & Castro Street sowie eine tiefliegende Station Laguna Honda (später Forest Hill). Die Gegend um das einst beeindruckende West Portal begann sich erst zu entwickeln, als die Linie K am 3. Februar 1918 erstmals durch den Tunnel fuhr. Inzwischen war die Strecke auf der Market Street durchgehend von der Van Ness Avenue zum Fährhafen viergleisig ausgebaut worden, wobei nun die inneren Gleise von den Trams der *United Railroads* und die äußeren von der städtischen Straßenbahn genutzt wurden.

Im Westen wurden Verträge mit *United Railroads* abgeschlossen, um einige ihrer bestehenden Strecken, die dieses Gebiet über lange Umwege erreichten, mitbenutzen zu dürfen. Die Linie K wurde daraufhin entlang der Ocean Avenue bis

now being used by United Railroads and the outer by the Municipal Railway.

In the west, agreements were achieved with United Railroads to share some of their existing routes, which reached this area via lengthy detours. The K line was thus extended along Ocean Avenue to Brighton Avenue, and the L line was introduced along Taraval Street to 33rd Avenue. The M line followed on 6 October 1925, but with the area along 19th Avenue staying undeveloped for several decades, it remained a shuttle service between West Portal and Broad Street & Plymouth Avenue in the Ocean View District for many years. It was sometimes replaced by buses between 1939 and 17 December 1944, when through service to downtown through the Twin Peaks Tunnel was established.

The construction of yet another tunnel to allow for a direct route from the Market Street corridor to the Sunset District south of Golden Gate Park began in June 1926. The 1.29 km tunnel under Buena Vista Park links Duboce Avenue to Carl Street. The 'Sunset Tunnel' was opened together with the N-Judah line on 21 October 1928, completing the network still in use today in the western districts of San Francisco. For many decades, it was also the Municipal Railway's last major addition, and only four years later, a first, though short section of the original line A on 10th Avenue was abandoned. In 1939, a short loop was added in downtown to link the Terminal Building, the terminus of the transbay railways. The loop was shared by Muni and the former United Railroads, which had become the 'Market Street Railway' (MSRy). 1941 saw the introduction of Muni's first trolleybus route on Howard Street and South Van Ness Avenue, although the MSRy had been operating trolleybuses since 1935.

The next important date for public transport in San Francisco was the acquisition by the City of the still larger

zur Brighton Avenue verlängert, und die Linie L wurde auf der Taraval Street bis zur 33rd Avenue eingerichtet. Die Linie M folgte am 6. Oktober 1925, aber da das Gebiet entlang der 19th Avenue über mehrere Jahrzehnte ohne Bebauung blieb, verkehrte sie jahrelang nur als Shuttle zwischen West Portal und Broad Street & Plymouth Avenue im Stadtteil Ocean View. Sie wurde ab 1929 manchmal auch durch Busse ersetzt, bis sie schließlich ab dem 17. Dezember 1944 ebenfalls durch den Twin Peaks Tunnel in die Innenstadt durchgebunden wurde.

Der Bau eines weiteren Tunnels begann im Juni 1926, mit dem Ziel, eine direkte Strecke von der Market Street zum Sunset District südlich des Golden Gate Park zu schaffen. Der 1,29 km lange Tunnel unter dem Buena Vista Park verbindet die Duboce Avenue mit der Carl Street. Der ‚Sunset Tunnel‘ wurde zusammen mit der Linie N-Judah am 21. Oktober 1928 eröffnet, womit das heute noch befahrene Netz in den westlichen Bezirken von San Francisco vollständig war. Jahrzehntelang war es auch die letzte wichtige Ergänzung der *Municipal Railway* und nur vier Jahre später wurde in erster, wenn auch kurzer Abschnitt auf der 10th Avenue der ursprünglichen Linie A aufgegeben. Im Jahr 1939 kam in der Innenstadt eine kurze Schleife hinzu, um das Terminal Building, die Endstation des *Key System*, anzubinden. Die Schleife wurde gemeinsam von der Muni und den ehemaligen *United Railroads* befahren, die mittlerweile zur *Market Street Railway* (MSRy) geworden waren. 1941 wurde die erste städtische Obuslinie auf der Howard Street und der South Van Ness Avenue eingerichtet, allerdings hatte die MSRy bereits seit 1935 Obusse betrieben.

Der nächste Meilenstein für den öffentlichen Nahverkehr in San Francisco war die Übernahme der noch größeren *Market Street Railway* durch die Stadt am 29. September 1944, ein bedeutender Schritt in Richtung eines einheitlichen Netzes. Die MSRy brachte 440 (plus 38 Kabelbahnen), die Muni hingegen nur 238 Fahrzeuge in den gemeinsamen Fuhrpark ein. Als Ergebnis dieser Fusion wurden viele Streckenläufe geändert, um zuvor konkurrierenden Parallelverkehr abzuschaffen. Wie in allen anderen Städten der USA war jedoch die Nachkriegszeit von einem raschen Anstieg der privaten Pkw-Nutzung und einer allgemeinen Tendenz geprägt, die altmodische Straßenbahn durch Busse zu ersetzen. Im Fall von San Francisco wurden auch die flexibleren und leistungsstärkeren Obusse eingeführt, da sie in der Lage waren, die starken Steigungen zu überwinden, vor allem auf den von der MSRy geerbten Kabelbahnstrecken. Bis Ende des Jahres 1949 waren alle Linien der ehemaligen MSRy verschwunden und nach 1951 betrieb Muni nur noch die Linien B (Geary), C (Geary-California), J, K, L, M und N, vor allem deswegen, weil die Umstellung auf Busbetrieb durch die Tunnel eine besondere Herausforderung

Ⓚ Ⓜ **St Francis Circle > West Portal**

Market Street Railway on 29 September 1944, a significant step towards an integrated system. The MSRy added 440 cars (plus 38 cable cars) to the Muni fleet of only 238. As a result of this merger, many streetcar routes were modified to eliminate the parallel running of previously competing lines. Like in all other U.S. cities, however, the postwar period saw a rapid increase in private car use and a general trend towards replacing old-fashioned streetcars with buses. In the case of San Francisco, the more flexible and powerful trolleybuses were also introduced as they were able to negotiate the city's steep roads, especially on cable car routes inherited from the MSRy. By the end of 1949, all the former MSRy lines had disappeared, and after 1951, Muni only retained lines B (Geary), C (Geary-California), J, K, L, M and N, largely because conversion to bus operation through the tunnels would have posed quite a challenge. At the same time, a proposal to put the remaining streetcars into a Market Street Subway was once again presented. In 1956, the Geary Street lines were abandoned, too, with the intention that this corridor would be served by the Golden Gate branch of the proposed BART system, which never materialised. New and second-hand PCC cars were purchased for the five remaining lines to replace prewar rolling stock.

The tide turned in 1962, Muni's 50th anniversary, when voters approved the ambitious BART project (see p. 41), which would have a rather positive effect on Muni's future. Through downtown San Francisco, a 4-track bi-level rapid transit tunnel was to be shared by BART and Muni, while additionally, a two-track underground extension was to be

Ⓝ **Ocean Beach**

Ⓝ **Duboce & Church**

Maurits van den Toorn, 1996

Ⓛ **Ulloa & Forest Side > West Portal** – Boeing #1238

dargestellt hätte. Gleichzeitig wollte man die verbleibenden Straßenbahnen in einen Tunnel unter der Market Street verlegen. Im Jahr 1956 wurden auch die Linien auf der Geary Street aufgegeben, wohl auch mit der Perspektive, dass dieser Korridor durch den Golden Gate-Ast des geplanten BART-Systems, der jedoch nie verwirklicht wurde, erschlossen werden würde. Neue und gebrauchte PCC-Wagen wurden für die fünf übriggebliebenen Linien gekauft, um die Vorkriegsfahrzeuge zu ersetzen.

Die Trendwende kam im Jahr 1962 zum 50. Geburtstag der *Municipal Railway*, als die Wähler das ehrgeizige BART-Projekt (siehe S. 41) befürworteten, was einen ziemlich positiven Effekt auf die Zukunft der Muni haben sollte. Durch die Innenstadt von San Francisco wurde ein viergleisiger doppelstöckiger Tunnel für BART und Muni geplant, außerdem eine zweigleisige unterirdische Verlängerung entlang der oberen Market Street von der Van Ness Avenue bis in den Stadtteil Castro mit Anschluss an den bestehenden Twin Peaks Tunnel, der wiederum an seinem westlichen Ende bis zum St Francis Circle erweitert werden sollte. Dadurch sollte eine städtische Schnellbahnlinie von Embarcadero bis St Francis Circle (und eventuell bis zur SF State University) geschaffen werden, während die übrigen Straßenbahnlinien auf Zubringerbusbetrieb umgestellt werden sollten. Beeinflusst durch ähnliche Projekte in mehreren europäischen Städten, wie Brüssel oder Köln, entschied Muni jedoch, die U-Bahnhöfe und Tunnel zwar groß genug für Schnellbahnzüge zu errichten, diese jedoch zunächst im Vorlaufbetrieb mit PCC-Wagen, also als „Premetro", zu nutzen. In der Zwischenzeit hatte BART begonnen, die Tunnel unter der Market Street im Schildvortrieb als vier eingleisige Tunnelröhren mit Mittelbahnsteigen dazwischen aufzufahren. Das hätte bedeutet, dass die Einrichtungswagen, die nur auf einer Seite Türen haben, wie in Zürich im Tunnel auf der linken Seite hätten fahren müssen. Im Jahr 1968 fiel schließlich die endgültige Entscheidung, neue Zweirichtungs-Gelenkwagen für den Tunnelbetrieb anzuschaffen.

built along upper Market Street from Van Ness Avenue to the Castro to link up with the existing Twin Peaks Tunnel, which at its western end was to be extended to St Francis Circle. This would have created a single municipal rapid transit line from Embarcadero to St Francis Circle (and possibly to S.F. State University), while the remaining streetcar routes would have been converted to bus feeder lines. Influenced by similar projects under development at that time in several European cities like Brussels or Cologne, however, Muni decided to have underground stations and tunnels built large enough to accommodate rapid transit trains in the future, but to operate them initially with PCC streetcars, a concept known as 'premetro'. In the meantime, BART had started tunnelling under Market Street with TBMs, resulting in four single-track tubes with island platforms between them. This would force single-ended PCC vehicles with doors on only one side to run on the left in the tunnel (as they do in Zürich). In 1968, the final decision was taken to purchase a new type of double-ended, articulated light rail vehicle for tunnel operation.

In 1972, Eureka Valley station, located at the eastern end of the Twin Peaks Tunnel between Eureka and Diamond Streets, was closed to allow for temporary ramps at this location when cut-and-cover construction began on the Castro — Van Ness segment. Embarcadero station was initially intended to be a Muni-only station, but as the area became increasingly developed with high-rise office buildings, a BART station was placed there, too. This became possible financially after the proposed tunnel extension west of West Portal had been cancelled.

While tunnel construction was still underway, surface routes were readied for the new cars and the K and M lines were extended to BART's Balboa Park station. Early efforts to put existing surface sections on a dedicated right-of-way separated from road traffic by a concrete curb, like on the inner section of Judah Street, were soon frustrated by

Ⓛ **West Portal** – Abzweig in die Ulloa Street | *turning into Ulloa Street*

ⓀⓁⓂⓉ **West Portal**
– halbunterirdischer Bahnhof | *partly underground station*

Im Jahr 1972 wurde die Station Eureka Valley am östlichen Ende des Twin Peaks Tunnel zwischen Eureka und Diamond Street geschlossen, damit an dieser Stelle provisorische Rampen gebaut werden konnten, als der Bau des Abschnitts Castro – Van Ness in offener Bauweise begann. Die Station Embarcadero war ursprünglich nur für die Muni vorgesehen, aber da das Gebiet zunehmend mit hohen Bürotürmen bebaut wurde, ordnete man dort auch eine BART-Station an. Das war finanziell möglich, nachdem die geplante Verlängerung des Tunnels westlich von West Portal gestrichen worden war.

Während der Tunnelbau noch im Gange war, wurden die oberirdischen Strecken für die neuen Wagen vorbereitet und die Linien K und M bis zur BART-Station Balboa Park verlängert. Frühe Bemühungen, bestehende Abschnitte auf einen eigenen Gleiskörper zu verlegen oder durch einen Bordstein vom Straßenverkehr zu trennen, wie es auf dem inneren Abschnitt entlang der Judah Street getan wurde, stießen auf den Widerstand der Anwohner, weshalb die Außenstrecken auch heute noch an die Straßenbahn des frühen 20. Jahrhunderts erinnern. Auf dem äußeren Teil der Judah Street wurden die Gleise zumindest als ÖPNV-Trasse abmarkiert. Die einzigen Abschnitte im Westen der Stadt mit einer stadtbahnartigen Trassierung auf eigenem Gleiskörper sind: von St Francis Circle bis 19th & Junipero Serra (2 km) auf der Linie M, einschließlich der einzigen zwei Stationen mit Hochbahnsteigen auf voller Länge; etwa 300 m südlich von St Francis Circle auf der Linie K; die oben erwähnte Steilstrecke am Rand des Mission Dolores Park auf der Linie J; 1,2 km auf der später gebauten Verlängerung der Linie J entlang der San Jose Avenue zwischen Randall Street und Diamond & Joost in der Nähe des U-Bahnhofs Glen Park.

protests from neighbours, and therefore most outer routes boast an early 20th century streetcar feel. The outer section of Judah Street was at least marked off and designated as a transit-only lane. The only sections in the western suburbs with a light rail-style dedicated right-of-way are: from St Francis Circle to 19th & Junipero Serra (2 km) on the M line, including the only two stations with full-length high platforms; some 300 m south of St Francis Circle on the K line; the above-mentioned climb near Mission Dolores Park on the J line; a 1.2 km segment on the more recently built extension of the J line along San Jose Avenue between Randall Street and Diamond & Joost, near Glen Park station.

In 1973, the year BART started operating through the San Francisco subway, Muni finally ordered 100 new light rail vehicles from Boeing-Vertol, a joint order placed with Boston's MBTA for their Green Line. The manufacturing of the cars was delayed by several years due to Boeing's lack of experience in building modern rolling stock. After extensive tests and many modifications, the production cars started arriving in November 1978.

Ⓜ The Emergence of Muni Metro
With the opening of the Muni subway repeatedly postponed for various reasons, the new light rail cars finally started passenger service on the extended K line between West Portal and Balboa Park on 23 April 1979. Regular service through the Market Street tunnel began, without ceremony, on 18 February 1980, but just for N line passengers. With the three lines coming through the Twin Peaks Tunnel having also been extended underground to Embarcadero by June 1980, the J line was the last to be upgraded to 'Metro' on 17 June

ⓀⓁⓂⓉ **Castro**

ⓀⓁⓂⓉ **Church**

ⓙⓀⓁⓂⓃⓉ **Civic Center**

ⓙⓀⓁⓂⓃⓉ **Van Ness**

Im Jahr 1973, als die BART-Strecke durch San Francisco in Betrieb genommen wurde, bestellte Muni schließlich 100 neue Stadtbahnwagen bei Boeing-Vertol, eine gemeinsame Bestellung mit Bostons MBTA für deren Green Line. Die Fertigung der Fahrzeuge verzögerte sich mehrere Jahre, da Boeing keine Erfahrung im Bau von modernen Schienenfahrzeugen hatte. Nach intensiven Tests und vielen Anpassungsarbeiten begann die Lieferung der Serienfahrzeuge im November 1978.

〰️〰️ Die Geburt der Muni Metro

Da die Inbetriebnahme der Muni Metro aus verschiedenen Gründen wiederholt verschoben werden musste, begann der Einsatz der neuen Stadtbahnwagen schließlich am 23. April 1979 auf der verlängerten Linie K zwischen West Portal und Balboa Park. Der regelmäßige Betrieb durch den Market Street Tunnel wurde ohne jede Eröffnungsfeierlichkeit am 18. Februar 1980 für die Fahrgäste der Linie N aufgenommen. Nachdem die drei Linien, die durch den Twin Peaks Tunnel fahren, bis Juni 1980 ebenfalls durch den neuen Tunnel bis Embarcadero verlängert worden waren, war die Linie J am 17. Juni 1981 die letzte, die zur „Metro" erhoben wurde. Bis September 1982 wurden alle PCC-Wagen in den Ruhestand geschickt. Die provisorischen Rampen westlich der Station Castro blieben bestehen und könnten im Falle von Störungen im Market Street Tunnel genutzt werden. Die oberirdischen Gleise auf der Market Street wurden ebenfalls erhalten, was im Jahr 1995 die Einführung der Linie F ermöglichte (siehe S. 66). Weitere Verbindungen zwischen den oberirdischen Gleisen in der Market Street und der unterirdischen Strecke bestehen am Tunnelmund nahe der Station Folsom auf der Linie N/T sowie an mehreren Stellen im Stadtteil Castro, z.B. entlang der 17th Street zwischen der Linie J auf der Church Street und der Schleife der Linie F.

Wie die MBTA in Boston war auch Muni mit den Boeing-Fahrzeugen aufgrund ihrer geringen Zuverlässigkeit sehr unzufrieden und beschloss daher bald, sie durch neue Fahrzeuge der italienischen Firma Breda zu ersetzen. Diese wurden zwischen 1995 und 2001 ausgeliefert. Gleichzeitig wurde das Netz erstmals seit Jahrzehnten wesentlich erweitert, nämlich 2,5 km von Embarcadero über eine Rampe (Ferry Portal) auf der gleichnamigen Straße und vorbei am neuen Baseballstadion der Giants bis zum Kopfbahnhof von Caltrain. Der neue Abschnitt wurde im Januar 1998 eröffnet und für die ersten sechs Monate von der Shuttle-Linie E zwischen Embarcadero und Caltrain Depot bedient. Die oberirdische Strecke und alle ihre Stationen haben modernen Stadtbahnstandard, d.h. einen eigenen Gleiskörper und Hochbahnsteige auf voller Länge. Das Projekt umfasste auch den Bau einer unterirdischen Abstell- und Kehranlage östlich

1981. By September 1982, the PCC cars had all been retired from service. The temporary ramps west of Castro station remained intact and could be used in case of disruption in the Market Street Tunnel. The surface tracks on Market Street were also maintained, which allowed the introduction of the F line in 1995 (see p. 66). Other links between the Market Street surface tracks and the subway are available at the Ferry Portal close to Folsom station on the N/T line as well as at various points in the Castro area, e.g. along 17th Street between the J line on Church Street and the F line loop.

Like Boston's MBTA, Muni was not satisfied with the unreliable Boeing cars, and soon decided to replace them with new rolling stock from Breda of Italy, which was delivered between 1995 and 2001.

The introduction of new rolling stock went hand in hand with the first real extension of the system in many decades. This went from the end of the Market Street tunnel via a ramp on The Embarcadero, referred to as the Ferry Portal, past the Giants' new ballpark to Caltrain's San Francisco terminus (2.5 km). The new section opened in January 1998, and for the first six months it was served by the E line shuttle between Embarcadero and the Caltrain Depot. The surface route and all its stations were built to modern light rail standards, with a reserved right-of-way and full-length high platforms for level boarding. The project included the construction of an underground train storage and turnback area east of Embarcadero station, as well as the installation of a new communications-based train control system (CBTC) from Alcatel on the subway section to replace the former

ⓙⓀⓁⓂⓃⓉ **Powell** – gelegentlicher | *temporary* "S Shuttle"

Ⓙ Ⓚ Ⓛ Ⓜ Ⓝ Ⓣ **Embarcadero**

der Station Embarcadero sowie die Installation eines neuen computergestützten Zugsicherungssystems (CBTC) von Alcatel auf dem U-Bahn-Abschnitt, das das frühere Signalsystem mit festen Blöcken ersetzte. Dadurch können die Züge im Tunnel in kürzeren Abständen verkehren, auch wenn sich nur jeweils ein Zug in einem Bahnhof befinden darf. Früher wendeten die Züge über einen Gleiswechsel vor der Endstation Embarcadero, da es dahinter keine Kehrgleise gab, was zu Engpässen im viel befahrenen Tunnel führte. Um die Anzahl der „Züge" im Tunnel zu reduzieren, wurden einzelne Wagen auf dem Weg Richtung Innenstadt vor Einfahrt in den Tunnel planmäßig gekuppelt. Stadtauswärtige Züge wurden an den Portalen getrennt und die einzelnen Wagen fuhren auf ihren jeweiligen Strecken weiter.

Im folgenden Jahrzehnt kam die Verlängerung des zuletzt eröffneten Abschnitts um 8 km nach Süden entlang der Third Street hinzu, die jetzt von der Linie T bedient wird. Ausgehend vom Caltrain Depot verläuft sie durch Mission Bay, ein großes Sanierungsgebiet im ehemaligen Hafen, wo auch der neue Metro East-Betriebshof beheimatet ist. Es geht weiter nach Süden durch Bayview und dann auf dem Bayshore Boulevard ins Visitacion Valley in der Nähe des Caltrain-Bahnhofs Bayshore an der Stadtgrenze von San Francisco. Wie bei der vorherigen Erweiterung wurden die Gleise vom Straßenverkehr durch eine niedrige Bordsteinkante aus Beton abgetrennt und alle Stationen haben Stadtbahnstandard. Im Gegensatz zu den unterirdischen Bahnhöfen und den Stationen auf der vorherigen Erweiterung, die etwa 95-100 m lange 4-Wagen-Züge aufnehmen können, sind die oft versetzt angeordneten Bahnsteige auf der Linie T nur lang genug für 2-Wagen-Züge. Auf einem kurzen Abschnitt zwischen Kirkwood und Shafter Avenue sowie auf der Brücke über den Mission Creek an der

fixed-block signalling system. This allowed more trains to enter the subway at shorter intervals, although only one train can be inside a station at any time. Trains had previously arrived at Embarcadero station via a crossover to the west of the station, but the lack of reversing sidings beyond the station led to some capacity constraints in the busy tunnel. To reduce the number of 'trains' in the subway, single cars from the western suburbs were scheduled to couple before entering the tunnels. Outbound trains would uncouple at the portals and the single cars would continue on their respective routes.

The following decade saw the previous section being extended by 8 km south along Third Street, now served by the T line. Starting from the Caltrain Depot, it runs through Mission Bay, a large redevelopment area of the former port that contains Muni's new Metro East operating and maintenance facility. The line continues south through the Bayview and then along Bayshore Boulevard to Visitacion Valley, near Caltrain's Bayshore station at the city/county border of San Francisco. As with the previous extension, the tracks are separated from road traffic by a low concrete curb and all stations have an L.A.-style light rail standard. Unlike the underground stations and those along the previous extension, which are approximately 95-100 m long to accommodate 4-car trains, the T line has platforms only long enough for 2-car trains, many of them offset at road intersections. On a short section between Kirkwood and Shafter Avenues, however, as well as on the bridge over Mission Creek on 4th Street just south of the Caltrain Depot, the T line has to share the roadway with private cars.

From the junction at 4th & King Streets, a 2.7 km northern extension has been under construction since sum-

Ⓝ Ⓣ **2nd & King** — *Giants Baseball Park*

Ⓝ **Caltrain Depot** — Endstelle | *terminus*

4th Street südlich des Caltrain Depot müssen sich die Muni Metro und der Autoverkehr die Fahrbahn teilen.

Ab der Kreuzung 4th & King Street ist seit Sommer 2012 eine 2,7 km lange Nordverlängerung im Bau. Da diese Strecke größtenteils unterirdisch wird, trägt das Projekt die Bezeichnung „**Central Subway**". Die Stadtbahn wird unter der Autobahn I-80 zwischen Bryant und Harrison Street in den Tunnel unter der 4th Street einfahren und dann über die Stockton Street die Endstation an der Stockton & Washington Street in Chinatown erreichen. Es wird eine oberirdische und drei unterirdische Stationen geben, an der Station Union Square/Market Street wird man zur BART/Muni-Station Powell umsteigen können. Für die U-Bahnhöfe Union Square/Market Street und Yerba Buena/Moscone wird die offene Bauweise angewandt, die Station Chinatown wird hingegen unter der Erde per NÖT (Neue Österreichische Tunnelbauweise) aufgefahren. Die Streckentunnel werden von Tunnelbohrmaschinen als zwei eingleisige Röhren erstellt. Hinter der Station Chinatown werden die Tunnel bis zu einer Baugrube an der Columbus Avenue & Union Street weiterführen, so dass ein Tunnelstutzen entsteht, der in Zukunft für eine mögliche Erweiterung der Central Subway durch North Beach (Columbus Avenue) in Richtung Fisherman's Wharf verwendet werden kann. Die Central Subway bis Chinatown soll im Jahr 2019 eröffnet werden.

mer 2012. As this route will be mostly underground, it has been dubbed the '*Central Subway*'. The tracks will enter the tunnel beneath the I-80 freeway between Bryant and Harrison Streets before proceeding under Fourth Street and Stockton Street to a terminus at Stockton & Washington in Chinatown. There will be one surface and three underground stations, with Union Square/Market Street station providing transfer to BART's and Muni's shared Powell station. Whereas the cut-and-cover method is being used to excavate Union Square/Market Street and Yerba Buena/Moscone stations, the Chinatown station will be built below ground applying NATM (New Austrian Tunnelling Method). The running tunnels will be driven by tunnel boring machines as two single-track tubes. Beyond Chinatown station, the tunnels will continue to a pit at Columbus Avenue & Union Street, creating a stub which may be used in the future for a proposed extension of the Central Subway through North Beach (Columbus Avenue) towards Fisherman's Wharf. The Central Subway to Chinatown is planned to open in 2019.

Einstieg bei abgesenkten Stufen
Boarding with lowered steps

Stufenloser Einstieg an Hochbahnsteigen
Stepfree boarding at high-level platforms

Balboa Park – Boeing-Flotte im Betriebshof | *Boeing fleet in rail yard*

Maurits van den Toorn, 1996

ⓣ 4th & King – Breda-Wagen | *Breda cars*

Muni Metro-Fahrzeuge

Nachdem die ursprüngliche, von Boeing-Vertol aus Philadelphia in den späten 1970er Jahren gelieferte Flotte wiederholt Probleme verursacht hatte, bestellte Muni im Jahr 1991 bei AnsaldoBreda in Italien zunächst 52 völlig neue Wagen, welche die älteren Fahrzeuge zwischen 1996 und 2002 nach und nach ersetzten. Im Gegensatz zu BART hat Muni die Normalspurweite von 1435 mm.

Die Breda-Flotte umfasst heute 151 Hochflur-Gelenkfahrzeuge (nummeriert von 1400 bis 1551), die über Kupplung 22,86 m lang, 2,74 m breit und 3,5 m hoch sind. Die Fahrerkabine ist leicht verjüngt, aber weniger als bei den Boeing-Wagen, die aufgrund der so entstandenen Lücke an Hochbahnsteigen die vordere Tür nicht benutzen konnten. Alle vier Türen auf jeder Seite sind mit beweglichen Stufen ausgerüstet, die an den westlichen oberirdischen Abschnitten abgesenkt werden, aber im Tunnel, auf der Third Street-Route sowie auf der Linie M an den Stationen Stonestown und SF State angehoben sind. Der Wagenfußboden liegt 864 mm über Schienenoberkante.

Die Breda-Wagen können bis zu 4-Wagen-Züge bilden, aber in der Regel sind nur Einzelwagen oder Doppeltraktionen im Einsatz. Sie fahren im Tunnel wie eine moderne Metro mit computergestützter Zugsicherung (CBTC), aber manuell auf Sicht auf den oberirdischen Abschnitten, wo es unzählige Haltestellen gibt, außerdem muss häufig an STOP-Schildern angehalten werden. Die beiden Enddrehgestelle sind angetrieben, während das mittlere Laufwerk unter dem Gelenk nicht motorisiert ist. Die Züge erreichen eine Höchstgeschwindigkeit von 80 km/h. Die Stromversorgung mit 600 V Gleichstrom erfolgt über die Oberleitung mithilfe eines Einholmstromabnehmers.

Muni hat zwei Betriebshöfe, einen älteren an der Station Balboa Park und einen neueren in Mission Bay auf der Third Street-Verlängerung.

Muni Metro Rolling Stock

After the original fleet delivered in the late 1970s by Boeing-Vertol of Philadelphia was beset with problems, Muni placed an initial order for 52 completely new cars with AnsaldoBreda of Italy in 1991, gradually replacing the older stock between 1996 and 2002. Unlike BART, Muni Metro has 1435 mm standard gauge.

The Breda fleet now comprises 151 articulated high-floor vehicles (numbered 1400-1551), which are 22.86 m long (including couplers), 2.74 m wide and 3.5 m high. The driver's cab section is tapered, but less than with the Boeing cars, which due to the resulting gap could not use the front doors at high-level stations. All four doors on each side are equipped with moveable steps, which remain lowered on the western surface sections, and raised in the tunnel and on the Third Street route; on the M line they are also raised at the Stonestown and SF State stations. The car floor is 864 mm above the top of the rail.

The Breda cars can form up to 4-car trains, but normally only single cars or 2-car trains are in service. They operate like a state-of-the-art metro with CBTC in the subway, but are manually driven under 'line-of-sight' rules on surface sections, where 'car stops' are frequent and regular STOP signs are also abundant. The two end bogies are powered, whereas the centre bogie under the articulation is not motorised. The trains reach a maximum speed of 80 km/h. They draw 600 V dc from an overhead catenary with a pantograph.

Muni has two maintenance facilities, an older one at Balboa Park and a newer one at Mission Bay on the Third Street extension.

Innenansicht eines Breda-Wagens | *Inside a Breda car*

ⓜ Stonestown – Breda-Doppeltraktion | *Breda 2-car train*

PCC-Wagen **1061** (ex Philadelphia, im Anstrich der südkalifornischen *Pacific Electric*) biegt am Fährhafen in den Boulevard ‚The Embarcadero' ein.
*PCC car no. **1061** (ex Philadelphia in Southern California Pacific Electric livery) turning into The Embarcadero boulevard opposite the Ferry Building.*

STREETCAR LINE Ⓕ – Market & Wharves

Zwischen 1980 und 1982 wurden alle übriggebliebenen Straßenbahnlinien auf Muni Metro-Betrieb umgestellt und somit in den Market Street Tunnel verlegt, trotzdem blieben zwei der einst vier Gleise an der Oberfläche entlang San Franciscos wohl wichtigster Straße erhalten. Da die beliebten Cable Cars 1982-84 für eine Generalüberholung außer Betrieb waren, kehrte die alte Straßenbahn im Sommer 1983 anfangs als Ersatztouristenattraktion auf die Market Street zurück, was dann bis 1987 wiederholt wurde. Muni beschloss schließlich, daraus eine dauerhafte Museumsstraßenbahnlinie mit Fahrzeugen sowohl aus San Francisco als auch aus anderen Städten der ganzen Welt zu machen.

Nach einer Gleiserneuerung wurde die Linie F am 1. September 1995 zwischen dem Stadtteil Castro und dem jetzt bereits abgerissenen Transbay Terminal, mit einer Schleife über die 1st, Mission und Fremont Street, in Betrieb genommen. Zunächst verkehrten nur PCC-Wagen mit unterschiedlichen Anstrichen, die an die verschiedenen Einsatzorte dieses Typs in ganz Nordamerika erinnern sollten. Aber nach dem unmittelbaren Erfolg der Linie wurden auch Peter Witt-Wagen aus Mailand (Italien) in den Wagenpark aufgenommen. Später kamen Fahrzeuge aus Porto (Portugal), Blackpool (Großbritannien), Melbourne (Australien), Kobe und Hiroshima (Japan) sowie aus Brüssel (Belgien – in Züricher Lackierung!) hinzu.

Entlang des Embarcadero, der Straße am Ostufer von San Francisco, wurde in den 1960er Jahren eine doppelstöckige Hochstraße errichtet, die glücklicherweise beim Erdbeben von 1989 so stark beschädigt wurde, dass die Stadt beschloss, diesen hässlichen „Embarcadero Skyway" nicht wiederaufzubauen, sondern stattdessen einen modernen Boulevard

Although Market Street became a streetcar-free corridor when the remaining routes were gradually upgraded to Muni Metro standard and diverted through the subway between 1980 and 1982, two of the four tracks remained in place along most of San Francisco's important thoroughfare. With the popular cable car system closed down for a major overhaul from 1982 to 1984, streetcars initially returned to Market Street as an alternative for tourists. The temporary summer-only service in 1983 was then repeated until 1987, and eventually Muni decided to make it a permanent line, to be operated with heritage trams from San Francisco as well as from other cities around the world.

After track renewal, the F line was introduced on 1 September 1995 between the Castro and the recently demolished Transbay Terminal, with a loop following 1st, Mission and Fremont Streets. Initially, only PCC cars in liveries reminiscent of those once in use in various North American cities were in operation, but thanks to the immediate success of the line, Peter Witt-style cars from Milan (Italy) were added to the fleet. The line later became a working museum, with vehicles from Porto (Portugal), Blackpool (UK), Melbourne (Australia), Kobe and Hiroshima (Japan) as well as Brussels (Belgium — running in Zürich livery!) contributing to the diverse vintage rolling stock.

Along The Embarcadero, the boulevard along the eastern waterfront, a double-deck elevated freeway called the 'Embarcadero Skyway' was built in the 1960s, but fortunately, this eyesore was badly damaged in the 1989 earthquake, and the City decided not to rebuild it. Instead, a modern boulevard was laid out along the bay, which was gradually transi-

Wagen **1856** (Peter Witt, ex Mailand) am Pier 39 von Fisherman's Wharf
Car no. 1856 (Peter Witt, ex Milan) at Pier 39 of Fisherman's Wharf

Wagen **228** („Boot-Tram", ex Blackpool), Turm des Fährhafengebäudes rechts
Car no. 228 ("boat tram", ex Blackpool), Ferry Building tower on the right

anzulegen und das ehemalige Hafen- in ein Erholungsgebiet umzuwandeln. Dieser Boulevard erhielt auf dem Mittelstreifen Straßenbahnschienen, so dass für Touristen neben den überfüllten Cable Cars eine zweite Route von der Market Street in Richtung Fisherman's Wharf geschaffen werden konnte. Die frühere Schleife am Transbay Terminal wurde aufgegeben und die Linie F stattdessen im März 2000 über das Ferry Building zum Fisherman's Wharf verlängert, wo sie in einer langen Schleife über die Jefferson, Jones and Beach Street wendet.

Im Gegensatz zu den Cable Cars ist die 8,3 km lange Linie F voll in das Muni-Tarifsystem integriert. Laut Fahrplan herrscht ein 5-Minuten-Takt, aber während der Hauptsaison können die Wartezeiten länger sein. Wie die Muni Metro verwendet auch die Linie F eine Oberleitung mit 600 V Gleichstrom, aber mit einem Stangenstromabnehmer (engl. ‚Trolley'). Auf einigen Abschnitten benutzen die Straßenbahnen einen Draht der zweipoligen Obusoberleitung (der zweite dient dem Obus als Rückleiter, was im Fall von Straßenbahnen über die Gleise funktioniert). Die Linie F ist durch kurze Hochbahnsteige und Überbrückungsplatten behindertengerecht zugänglich.

Die Einrichtung einer Linie E von Fisherman's Wharf entlang des Embarcadero zum Caltrain Depot war von Anfang an geplant, aber bisher nicht möglich, da es nicht genügend Zweirichtungsfahrzeuge gibt und an der 4th & King Street keine Wendeschleife vorhanden ist. Die jetzt nur zu besonderen Anlässen betriebene Linie könnte dauerhaft werden, sobald weitere Zweirichtungsfahrzeuge angeschafft und restauriert worden sind.

Benannt nach der *Market Street Railway Company*, einst der größte, private Straßenbahnbetreiber in San Francisco, ist der gemeinnützige Verein „Market Street Railway" heute verantwortlich für die Restaurierung der Fahrzeuge und unterstützt gleichzeitig Muni bei der Wartung. Der Verein hat ein kleines Museum in der Nähe des Fährhafens und auf seiner Website findet man eine vollständige Liste des aktuellen Fuhrparks. (www.streetcar.org)

tioning from industrial to recreational uses. This boulevard layout included a pair of streetcar tracks along the median, which would allow for a second route for tourists (in addition to the overcrowded cable cars) wishing to go from Market Street towards the Fisherman's Wharf area. The former loop at the Transbay Terminal was abandoned, and in March 2000 the F line was instead extended down to the Ferry Building and on to Fisherman's Wharf, where it turns back in a long loop following Jefferson, Jones and Beach Streets.

Unlike the cable cars, the 8.3 km F line is fully integrated into Muni's fare system. According to the timetable, it runs about every 5 minutes, but during the busy tourist season, waiting times can be longer. Like Muni Metro, the F line uses a 600 V dc overhead power supply, but with an old-style trolley pole. On some sections, the streetcars share one of the two trolleybus wires (the second is required as the return part of the electrical path, which in the case of streetcars is via the tracks). The F line is fully accessible via short raised platforms and bridge plates.

Although the addition of an E line running along The Embarcadero from Fisherman's Wharf to the Caltrain Depot has been planned from the beginning, it has remained impossible due to the fact that not enough double-ended vehicles are available and there is no terminal loop at 4th & King Streets. Now operated only on special occasions, a permanent service may be established as soon as more bidirectional cars have been acquired and restored.

Taking its name from the Market Street Railway Company, once San Francisco's largest, though privately owned streetcar operator, the 'Market Street Railway' nonprofit association is in charge of restoring the vehicles and supports Muni in maintaining them. They have a small museum near the Ferry Building, and their website provides a full list of the present fleet (www.streetcar.org).

Maurits van den Toorn

Zweirichtungswagen Nr. 496 aus Melbourne auf der zeitweise verkehrenden Linie E nahe des Caltrain-Bahnhofs
– Double-ended Melbourne car no. 496 near the Caltrain station on line E, which is operated on special occasions.

(1) Trolleybus #5502 + PCC #1075 (1946, ex Minneapolis-St. Paul/Newark) @ Market & 5th – im Anstrich von Cleveland | *in Cleveland livery*

(2) Peter Witt #1818 (1928, ex Milano) @ Market & 5th – im Mailänder Anstrich der 1930er bis 1970er Jahre – *in 1930s to 1970s Milan livery*

(3) PCC #1010 (1948, San Francisco Municipal Railway) @ Beach & Mason – mit 'Magic Carpets'-Anstrich | *in 'Magic Carpets' livery*

(4) PCC #1074 (1946, ex Minneapolis-St. Paul/Newark) @ Market & Castro – im Anstrich von Toronto | *in Toronto livery*

⑤ PCC **#1059** (1948, ex Philadelphia) @ The Embarcadero & Market
– im Anstrich von Boston | *in Boston livery*

⑥ PCC **#1062** (1948, ex Philadelphia) @ Market & Drumm
– im Anstrich von Louisville und mit dem Fährhafengebäude im Hintergrund
– *in Louisville livery and with the Ferry Building in the background*

⑦ PCC **#1057** (1948, ex Philadelphia) @ Castro & Market
– im Anstrich von Cincinnati und den Twin Peaks im Hintergrund
– *in Cincinnati livery and with the Twin Peaks in the background*

⑧ PCC **#1050** (1948, ex Philadelphia) @ Market & 16th & Noe
– im Anstrich der San Francisco Municipal Railway der 1950er Jahre
– *in San Francisco Municipal Railway 1950s livery*

Wagen **15**, Nachbau eines Fahrzeugs der ursprünglichen *Market Street Railway* (1893-1902), am Union Square (Powell & Geary)
*Car no. **15**, replica of a vehicle built for the original Market Street Railway (1893-1902), seen here at Union Square (Powell & Geary)*

CABLE CARS

San Francisco hat gewiss auch viele andere Sehenswürdigkeiten, aber keine steht so für diese Stadt wie die *Cable Cars*, die Kabelstraßenbahnen. Das heutige Netz besteht aus drei Routen, in Nord-Süd-Richtung die Linien Powell & Mason und Powell & Hyde sowie die Ost-West-Linie auf der California Street, nur ein kleiner Rest eines einst viel größeren Netzes.

Nachdem die erste Kabelbahn 1873 von der *Clay Street Hill Railroad* eröffnet worden war, bauten insgesamt acht verschiedene Unternehmen Kabelbahnen in der ganzen Stadt, jeweils mit unterschiedlichen Spurweiten von 3 ½ bis 5 Fuß (1067 bis 1524 mm). Gemeinsam erreichten sie ihre maximale Ausdehnung in den frühen 1890er Jahren. Das schwere Erdbeben von 1906 zerstörte viele Strecken und einige davon wurden danach nicht mehr als Kabelbahnen wiederaufgebaut, sondern für elektrischen Straßenbahnbetrieb umgebaut. Im Laufe der Jahre gingen die meisten Unternehmen in der *Market Street Railway* auf, bis auf die *California Street Cable Railroad* (kurz *Cal Cable*), die seit ihrer Eröffnung im Jahr 1878 bis 1952 unabhängig blieb, dann wurde sie von der *Municipal Railway* übernommen. Die heutige Strecke auf der Hyde Street (die damals weiter nach Süden über die Jones und O'Farrell Street führte) gehörte auch zu *Cal Cable*. Die anderen heute noch bestehenden Routen stammen aus dem Jahr 1888 und wurden von der *Ferries and Cliff House Railway* errichtet, die bereits 1893 zur *Market Street Railway* kam. Letztere fusionierte schließlich im Jahr 1944 mit der *Municipal Railway*.

Der Widerstand gegen die anstehende Stilllegung des ziemlich veralteten Systems begann sich bereits in den späten 1940er Jahren zu organisieren. So kam es zur Idee, wenigstens ein auf Touristen ausgerichtetes Kernnetz zu erhalten und den Rest stillzulegen, was 1954 auch so beschlossen wurde. Für die heutigen Linienführungen mussten neue Verbindungen gebaut werden, um die von der *Cal Cable* geerbte Hyde

San Francisco certainly has many other attractions, too, but for most tourists the cable cars are probably the city's best-known icon. Today's system comprises three routes, the north-south Powell & Mason and Powell & Hyde lines, and the east-west California Street line. This is, however, only a small remainder of a once much larger network.

After the first cable car line was opened in 1873 by the 'Clay Street Hill Railroad', a total of eight different companies built cable cars across the city using track gauges ranging from 3 ½' to 5' (1067 to 1524 mm). Together they reached their maximum expansion in the early 1890s. The severe 1906 earthquake destroyed many routes, and some were not rebuilt as cable cars but instead became electric streetcars. Most companies were consolidated in the 'Market Street Railway' over the years, although the 'California Street Cable Railroad' (Cal Cable) remained independent from its opening in 1878 until 1952, when it was absorbed by the Municipal Railway. The present line on Hyde Street belonged to Cal Cable, too; it used to continue south to Jones and O'Farrell Streets. The other surviving routes date from 1888 and were built by the 'Ferries and Cliff House Railway'. In as early as 1893, this was taken over by the 'Market Street Railway', which eventually merged with the Municipal Railway in 1944.

Opposition to the expected closure of this rather outdated system began to grow in the late 1940s. This led to proposals to at least maintain a core system for tourists while closing down the rest, a plan approved in 1954. The establishment of the routes we know today required some rebuilding to link the Hyde Street line from the Cal Cable to the Powell line via Jackson and Washington Streets, over sections of an east-west line which was abandoned at the same time. At Beach Street, at the lower end of Hyde

Zweirichtungswagen **57**, Nachbau eines Fahrzeugs der *California Street Cable Railroad Company* aus der Zeit um 1891, am unteren Ende der California Street
*Double-ended car no. **57**, replica of a vehicle built for the California Street Cable Railroad Company around 1891, seen here at the lower end of California St*

Street-Linie an die Powell-Linie über gleichzeitig aufgegebene Ost-West-Gleise auf der Jackson und Washington Street anzuschließen. Am unteren Ende der Hyde Street, an der Beach Street, wurde eine Drehscheibe eingebaut, da auf der Powell Street nur Einrichtungswagen zum Einsatz kamen. Um alle Linien auf ein Maschinenhaus und Depot konzentrieren zu können, wurde die California Street-Linie im Jahr 1957 umgebaut, denn sie verwendete bis dahin einen anderen Greifmechanismus und hatte einen nicht ganz mittigen Kabelschlitz. Noch heute setzt die California Street-Linie Zweirichtungswagen ein und braucht daher an ihren Endpunkten anders als die Powell-Linien keine Drehscheiben. Mit 9,2 m sind diese Wagen auch etwas länger als die 8,6 m langen Fahrzeuge auf den Powell Street-Linien. Beide Typen sind 2,4 m breit und haben eine Spurweite von 1067 mm.

In dieser Form überlebten die Cable Cars mehrere Jahrzehnte und wurde sogar mit ansteigendem Tourismus noch beliebter. Zwischen September 1982 und Juni 1984 wurde das gesamte System für eine Generalüberholung geschlossen, dabei wurden Schienen und Kabelkanäle ersetzt und die Fahrzeuge instandgesetzt. Jeder der heute 40 Wagen wird von zwei Männern betrieben, einem ,Gripman' und einem Begleiter, der den Fahrer bergab mit einer Handbremse unterstützt. Um das Fahrzeug in Bewegung zu setzen, wird das kontinuierlich laufende unterirdische Kabel mit einem klauenartigen Mechanismus gefasst, der über den Griffhebel im Vorderteil des Fahrzeugs betätigt wird. Das Maschinenhaus an der Washington & Mason Street in Nob Hill beherbergt ein kleines Museum, das das ausgeklügelte System im Detail erklärt.

Im Gegensatz zur Linie F benötigt man für die Cable Cars einen besonderen Fahrschein, der nicht weniger als 6,00 $ für eine einfache Fahrt kostet, allerdings erlauben die im Tourist Office angebotenen ,Muni Visitor Passports' auch beliebige Fahrten mit den Cable Cars.

Street, a turntable was added as the Powell Street line used single-ended cars. In order to concentrate all the lines in one powerhouse and barn, the California Street line was rebuilt in 1957; it had been operated with a different grip mechanism and with a slightly offset cable slot. Still today, however, the California Street line uses double-ended cars and therefore, unlike the Powell Street lines, does not require turntables at its termini. At 9.2 m, these cars are slightly longer than the 8.6 m cars on the Powell Street lines. Both types are 2.4 m wide and run on 1067 mm gauge tracks.

The cable cars survived in this form for several decades and became even more popular as tourism increased. Between September 1982 and June 1984, the entire system was closed to allow for a complete overhaul, with tracks and cable channels being replaced and the vehicles repaired. Each of the 40 cars in the present fleet is operated by two men, a gripman and a conductor, who assists the former with a hand brake on downhill sections. To put the car in motion, the continuously moving underground cable is gripped by a clamp-like mechanism that is operated via a grip lever in the front of the car. The powerhouse at Washington & Mason Streets on Nob Hill accommodates a small museum that displays and explains in detail how the sophisticated mechanism works.

Unlike the F line, the cable cars require a special fare of no less than $6.00 for a single ride, but the Muni Visitor Passports sold at the Tourist Office allow unlimited travel on cable cars, too.

(1) Wagen 20 (gebaut 1893, heute im Kleid von 1888, als die erste Kabelbahn entlang der Clay Street fuhr) auf der Steilstrecke entlang der Hyde Street, mit Blick über die San Francisco Bay und mit Alcatraz im Hintergrund
– *Car no. 20 (built in 1893, now in 1888 livery honouring the first cable cars on Clay Street) on the steep route along Hyde Street, with San Francisco Bay and Alcatraz Island in the background*

(2) Wagen 22 (wie Wagen 20 gebaut 1893) am Maschinenhaus und Cable Car Museum an der Ecke Washington & Mason
– *Car no. 22 (like no. 20 built in 1893) running past the powerhouse and Cable Car Museum at Washington & Mason*

(3) Blick ins Maschinenhaus, von wo aus die verschiedenen Kabelumläufe angetrieben werden.
– *View inside the powerhouse from where the different cables are operated.*

(4)

④ Wagen 13 (Nachbau von 1991 in den Farben der *United Railroads* nach dem Erdbeben von 1906) auf der Steilstrecke entlang der Powell Street, Ecke Bush Street
– *Car no. 13 (replica built in 1991 boasting a United Railroads post-1906 earthquake livery) on the steep route along Powell Street, at the corner of Bush Street*

⑤ Wagen 49 (Nachbau eines Cal Cable-Fahrzeugs von 1891) auf dem höchsten, kurzzeitig relativ flachen Abschnitt der California Street Line (Ecke Taylor Street mit Grace Cathedral)
– *Car no. 49 (replica of a Cal Cable vehicle from 1891) on the highest, though here rather flat section of the California Street Line (at the corner of Taylor Street with Grace Cathedral)*

⑥ Originaler Cal Cable-Wagen 56 von 1913 hält mitten auf der Kreuzung California & Powell, mit Umsteigemöglichkeit zu den anderen Linien.
– *Original Cal Cable vehicle no. 56 from 1913 stopping in the middle of the road intersection at California & Powell, allowing interchange with the other cable car lines.*

(5)

(6)

Almaden – südliche Endstation der kurzen Shuttle-Linie | *southern terminus of the short shuttle line*

SAN JOSÉ, CA

San Jose liegt am südöstlichen Zipfel der San Francisco Bay Area. Es ist die Hauptstadt des Santa Clara County, des weltweit bekannten Silicon Valley, wo unter anderem Google, Apple, Adobe, eBay oder Intel beheimatet sind. Mit einer Einwohnerzahl von 970.000 in der eigentlichen Stadt (457 km²) ist San Jose nach Los Angeles und San Diego die drittgrößte Stadt in Kalifornien. Im Santa Clara County, das außerdem Städte wie Campbell, Milpitas, Mountain View, Palo Alto, Santa Clara und Sunnyvale umfasst, leben rund 1,7 Mio. Menschen.

San Jose ist ein Halt des täglich verkehrenden Amtrak-Zugs „Coast Starlight" von Seattle nach Los Angeles. Von San Jose fahren außerdem sieben „Capitol Corridor"-Züge pro Tag über Oakland nach Sacramento und mehr als 40 Caltrain-Züge nach San Francisco (siehe S. 52), von denen drei nachmittags nach Süden bis Gilroy durchgebunden werden (morgens umgekehrt). Der ACE (Altamont Commuter Express) aus Stockton über Pleasanton und Fremont bietet nur vier Fahrten morgens nach San Jose und nachmittags vier zurück. San Jose liegt außerdem an der künftigen Hochgeschwindigkeitsstrecke von San Francisco nach Los Angeles. Mittelfristig wird die Stadt auch durch die BART Silicon Valley-Verlängerung mit Oakland und San Francisco verbunden sein.

Der öffentliche Nahverkehr im Santa Clara County (3.343 km²), d.h. Stadtbahn und Busse, liegt in der Hand von *Santa Clara Valley Transportation Authority* (VTA). VTA ist auch mitverantwortlich für Caltrain.

VTA verfügt über ein einfaches Tarifsystem, mit Einzelfahrten für 2,00 $ (ohne Umsteigen!) und Tageskarten für 6,00 $. Die für die gesamte Bay Area entwickelte Smartcard ‚Clipper' kann auch auf dem VTA-Netz genutzt werden.

San Jose lies at the southeastern tip of the San Francisco Bay Area; it is the county seat of Santa Clara County, an area known around the world as Silicon Valley, home to major IT corporations like Google, Apple, Adobe, eBay and Intel, besides hundreds of smaller companies. With a population of 970,000 in the city proper (457 km2), it is the third largest in California after Los Angeles and San Diego. Santa Clara County, which contains the cities of Campbell, Milpitas, Mountain View, Palo Alto, Santa Clara and Sunnyvale, is home to some 1.7 million people.

San Jose is a stop on Amtrak's daily "Coast Starlight" from Seattle to Los Angeles. It is also the departure point for 7 daily "Capitol Corridor" trains to Sacramento via Oakland, and more than 40 Caltrain services to San Francisco (see p. 52), three of which run south to Gilroy in the afternoon (and depart from there in the morning). The ACE (Altamont Commuter Express) from Stockton via Pleasanton and Fremont provides only four trips to San Jose in the morning, and four back in the afternoon. San Jose will also be served by the planned California High Speed Rail from San Francisco to Los Angeles. In the mid-term future, it will also be linked to Oakland and San Francisco via BART's Silicon Valley extension.

Public transport, i.e. light rail and bus service, in Santa Clara County (3,343 km2) is provided by the Santa Clara Valley Transportation Authority (VTA). VTA is also co-responsible for Caltrain.

VTA operates a simple fare system, with single fares being $2.00 (no transfer!), and a day pass available at $6.00. 'Clipper', the smartcard designed for the entire Bay Area, also works on VTA services.

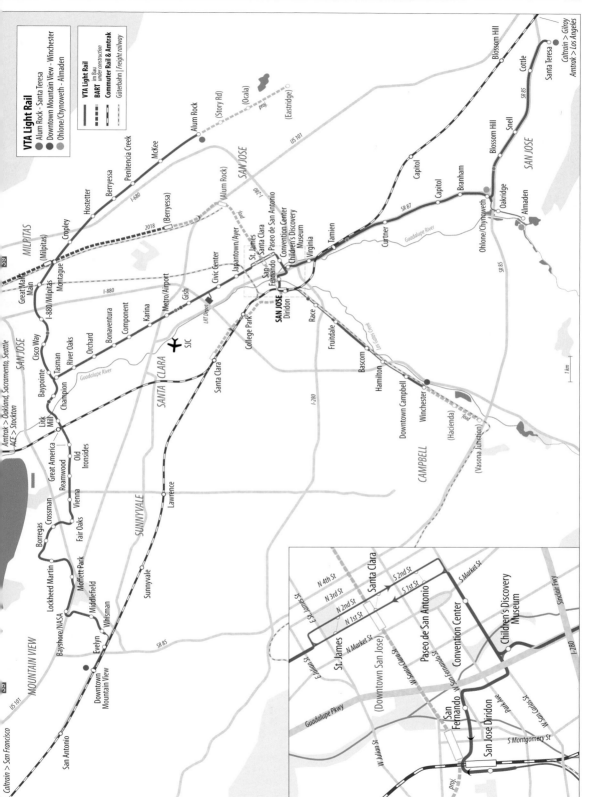

VTA Light Rail
- Alum Rock - Santa Teresa
- Downtown Mountain View - Winchester
- Ohlone/Chynoweth - Almaden

VTA Light Rail
BART *im Bau / under construction*
Commuter Rail & Amtrak
Güterbahn | *Freight railway*

Santa Clara – nach Süden durch das Stadtzentrum führende Strecke in der 1st Street | *southbound route through the city centre on 1st Street*

◉ VTA Light Rail

Auch wenn es nicht den Anschein hat, so wurde die Stadtbahn von San Jose bereits im Jahr 1987 in Betrieb genommen und gehört somit eigentlich zu den älteren Stadtbahnen in den USA. Während Städte wie Sacramento und Denver weiterhin ausschließlich Hochflurfahrzeuge einsetzen, die an Niedrigbahnsteigen halten, hat San Jose in den frühen 2000er Jahren alle älteren Wagen durch neue behindertengerechte Niederflurwagen ersetzt, so dass der Standard heute dem der moderneren Systeme in Seattle, Minneapolis oder Phoenix entspricht.

Die VTA-Stadtbahnstrecken weisen für dieses Verkehrsmittel typische Trassierungen auf: straßenbündige Strecken durch die Innenstadt, meist eigener Gleiskörper durch die inneren Vorstädte sowie lange, völlig kreuzungsfreie Abschnitte im Mittelstreifen von Autobahnen auf Außenstrecken.

Das heutige Netz besteht aus zwei Hauptlinien mit einer gemeinsamen Stammstrecke, dazu kommt eine kurze Shuttle-Linie. Auch wenn sie auf Netzplänen in unterschiedlichen Farben dargestellt sind, werden in San Jose Bezeichnungen wie „Blue Line" bislang in offiziellen Dokumenten nicht verwendet, die Linien werden nur durch ihre Endpunkte und im Fahrplan mit einer 3-stelligen Liniennummer unterschieden:

● **Alum Rock – Santa Teresa Line** (902, 40 km, 36 Haltest.)
● **Mountain View – Winchester Line** (901, 34,8 km, 38 Hst.)
● **Ohlone/Chynoweth – Almaden Shuttle** (900, 2 km, 3 Hst.)

Interessanterweise sind auf offiziellen Netzplänen die Fahrtziele auch durch ein Bildsymbol ausgewiesen:
Mountain View durch einen Baum, Alum Rock durch eine

Although it appears to be of a more recent type, the VTA light rail system opened back in 1987, and thus actually belongs to the first batch of cities to introduce this form of urban rail transport in the U.S. While cities like Sacramento and Denver continue operating exclusively with high-floor vehicles and low-level platforms, San Jose replaced its entire original rolling stock in the early 2000s to offer a fully accessible system with new low-floor trains, placing it in line with more recent systems like Seattle, Minneapolis or Phoenix.

The VTA light rail routes feature alignments typical for this form of transport, with a mix of on-street running in the downtown area, mostly reserved rights-of-way through the inner suburbs and long grade-separated sections in the median of freeways in outer areas.

The present system consists of two main lines sharing the same central trunk route, plus a short shuttle. Although colour-coded on maps, terms like 'Blue Line' have not been used in official documents so far; rather, the lines are identified on schedules by their end points and a 3-digit number:

● *Alum Rock – Santa Teresa Line (902, 40 km, 36 stops)*
● *Mountain View – Winchester Line (901, 34.8 km, 38 stops)*
● *Ohlone/Chynoweth – Almaden Shuttle (900, 2 km, 3 stops)*

Interestingly, on official maps the final destinations can also be identified by a pictorial symbol:
Mountain View by a tree, Alum Rock by a rising sun, Santa Teresa by a river, Almaden by grapes and Winchester by a bird.

Alum Rock

Japantown/Ayer

aufgehende Sonne, Santa Teresa durch einen Fluss, Almaden durch Trauben und Winchester durch einen Vogel.

Die Bahnen fahren von 4:00 Uhr bis etwa Mitternacht, bis 19:00 Uhr alle 15 Minuten, danach alle 20-30 Minuten. Auf der grünen Linie herrscht jedoch während der Mittagszeit und am Wochenende nur ein 30-Minuten-Takt. Auf der blauen Linie gibt es drei zusätzliche ‚Peak Commuter Express Service'-Züge zwischen Baypointe und Santa Teresa in der Hauptlastrichtung, wobei die Stationen zwischen Convention Center und Ohlone/Chynoweth ohne Halt durchfahren werden.

● Entwicklung der Stadtbahnstrecken

Die erste Stadtbahnlinie von San Jose verlief vom Betriebshof in der Nähe des Civic Center Richtung Norden entlang der North 1st Street zur Station Tasman, wo sie nach Westen abbog und entlang des West Tasman Drive zur ursprünglichen Endstation Old Ironsides führte. Die Station Great America erschließt den gleichnamigen Vergnügungspark und auch das Santa Clara Convention Center. Der gleichnamige Bahnhof hingegen befindet sich etwa 700 m weiter östlich und näher an der Stadtbahnhaltestelle Lick Mill, obwohl es dort keine direkte Umsteigemöglichkeit gibt. Die Station Champion wurde erst später eingefügt, als das Gebiet durch Cisco Systems entwickelt wurde. Die gesamte Strecke von 1987 liegt auf einem eigenen Gleiskörper in der Mitte der beiden bereits erwähnten Straßen, wobei viele Haltestellen entlang der North 1st Street versetzte Bahnsteige aufweisen, mit Halt jeweils nach der Kreuzung. Der Stadtbahnbetriebshof ist über die West Younger Avenue angeschlossen.

Die erste Linie wurde nur wenige Monate später nach Süden in die Innenstadt verlängert. Die Stadtbahn fährt Richtung Süden weiter auf der 1st Street, und obwohl die Straße

SAN JOSE VTA Light Rail

67.5 km
62 Haltestellen | stations

11 Dec 1987: Old Ironsides – Civic Center
17 June 1988: Civic Center – Convention Center
17 Aug 1990: Convention Center – Tamien
25 Apr 1991: Tamien – Santa Teresa & Almaden
24 Mar 1994: + Champion station
20 Dec 1999: Old Ironsides – Downtown Mountain View
 Tasman – Baypointe
17 May 2001: Baypointe — I-880/Milpitas
24 June 2004: I-880/Milpitas – Alum Rock
29 July 2005: Convention Center – San Jose Diridon
01 Oct 2005: San Jose Diridon – Winchester

Trains operate from 04:00 until around midnight, every 15 minutes until 19:00, then every 20-30 minutes. On the green line, however, service is reduced to trains every 30 minutes during midday and on weekends. On the blue line, three additional 'Peak Commuter Express Service' trains run between Baypointe and Santa Teresa, skipping stops between Convention Center and Ohlone/Chynoweth; they travel north in the morning peak, and south in the afternoon.

● Light Rail History and Routes

San Jose's initial light rail line ran north from the train depot near Civic Center along N 1st Street to Tasman station, where it turned west and continued along W Tasman Drive to its original terminus at Old Ironsides. The Great America stop serves a theme park of that name as well as the Santa Clara Convention Center. The railway station of the same name is located some 700 m further east and closer to the Lick Mill light rail stop, although there is no direct interchange. Champion station was only added later when the area was developed by Cisco Systems. The entire 1987 route runs on a reserved right-of-way in the median of the two roads mentioned above, with many stops along N 1st Street featuring offset platforms and trains stopping after having passed the respective road intersections. The LRT maintenance yard is accessible via W Younger Avenue.

The original line was extended south into downtown only a few months later. Trains continue south on 1st Street, and although the street gets narrower as it approaches the city centre, a slightly raised right-of-way remains reserved for light trains in the centre of the roadway. Some 250 m south of Japantown/Ayer station, the trains descend into a 300 m open trench, primarily built to avoid an intersection with a crossing freight line, but at the same time they dive under Bassett Street. One block after returning to street level, southbound trains turn east into Devine Street, crossing the northbound track, which remains on 1st Street, before turning right into 2nd Street. The parallel routes and stations in the city centre are separated from the roadway by a row of trees and embedded into a wide sidewalk paved with stones. The two tracks rejoin just before arriving at Convention Center station on San Carlos Street, the southern terminus for two years.

While the 1987/88 starter line resembles a typical European modern tram line, the southern extension, opened in two stages in 1990/91, has more of a metro-style alignment. Just after Children's Discovery Museum station, trains leave the downtown area and enter the freeway median of Guadalupe Parkway (SR 87), with stations accessible from either underpasses (Tamien, Curtner, Capitol) or road bridges

Ohlone/Chynoweth

Convention Center

schmaler wird, steht ihr eine leicht erhöhte eigene Trasse zur Verfügung. Etwa 250 m südlich von Japantown/Ayer erreicht die Stadtbahn einen 300 m langen offenen Einschnitt, der vor allem zum Unterfahren einer kreuzenden Güterbahnstrecke gebaut wurde, aber gleichzeitig auch eine niveaugleiche Kreuzung an der Bassett Street umgeht. Wieder auf Straßenebene schwenkt das nach Süden führende Gleis nach einem Häuserblock nach Osten in die Devine Street, kreuzt dabei das Gleis Richtung Norden, welches auf der 1st Street bleibt, und biegt dann rechts in die 2nd Street ein. Die parallelen Gleise und Stationen in der Innenstadt sind von der Fahrbahn durch eine Baumreihe getrennt und in einen breiten, gepflasterten Bürgersteig eingebettet. Die beiden Gleise treffen kurz vor der Haltestelle Convention Center in der San Carlos Street wieder aufeinander. Hier war zwei Jahre lang die südliche Endstation.

Während die 1987/88 eröffnete Strecke einer modernen europäischen Straßenbahn ähnelt, hat die südliche Verlängerung von 1990/91 eher eine metromäßige Trassierung. Gleich nach der Haltestelle Children's Discovery Museum verlässt die Stadtbahn die Innenstadt und schwenkt auf den Mittelstreifen des Guadalupe Parkway (SR 87), wobei die Stationen auf diesem Abschnitt entweder von Unterführungen (Tamien, Curtner, Capitol) oder Straßenbrücken (Virginia, Branham) aus zugänglich sind. Bevor diese Autobahn in den querenden West Valley Freeway (SR 85) einmündet, verlässt die Stadtbahn den Mittelstreifen, um die Umsteigestation Ohlone/Chynoweth zu erreichen. Von hier aus pendelt ein Einzelwagen vom Gleis Richtung Süden alle 15 Minuten auf der eingleisigen Strecke nach Almaden und schließt dabei vor allem die Oakridge Mall an. Die Hauptstrecke nach Santa Teresa hingegen schwenkt nach Osten und verläuft nun im Mittelstreifen des West Valley Freeway. Kurz vor Erreichen der Endstation Santa Teresa taucht die Stadtbahn unter den südlichen Fahrbahnen der Autobahn hindurch. Es gibt hier drei Zwischenstationen, von denen Snell und Cottle von einer Straßenbrücke und Blossom Hill durch eine Unterführung zugänglich sind. Eine Fahrt auf der 16,4 km langen Schnellbahnstrecke von Santa Teresa zum Convention Center dauert nur 23 Minuten.

Die Linie Old Ironsides – Santa Teresa blieb acht Jahre lang unverändert, bis im Jahr 1999 eine Verlängerung nach Mountain View in Betrieb genommen wurde. Dieses Projekt umfasste auch eine kurze Verlängerung in die entgegengesetzte Richtung bis Baypointe, wo eine dreigleisige Anlage gebaut wurde, um ein bequemes Umsteigen zwischen der ursprünglichen „Guadalupe"-Linie (Nord-Süd) und der zukünftigen „Tasman"-Linie (Ost-West) zu ermöglichen. Die Mountain View-Verlängerung ähnelt der ursprünglichen Linie, mit eigenem Gleiskörper in der Mitte städtischer Straßen. Sie verläuft zunächst entlang des West Tasman Drive, dann nach Norden

(Virginia, Branham). Before the freeway merges with the West Valley Freeway (SR 85), LRT trains leave the median to serve the Ohlone/Chynoweth interchange: from the southbound track, a single car shuttles every 15 minutes on the single-track line to Almaden, mostly to provide access to the Oakridge Mall. The main route to Santa Teresa turns east and then runs in the median of West Valley Freeway. Just before arriving at the Santa Teresa terminus, the trains dive under the eastbound road lanes to leave the freeway corridor. There are three intermediate stations, with Snell and Cottle accessible from a road bridge, and Blossom Hill via a pedestrian underpass. A ride on the 16.4 km express route from Santa Teresa to Convention Center only takes 23 minutes.

The Old Ironsides – Santa Teresa line remained the same for 8 years until an extension to Mountain View was added in 1999; this project also included a short extension in the opposite direction to Baypointe, where a three-track station was built to provide convenient interchange between the original 'Guadalupe' corridor (north-south) and the future 'Tasman' corridor (east-west). The Mountain View extension is similar to the original line, with trains running on a reserved right-of-way in the centre of urban roads. Starting along West Tasman Drive, they turn north into Fair Oaks Avenue, cross the Southbay Freeway and get to Java Drive before turning south into Mathilda Avenue where the route gets aligned along the western side of the road. Trains then continue west along the northern side of Moffett Park Drive and Manila Drive, before reaching Bayshore NASA station, after which they take a sharp, almost 180 degree turn south to dive under the Bayshore Freeway. The following section down to the Caltrain route runs away from urban roads through a mix of commercial areas and new housing estates on a corridor once occupied by a railway track leading to NASA's Moffett Airfield. Just after Whisman station, the line becomes single-track and continues alongside Caltrain's route to San Francisco up to the double-track Downtown Mountain View terminus, which lies adjacent to the Caltrain station. In 1999, when the Mountain View branch opened, trains ran from Mountain View to Baypointe, and from 2001, they continued to I-880/Milpitas. In 2004, they were cut back to Baypointe, when the Alum Rock extension started being served by trains from Santa Teresa. Since 2005, the two lines have shared the route into downtown, from where trains from Mountain View continue southwest on the Winchester branch.

The Alum Rock branch runs along East Tasman Drive, which becomes Great Mall Parkway after crossing I-880. About 1 km east of I-880/Milpitas station, the trains climb

Japantown/Ayer > Civic Center

San Jose Diridon

Downtown Mountain View

Civic Center

Great Mall/Main

in die Fair Oaks Avenue, über den Southbay Freeway bis zum Java Drive und dann nach Süden in die Mathilda Avenue, wo die Trasse nun in westlicher Seitenlage ist. Die Stadtbahn fährt weiter an der Nordseite des Moffett Park Drive und Manila Drive nach Westen und erreicht die Station Bayshore NASA. Danach biegt sie scharf, fast 180 Grad nach Süden ab und taucht unter dem Bayshore Freeway hindurch. Der folgende Abschnitt bis zur Caltrain-Strecke verläuft abseits von städtischen Straßen durch einen Mix aus Gewerbegebieten und neuen Wohnsiedlungen und nutzt dabei einen Korridor, auf dem einst ein Anschlussgleis zum NASA Moffett Airfield lag. Kurz nach der Haltestelle Whisman wird die Strecke eingleisig und führt neben den Caltrain-Gleisen Richtung San Francisco bis zur zweigleisigen Endstelle Downtown Mountain View direkt neben dem Caltrain-Bahnhof. Nach Inbetriebnahme dieser Neubaustrecke im Jahr 1999 fuhren die Züge von Mountain View bis Baypointe, ab 2001 dann weiter bis I-880/Milpitas. Sie wurden 2004 wieder bis Baypointe zurückgenommen, da der neue Ast nach Alum Rock mit der älteren Strecke nach Santa Teresa verknüpft wurde. Seit 2005 fahren beide Linien gemeinsam durch die Innenstadt, wobei die Züge aus Mountain View nach Südwesten auf den Winchester-Ast durchgebunden werden.

Der Alum Rock-Ast verläuft entlang des East Tasman Drive, der nach Überquerung der I-880 zum Great Mall Parkway wird. Etwa 1 km östlich von I-880/Milpitas erreicht die Stadtbahn eine 2,3 km lange Hochbahnstrecke über den Mittelstreifen des Great Mall Parkway, eine bei Stadtbahnen seltene und eher für BART typische Trassierung. Dadurch konnten jedoch sechs Straßenkreuzungen umgangen und zwei niveaugleiche Kreuzungen mit Güterbahnen vermieden werden. Auf diesem Abschnitt liegen zwei Hochbahnhöfe, Great Mall/ Main und Montague. Letzterer wird mittelfristig eine Umsteigemöglichkeit zu BART bieten, wobei die BART-Trasse hier unter der Straßenebene verlaufen wird. Der Rest der Stadtbahnstrecke führt ebenerdig auf einem eigenen Gleiskörper in Mittellage entlang desselben Straßenzugs, der jetzt Capitol Avenue heißt. Eine teilweise aufgeständerte Verlängerung weiter nach Südosten bis zum Eastridge Transit Center ist geplant.

Die bislang letzte Ergänzung der Stadtbahn von San Jose war die 8,2 km lange Verlängerung bis Winchester in der südwestlichen Nachbarstadt Campbell. Die Strecke zweigt von der bestehenden in der Nähe des Convention Center ab und führt zunächst durch einen 260 m langen Tunnel unter den Eisenbahngleisen am Bahnhof San Jose Diridon hindurch. Südlich der Stadtbahnhaltestelle an der Westseite des Bahnhofs wird die Strecke dann eingleisig, da auf der Trasse der ehemaligen *Southern Pacific Railroad* weiterhin Platz für ein Gütergleis der *Union Pacific* bleiben musste. Ausweichgleise sind zwischen Fruitdale und Bascom und von Downtown Campbell bis Winchester vorhanden. Neben dem Tunnel am Hauptbahnhof war eine eingleisige Brücke über die Hamilton Avenue mit einer gleichnamigen Haltestelle am südlichen Brückenende das wichtigste Bauprojekt auf diesem Ast. Eine 2,5 km lange Verlängerung bis Vasona Junction war von Anfang an geplant und könnte in Zukunft gebaut werden.

onto a 2.3 km viaduct erected above the median of Great Mall Parkway, a type of alignment rarely found on light rail systems and more typical of BART; in this way, the trains avoid six road intersections and two freight line crossings. The viaduct accommodates two elevated stations, Great Mall/Main and Montague. The latter will be a transfer point for BART in the mid-term future, with the BART tracks running below street level at this point. The rest of the light rail route continues at grade on a reserved right-of-way in the median of the same corridor, which is now called Capitol Avenue. A partly elevated extension further southeast to Eastridge Transit Center is planned.

The latest addition to San Jose's light rail system is the 8.2 km Winchester extension in the southwestern city of Campbell. The route diverges from the original line near Convention Center, and includes a short 260 m tunnel under the mainline tracks at San Jose Diridon station. Just south of the light rail stop on the western side of the railway station, the line becomes single-track as it follows an old Southern Pacific Railroad corridor which still accommodates a Union Pacific freight track. Two tracks for passing trains are available between Fruitdale and Bascom, and from Downtown Campbell to Winchester. Besides the tunnel at Diridon, the most important new structure on this branch is a single-track bridge over Hamilton Avenue, with a station of that name at its southern end. A 2.5 km extension to Vasona Junction has been planned from the beginning, and may still be built in the future.

UTDC-Wagen | *UTDC car (Bernhard Kußmagk, 1993)*

● Stadtbahnfahrzeuge

Die Stadtbahn von San Jose ist die einzige der neueren Generation in den USA, die in ihrer 25-jährigen Geschichte bereits ihren gesamten ursprünglichen Wagenpark ersetzt hat. Dieser bestand aus 50 Hochflur-Gelenkfahrzeugen von UTDC (Urban Transportation Development Corporation, jetzt Bombardier) aus Kanada. In den späten 1990er Jahren entschied VTA, neue Niederflurfahrzeuge anzuschaffen, um einen behindertengerechten Einstieg zu ermöglichen und so die bisher erforderlichen Rollstuhllifte loszuwerden. Die neuen Wagen wurden von der japanischen Firma Kinkisharyo gebaut, die einen Produktionsstandort in Massachusetts hat. Die elektrische Ausrüstung und das Antriebssystem stammen von Alstom. Die 6-achsigen Doppelgelenkwagen sind zu 70% niederflurig (Fußbodenhöhe 355 mm/889 mm), 27,43 m lang, 2,64 m breit und mit Fahrradaufhängevorrichtungen ausgestattet. Die Drehgestelle unter den erhöhten Endabschnitten sind angetrieben, während sich unter dem kurzen Mittelteil ein loses Fahrwerk befindet. 750 V Gleichstrom wird über eine Oberleitung zugeführt. Die Fahrzeuge verkehren normalerweise als Einzelwagen oder in Doppeltraktion, obwohl die meisten Bahnsteige rund 100 m lang sind (auf dem Winchester-Ast nur 75 m) und sogar 4-Wagen-Züge aufnehmen könnten. Nachdem das letzte der neuen Fahrzeuge im Jahr 2001 ausgeliefert worden war, verkaufte man die alten UTDC-Fahrzeuge nach Sacramento und Salt Lake City.

Der Stadtbahnbetriebshof befindet sich unweit der Strecke entlang der 1st Street zwischen den Haltestellen Civic Center und Gish.

● *Light Rail Rolling Stock*

The San Jose system is the only new-generation light rail system in the U.S. that, although only 25 years old, has already completely replaced its original rolling stock, which consisted of 50 articulated high-floor vehicles manufactured by UTDC (Urban Transportation Development Corporation; now Bombardier) of Canada. In the late 1990s, VTA decided to purchase a completely new fleet to provide level access for everyone by using low-floor technology, thus obviating the need for wheelchair lifts. The new cars were built by Kinkisharyo of Japan, which has a production plant in Massachusetts, with the electrical equipment and propulsion system supplied by Alstom. The 6-axle, double articulated vehicles are 70% low-floor (floor height 355 mm/889 mm), 27.43 m long, 2.64 m wide and are equipped with bicycle racks. The bogies under the raised end sections are powered, whereas a trailer truck is located under the short middle section. 750 V dc is supplied via an overhead catenary. The cars normally run as single or double units, although most platforms are around 100 m (on the Winchester branch only 75 m) long and could even accommodate 4-car trains. With the last of the new cars delivered in 2001, the old vehicles were sold to Sacramento and Salt Lake City.

The workshops for light rail vehicles are located off the 1st Street route between Civic Center and Gish stations.

Downtown Mountain View – dreisprachige Fahrgastinformation (Englisch, Spanisch und Vietnamesisch!) und Linienendsymbole – *trilingual passenger information (English, Spanish and Vietnamese!) and terminus symbols*

Kinkisharyo: stufenloser Einstieg | *stepfree boarding*

Kinkisharyo: 70% niederflurig | *70% low-floor*

South Pasadena – Kunstobjekte zieren die meisten Stationen in Los Angeles
– *public art is on display in almost all stations in Los Angeles*

LOS ANGELES, CA

Los Angeles ist bekannt als eine der größten Städte der Welt. Doch wie bei den meisten Ballungsräumen in den USA ist das, was man gemeinhin als Los Angeles bezeichnet, eine unendliche Anhäufung eigenständiger Städte, zwischen denen das eigentliche Los Angeles ein fast bizarres Gebilde darstellt. Unter den Nachbarstädten sind im Westen Santa Monica, Culver City und Beverly Hills, alle drei eigentlich Enklaven zwischen der Innenstadt von L.A. und dem ca. 20 km entfernten, teils zu L.A. gehörenden Strand, und im Osten und Süden Pasadena, Long Beach und Anaheim. Andererseits erstreckt sich L.A. rund 40 km nach Nordwesten ins San Fernando Valley und, wenn auch nur durch einen schmalen Korridor verbunden, 30 km nach Süden bis zum Hafen von San Pedro. Die eigentliche Stadtgemeinde hat eine Fläche von 1.302 km² mit rund 3,8 Mio. Einwohnern. Das durchgehend bebaute Gebiet reicht jedoch in Ost-West-Richtung von Malibu bis San Bernardino, eine Strecke von etwa 125 km, und etwa gleich weit von Nordwesten nach Südosten und umfasst das Los Angeles, Ventura, Orange, San Bernardino und Riverside County, eine Region, in der rund 18 Mio. Menschen leben. Eine weitere Ausdehnung des Ballungsraums ist kaum möglich, da das Becken von Los Angeles und das San Fernando Valley durch die relativ hohe Küstenkette, die San Gabriel Mountains im Norden und die San Jacinto Mountains im Osten, begrenzt ist, während der Pazifische Ozean im Südwesten eine natürliche Grenze bildet.

    Los Angeles kann mit den Zügen von Amtrak aus mehreren Richtungen erreicht werden: von Seattle, Sacramento und der San Francisco Bay Area täglich mit dem „Coast Starlight" über

Los Angeles is considered one of the largest cities in the world. However, like most conurbations in the U.S., what is commonly referred to as Los Angeles is a continuous cluster of independent cities, with L.A. proper assuming a rather bizarre form amid numerous smaller municipalities like the well-known Santa Monica, Culver City and Beverly Hills, which are actually enclaves in the 20 km stretch between downtown L.A. and the beaches, and Pasadena, Long Beach and Anaheim to the east and south. On the other hand, L.A. proper extends some 40 km northwest into the San Fernando Valley, and although only linked by a narrow corridor, 30 km south to the seaport at San Pedro. The city proper covers an area of 1,302 km2 with a population of roughly 3.8 million. The urbanised area, however, extends east-west from Malibu to San Bernardino, a distance of some 125 km, and similarly from the northwest to the southeast, including Los Angeles, Ventura, Orange, San Bernardino and Riverside Counties, a region home to some 18 million people. Further expansion of the metropolitan area is nearly impossible as the Los Angeles Basin and San Fernando Valley are bordered by the rather high peaks of the Coastal Ranges, the San Gabriel Mountains in the north and the San Jacinto Mountains in the east, with the Pacific Ocean constituting a natural limit in the southwest.

    Los Angeles can be reached by Amtrak trains from several directions: from Seattle, Sacramento and the San Francisco Bay Area daily on the "Coast Starlight" via San Luis Obispo (which is also served once a day by the "Pacific Surfliner");

San Luis Obispo (was auch einmal täglich durch den „Pacific Surfliner" angebunden ist); aus Chicago über Kansas City und Albuquerque täglich mit dem „Southwest Chief"; von New Orleans über Houston und Tucson drei Mal wöchentlich mit dem „Sunset Limited" (mit Kurswagen aus Chicago mit dem „Texas Eagle") und von San Diego sogar 11-mal täglich mit dem „Pacific Surfliner".

Metro (kurz für *Los Angeles County Metropolitan Transportation Authority*) ist zuständig für den öffentlichen Nahverkehr

Willowbrook

im Los Angeles County und betreibt in dieser Funktion die U-Bahn- und Stadtbahn-Linien sowie lokale und Express-Busse. Einige der eigenständigen Städte haben jedoch ihre eigenen Busse oft entlang derselben Routen, jedoch mit einem eigenen Tarif. Ein *Metro*-Ticket ist somit zum Beispiel nicht in den DASH-Bussen von Los Angeles oder den ‚Big Blue'-Bussen von Santa Monica gültig. Für alle Verkehrsmittel von *Metro* gibt es einen ‚Metro Day Pass' für nur 5,00 $, während eine Einzelfahrt (ohne Umsteigen) nur 1,50 $ kostet! Der Fahrpreis kann auch mit einer elektronischen Smartcard, der ‚TAP-Card' entrichtet werden. Für die Vorortszüge der Metrolink gelten eigene Fahrpreise.

from Chicago via Kansas City and Albuquerque daily on the "Southwest Chief"; from New Orleans via Houston and Tucson three times a week on the "Sunset Limited" (with direct coaches from Chicago running with the "Texas Eagle"); and from San Diego as often as 11 times a day on the "Pacific Surfliner".

Metro (short for Los Angeles County Metropolitan Transportation Authority) is responsible for public transport in L.A. County, and as such, operates the subway and light rail lines as well as local and express buses. Several of the independent cities, however, run their own buses often along the same routes, but without proper fare integration. A Metro ticket is thus not valid, for example, on Los Angeles' DASH buses or Santa Monica's Big Blue Buses. For all modes operated by Metro, a Metro Day Pass is available at only $5.00, while a single ride (without transfer) costs just $1.50! Fares can be paid with an electronic smartcard called the 'TAP card'. Different fares also apply for Metrolink commuter rail.

LOS ANGELES Innere Stadt | Inner City

LOS ANGELES

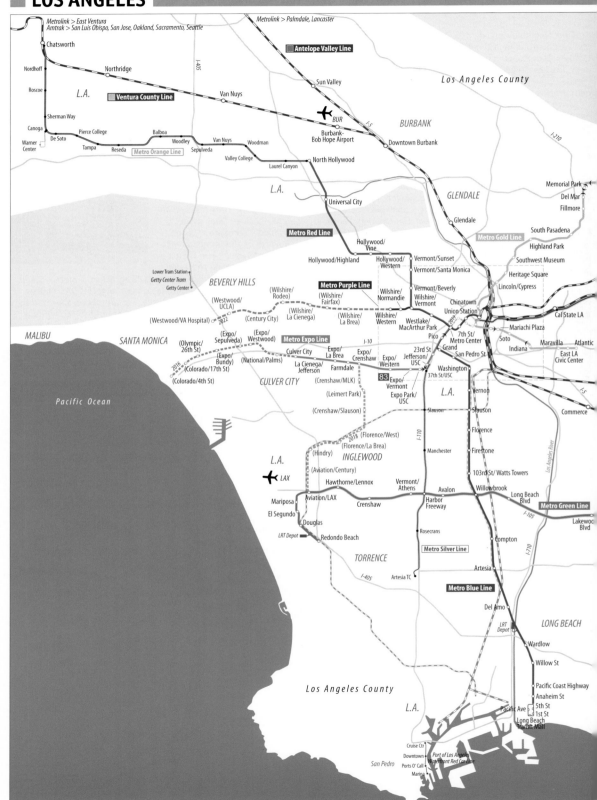

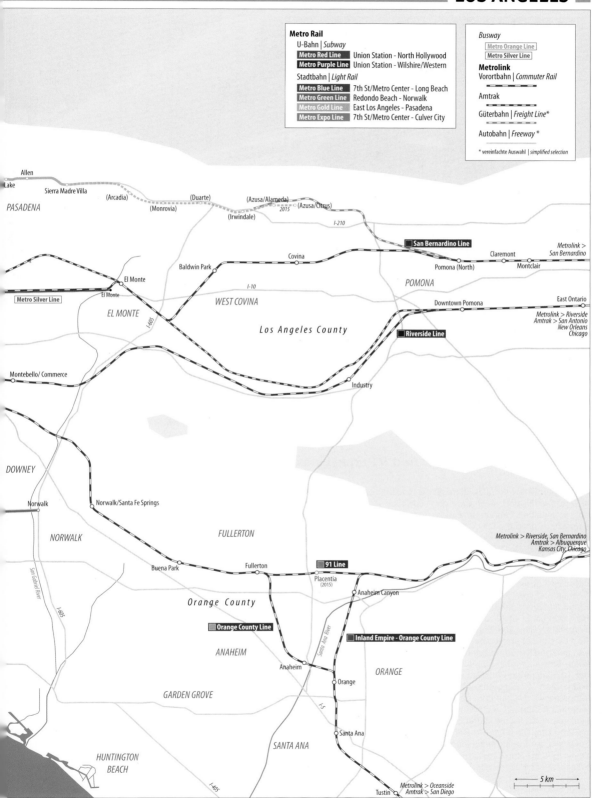

Metro Rail
U-Bahn | Subway
Metro Red Line Union Station - North Hollywood
Metro Purple Line Union Station - Wilshire/Western
Stadtbahn | Light Rail
Metro Blue Line 7th St/Metro Center - Long Beach
Metro Green Line Redondo Beach - Norwalk
Metro Gold Line East Los Angeles - Pasadena
Metro Expo Line 7th St/Metro Center - Culver City

Busway
Metro Orange Line
Metro Silver Line
Metrolink
Vorortbahn | Commuter Rail

Amtrak

Güterbahn | Freight Line*

Autobahn | Freeway *

* vereinfachte Auswahl | simplified selection

Allen
Lake
Sierra Madre Villa
(Arcadia)
(Duarte)
(Azusa/Alameda)
2015 (Azusa/Citrus)
(Monrovia)
(Irwindale)
PASADENA
I-210

San Bernardino Line
Covina
Pomona (North)
Claremont
Montclair
Metrolink >
San Bernardino

Baldwin Park
WEST COVINA
I-10
El Monte
Metro Silver Line
El Monte
EL MONTE
I-605
POMONA
Downtown Pomona
East Ontario
Metrolink > Riverside
Amtrak > San Antonio
New Orleans
Chicago

Los Angeles County
Riverside Line

Montebello/ Commerce
Industry

DOWNEY
Norwalk
Norwalk/Santa Fe Springs
NORWALK
FULLERTON
Metrolink > Riverside, San Bernardino
Amtrak > Albuquerque
Kansas City, Chicago

San Gabriel River
I-605
Buena Park
Fullerton
91 Line
Placentia
(2015)
Anaheim Canyon

Orange County
Orange County Line
Inland Empire - Orange County Line
ANAHEIM
Santa Ana River
Anaheim
ORANGE
Orange
GARDEN GROVE
I-5
Santa Ana
SANTA ANA
I-405

*HUNTINGTON
BEACH*
Metrolink > Oceanside
Amtrak > San Diego
Tustin

5 km

85

Wilshire/Western – noch einige Jahre westlicher Endpunkt der Purple Line
– for a few more years, the western terminus of the Purple Line

● ● SUBWAY – Metro Rail Red & Purple Lines

Das U-Bahn-Netz von L.A. umfasst die Red Line und die Purple Line. Die Green Line ist zwar auch völlig kreuzungsfrei, aber da sie dieselben Fahrzeuge wie die anderen Stadtbahnlinien einsetzt, wird sie als Teil des ‚Light Rail'-Netzes betrachtet.

Die Red Line und die Purple Line sind völlig unterirdisch und verbinden die Union Station auf der Ostseite der Innenstadt mit der als Koreatown bekannten Gegend entlang des Wilshire Boulevard (Purple Line) sowie mit dem Touristenmagneten Hollywood (Red Line) mit Stationen entlang der Vermont Avenue und des Hollywood Boulevard. Nach Hollywood/Highland fahren die Züge Richtung Nordwesten unter den Hollywood Hills weiter und erreichen zwei U-Bahnhöfe im San Fernando Valley, Universal City und North Hollywood. Die Red Line bietet somit eine kaum schlagbare Express-Fahrt von den nördlichen Vororten ins Zentrum von L.A., die 24 km lange Strecke wird in 30 Minuten zurückgelegt. Eine Fahrt auf der 10,3 km langen Purple Line dauert 13 Minuten. Jede Linie verkehrt alle 12 Minuten (alle 10 Minuten in den Hauptverkehrszeiten), d.h. auf dem gemeinsamen Abschnitt durch die Innenstadt fährt alle 5-6 Minuten eine Bahn. Die Betriebszeiten sind von 4:30 Uhr bis Mitternacht, Freitag und Samstag nachts bis 2:00 Uhr. Die beiden U-Bahn-Linien liegen vollständig innerhalb der Stadtgrenzen von L.A. Bis Ende 2006 wurden beide Äste als Red Line betrieben, die Beschilderung auf dem Wilshire-Ast ist aber weiterhin überwiegend rot statt violett.

Los Angeles ist noch immer als eine sehr autofreundliche Stadt bekannt, mit vielspurigen Autobahnen, die kreuz und

L.A.'s subway system consists of the Red and Purple Lines; the Green Line, despite being completely grade-separated, is considered a part of the city's light rail system as the same type of rolling stock is used as on the actual light rail lines.

The Red and Purple Lines are completely underground. They link Union Station on the east side of downtown with an area along Wilshire Boulevard known as Koreatown (Purple Line), and the tourist destination of Hollywood (Red Line) with stations along Vermont Avenue and Hollywood Boulevard. After Hollywood/Highland station, the trains head northwest under the Hollywood Hills to serve two stations in the San Fernando Valley, Universal City and North Hollywood. The Red Line thus provides a hard-to-beat express journey from the northern suburbs to downtown L.A., with the 24 km route taking just 30 minutes. A journey on the 10.3 km Purple Line takes 13 minutes. Each line operates every 12 minutes (10 minutes in peak hours), resulting in a train every 5-6 minutes on the shared downtown segment. Service hours are from 04:30 to midnight, extended until 02:00 on Friday and Saturday nights. The two subway lines run entirely within the L.A. city boundaries. Until late 2006, both subway branches were operated as the Red Line, and since then, signage on the Wilshire branch has remained predominantly red instead of purple.

Los Angeles is still famous for being a very car-friendly city, with multi-lane freeways criss-crossing the entire metropolitan region. But by the 1980s it had become clear

Universal City – gut sichtbare Metro-Stelen an allen Stationseingängen
– easily visible Metro poles at all station entrances

quer die gesamte Metropolregion erschließen. In den 1980er Jahren wurde aber sogar hier klar, dass mehr Straßen nicht die Lösung sein konnten, sondern dass ein Bahnnetz mit hoher Kapazität notwendig ist, vor allem im Zentrum von L.A. und in der dichter bebauten Westside. Der Bau der Red Line begann schließlich im September 1986 und dauerte bis Januar 1993, als das Teilstück im Zentrum von der Union Station bis Westlake in Betrieb genommen wurde. Dies war jedoch nicht die erste U-Bahn in L.A.: Im Jahr 1925 wurde die sogenannte ‚Hollywood Subway' (oder der ‚Belmont Tunnel') eröffnet, die es den elektrischen Straßenbahnen erlaubte, die Innenstadt durch einen 1,6 km langen zweigleisigen Tunnel von der Kreuzung Beverly/Glendale Boulevard zu erreichen. Die Endhaltestelle lag unterirdisch unter dem noch vorhandenen Subway Terminal Building auf der Westseite des Pershing Square. Der Straßenbahntunnel wurde von Bahnen der *Pacific Electric Railway* bis zum 19. Juni 1955 genutzt.

Alle U-Bahnhöfe wurden in offener Bauweise sehr großzügig errichtet. Durch ihre kunstvolle Ausgestaltung gehören sie zu den spektakulärsten in den USA, mit denen nur die beeindruckenden Gewölbestationen der Metro von Washington DC mithalten können. Der Abschnitt westlich der Station Westlake/MacArthur Park wurde auch offen errichtet, wobei der See während der Bauzeit abgepumpt wurde. Die übrigen Streckentunnel, die Erdbeben bis Stärke 7,5 standhalten müssen, wurden mit Tunnelbohrmaschinen (TBM) mit einem Durchmesser von 6,7 m bei einer durchschnittlichen Tiefe von 25 m in städtischen Gebieten und bis zu 200 m unter den Hollywood Hills aufgefahren. Neben den typischen Betontübbings wurden die Röhren mit einer speziellen Polyethylenmembran ausgekleidet, um das Eindringen von unterirdischen Gasen in den Tunnel zu verhindern. Unterirdische Methangase sind in den westlichen Bezirken von L.A. häufig, da dieses Gebiet einst ein wichtiges Ölfeld war und immer noch als kontaminierte Zone eingestuft wird. Die damit verbundenen Gefahren führten im Jahr 1998 nach einem Referendum zu einem U-Bahn-Bauverbot, doch 10 Jahre später gaben die Wähler in einer neuerlichen Abstimmung schließlich grünes Licht für eine Verlängerung der Purple Line.

Die sog. „Westside Subway Extension" erweitert die Purple Line Richtung Westen um ca. 14,5 km mit sieben neuen Stationen. Abgesehen von einem Schwenk zur Century City folgt die Strecke dem Wilshire Boulevard, verläuft durch die Stadt Beverly Hills und endet dann wieder in Los Angeles im Bezirk Westwood. In einer späteren Phase könnte sie bis Santa Monica verlängert werden.

Der Hollywood-Ast sollte einst weiter ins San Fernando Valley verlängert werden, aber schließlich wurde stattdessen die Bustrasse (*Busway*) für die Orange Line (siehe S. 112) als erschwinglichere Variante gebaut.

Am östlichen Ende enthielten die ursprünglichen Pläne eine Erweiterung Richtung East L.A., aber angesichts der geringeren Fahrgastprognosen und des vorübergehenden Tunnelbauverbots wurde hier schließlich eine weitgehend oberirdische Strecke als Teil der Gold Line umgesetzt.

even there that more roads were not the solution to traffic congestion, and that instead a high-capacity rail system was needed, especially in downtown L.A. and the more densely built-up Westside. Construction on the Red Line started in September 1986 and took until January 1993, when the downtown portion from Union Station to Westlake was inaugurated. This was not, however, the first subway in L.A.: opened in 1925, the so-called 'Hollywood Subway' (or 'Belmont Tunnel') allowed electric streetcars to enter the downtown area through a 1.6 km double-track tunnel starting at the intersection of Beverly & Glendale Boulevards and terminating underground under the Subway Terminal Building, which still stands on the west side of Pershing Square. The streetcar subway was used by Pacific Electric trains until 19 June 1955.

All the stations on the L.A. subway were built by cut-and-cover and feature large spaces, decorated with artwork, making the system by far the most spectacular in the U.S., rivalled only by the impressive vaults of the Washington DC Metro. The section just west of Westlake/MacArthur Park station was also built from the surface, in this case by completely draining the lake during construction. The remaining running tunnels, which had to be built to withstand earthquakes up to a magnitude of 7.5, were excavated using tunnel boring machines (TBMs) with a 6.7 m diameter at an average depth of 25 m in urban areas and up to 200 m under the Hollywood Hills. Besides the typical concrete linings, the tubes were isolated with a special polyethylene membrane to prevent subsoil gases from entering the tunnels. Underground methane gases are common in western L.A. as the area was once an important oil field and is still a contaminated zone. The dangers associated with this led to a subway tunnelling ban imposed by a referendum in 1998, although

LOS ANGELES Metro Rail – *Subway*

~25.5 km (unterirdisch | *underground*)
16 Bahnhöfe | *stations*

30 Jan 1993: Union Station – Westlake/MacArthur Park (4.8 km)
13 July 1996: Westlake/MacArthur Park – Wilshire/Western (3.2 km)
12 June 1999: Wilshire/Vermont – Hollywood/Vine (7.5 km)
24 June 2000: Hollywood/Vine – North Hollywood (10.0 km)
~ 2022: Wilshire/Western – Westwood/VA Hospital (14.5 km)

Seitenansicht eines U-Bahn-Wagens von Ansaldobreda
– *side view of an Ansaldobreda subway car*

10 years later, a new ballot measure to give Metro the green light to finally proceed with an extension of the Purple Line was approved by the majority of voters.

The 'Westside Subway Extension' will extend the Purple Line about 14.5 km westwards with seven new stations. Except for a detour to Century City, it will follow the busy Wilshire Boulevard corridor, running through the City of Beverly Hills before returning to L.A. and terminating in the Westwood area. In a future stage, it may be extended to Santa Monica.

The Hollywood branch was once planned to be extended further into the San Fernando Valley, but in the end the Orange Line Busway (see p. 112) was built as a more affordable option.

At the eastern end, the initial plans included an extension towards East L.A., but given the lower ridership projections and the temporary subway construction ban, it was eventually built as a primarily surface extension of the light rail Gold Line.

Ⓜ U-Bahn-Fahrzeuge

Die beiden U-Bahn-Linien werden mit einer Flotte von 104 Fahrzeugen des Typs A650 von Ansaldobreda aus Italien betrieben. Sie wurden in zwei Serien ausgeliefert, 30 Wagen zwischen 1988 und 1993 mit Gleichstrommotoren und 74 Wagen zwischen 1995 und 1997 mit Drehstrommotoren. Jeder Wagen ist 22,7 m lang, 3 m breit und klimatisiert. Der Fußboden liegt 1136 mm über Schienenoberkante. Es handelt sich um Doppeltriebwagen, die während der Hauptverkehrszeiten als 6-Wagen-Züge, sonst als 4-Wagen-Züge eingesetzt werden. Die Stromversorgung mit 750 V Gleichspannung erfolgt über eine seitliche Stromschiene. Die Höchstgeschwindigkeit beträgt 112 km/h und kann auf der langen Strecke zwischen Hollywood/Highland und Universal City voll ausgefahren werden.

Der U-Bahn-Betriebshof liegt südlich der Union Station am Santa Fe Drive, auf dem Gelände der ehemaligen La Grande Station, dem Hauptbahnhof der *Santa Fe*, bevor im Jahr 1939 die heutige Union Station eröffnet wurde.

Ⓜ Subway Rolling Stock

The two subway lines are operated with a fleet of 104 vehicles of A650 stock manufactured by Ansaldobreda of Italy. They were delivered in two batches, 30 cars between 1988 and 1993 equipped with a dc traction system, and 74 cars between 1995 and 1997 with ac drives. Each car is 22.7 m long, 3 m wide and air-conditioned. The train floor is 1136 mm above the rail top. They work as married pairs in 4-car trainsets during off-peak hours, and in 6-car sets during rush hour. 750 V dc is supplied via a third rail. The maximum speed of 112 km/h can be savoured on the long stretch between Hollywood/Highland and Universal City.

The subway maintenance yard is located south of Union Station on Santa Fe Drive on a site once used by La Grande Station, Santa Fe's main passenger terminal before today's Union Station opened in 1939.

Gegenüberliegende Seite | *Facing page*

① ② ③ **Union Station**

  ③ Relief von Cynthia Carlson mit dem Titel „L.A.: Stadt der Engel" (1993)
  – *relief mural by Cynthia Carlson called "L.A.: City of Angels" (1993)*

  ④ **Civic Center** – großzügiges Zwischengeschoss
  – *spacious mezzanine level*

Innenansicht eines 3 m breiten U-Bahn-Wagens von Ansaldobreda
– *interior view of a 3 m wide Ansaldobreda subway car*

U-Bahn-Betriebshof östlich der Innenstadt mit Skyline im Hintergrund
– *subway maintenance yard east of downtown with skyline in the background*

① Pershing Square – *"Neons for Pershing Square"* (1993)
– Installation mit Neonleuchten von Stephen Antonakos
– *neon sculptures by Stephen Antonakos*

② 7th Street/Metro Center
– harmonisch in ein klassisches Gebäude integrierter Eingang an der 7th Street; hier enden auf der Ebene -2 die Stadtbahnen der Blue & Expo Line, und auf der Ebene -3 kreuzt die U-Bahn.
– *entrance harmoniously integrated into a classic building on 7th Street; light rail trains of the Blue & Expo Lines terminate on level -2, while subway trains of the Red & Purple Lines cross on level -3.*

③ Wilshire/Vermont – *"No title"* (2004)
– typografische Zeichen von Bob Zoell; doppelstöckiger Verzweigungsbahnhof, oben zweigleisig stadteinwärts, unten eingleisig stadtauswärts.
– *typographic symbols by Bon Zoell; here the two lines diverge, on the upper level inbound on two tracks, and on the lower, outbound on a single track.*

④ **Westlake/MacArthur** – *"El Sol/La Luna"* (1993)
– Fliesenwandbild (Sonne/Mond) von Francisco Letelier
– *tile mural (Sun/Moon) by Francisco Letelier*

⑤ **Wilshire/Vermont** – *"Los Angeles Seen"* (1996)
– schwebende Objekte über den Gleisen von Peter Shire
– *objects floating above the tracks, created by Peter Shire*

⑥ **Wilshire/Normandie** – *"Festival of Masks Parade"* (1996)
– Wandbild von Frank Romero
– *mural by Frank Romero*

⑦ **Wilshire/Western** – *"People Coming People Going"* (1996)
– Fliesenwandbild von Richard Wyatt zeigt die Verschiedenartigkeit
  der Menschen in Los Angeles.
– *tile mural by Richard Wyatt depicting the diversity of people in Los Angeles.*

①

②

③

① Vermont/Beverley
– Felsblöcke von George Stone (1999) symbolisieren das Nebeneinander von Natur und moderner Architektur.
– *Rock formations by George Stone (1999) symbolise nature in juxtaposition with modern architecture.*

② Vermont/Santa Monica
– außergewöhnliche, linsenartige Überdachung des nördlichen Eingangs, ein Entwurf von Ellerbe Becket Architects
– *unusual lens-shaped roof over the north entrance, a design by Ellerbe Becket Architects*

③ Vermont/Santa Monica
– Bahnsteigebene
– *platform level*

④ **Vermont/Sunset** – *"Ecliptic/Illume"* (1999)
– fiktive Planetenkonstellation von Michael Davis
– *ficticious planet constellations by Michael Davis*

⑤ ⑥ ⑦ **Hollywood/Western**
– Erinnerung an die „Red Cars" der *Pacific Electric* in einer durch farbenfrohe Wandfliesen geprägten Station, ein Konzept, das sich an der Oberfläche in der Architektur eines Hauses fortsetzt.
– *tribute to the Pacific Electric 'Red Cars' in a station dominated by colourful tiling, a design also reflected in the architecture of a building just outside the station.*

① - ④ **Hollywood/Vine** – (*"Hooray for Hollywood"*, Gilbert Lujan, 1999)
– wahrscheinlich der beeindruckendste U-Bahnhof in den USA, ganz im Zeichen von Hollywood: Alte Filmprojektoren im Zwischengeschoss, stilisierte Palmen als Symbol der Scheinwelten, mit Filmrollen verkleidete Decken, Filmstreifen an den Wänden und viele weitere kleinere Details gibt es zu entdecken. Die klassischen Autos auf den Sitzbänken sind leider inzwischen verschwunden.
– *probably the most spectacular underground station in the U.S.A., all inspired by Hollywood: old movie projectors on the mezzanine level, stylised palm trees to create an illusory world, ceilings covered with film reels, film strips along the walls plus many other details waiting to be discovered. Unfortunately, the classic cars on the benches are no longer there.*

⑤

⑤ - ⑦ Hollywood/Highland

– Diese Station liegt direkt im Herzen von Hollywood, neben dem Dolby (vormals Kodak) Theatre, dem berühmten Walk of Fame und vielen anderen Touristenattraktionen. Der Entwurf des U-Bahnhofs mit seinen geschwungenen abstrakten Formen stammt von Sheila Klein in Zusammenarbeit mit Dworsky Associates Architects.

– *This station lies in the heart of Hollywood, next to the Dolby (formerly Kodak) Theatre, the famous Walk of Fame and many other tourist attractions. The design of the underground station, which features undulating abstract shapes, is by Sheila Klein, in collaboration with Dworsky Associates Architects.*

⑦

⑥

(1)

(2)

(1) - (4) **Universal City** – (*"Tree of Califas"*, Margaret Garcia, 2000)
– In diesem U-Bahnhof, der nach den benachbarten Universal Studios benannt
ist, dominieren im Gegensatz zur vorangegangenen Station gerade und gewin-
kelte Formen, die den Blick auf die Wandbilder an den Mittelstützen richten.
Diese nehmen Bezug auf ein wichtiges geschichtliches Ereignis (auf einer
Seite auf Spanisch, auf der anderen auf Englisch), denn in dieser Gegend
wurde 1847 der Vertrag unterzeichnet, durch den Kalifornien von Mexiko an
die USA überging.
– *Unlike the previous one, this station, named after the nearby Universal
Studios, is dominated by straight and angled shapes which draw the passenger's attention to the tiles on the central pillars, which tell the story of an
important historical event (in Spanish on one side and English on the other):
on this site, the treaty which relinquished control of California from Mexico
to the United States was signed in 1847.*

(3)

(4)

⑤

⑤ - ⑧ **North Hollywood** – (*"Kaleidoscope Dreams"*, Anne Marie Karlsen, 2000)
– Die nördliche Endstation der Red Line im San Fernando Valley ist von warmen
Orange-Tönen geprägt, die durch mehrere bunte Fliesenmosaike ergänzt
werden. Diese sollen die Träume und Sehnsüchte mehrerer Generationen von
Einwanderern in dieser Gegend widerspiegeln.
– *the northern terminus of the Red Line in the San Fernando Valley is
dominated by warm orange colours, enhanced with several tile mosaics
which depict the dreams and aspirations of generations of immigrants in
this area.*

⑥

⑦

⑧

1st Street (Garey St) – Gold Line auf dem Weg Richtung East L.A. vor der Skyline von Los Angeles
– *Gold Line train on its way to East L.A. in front of L.A.'s skyline*

●●●●● LIGHT RAIL – Metro Rail Blue, Green, Gold & Expo Lines

Das derzeitige Stadtbahnnetz von L.A. besteht aus vier Linien, wobei sich nur die Blue Line und die Expo Line einen 2 km langen Abschnitt auf der Flower Street in der Innenstadt von L.A. teilen. Alle Routen wurden jedoch nach den gleichen Parametern gebaut, so dass die Fahrzeuge zwischen den einzelnen Linien austauschbar sind und die Linienführungen in Zukunft angepasst werden können, sobald verschiedene Strecken baulich miteinander verbunden worden sind. Die Stadtbahn wird mit Hochflurfahrzeugen betrieben, die auch nur an Hochbahnsteigen halten. Das ist in den USA eher unüblich (das einzige andere System dieser Art ist das in Saint Louis) und folgt dem Beispiel von ähnlichen, etwa 10 Jahre früher eröffneten Betrieben in Kanada, nämlich in Edmonton und Calgary.

Angesichts der gleichmäßigen Ausdehnung der meisten Vororte von L.A., wo meist nur breite Autobahnen und seit langem bestehende Bahnstrecken eine gewisse Struktur erkennen lassen, war die Stadtbahn wahrscheinlich die beste Wahl, um eines Tages ein Bahnnetz für die gesamte Metropolregion schaffen zu können. Ein ähnliches System existierte im Großraum von Los Angeles bereits ab dem späten 19. Jahrhundert bis 1961 in der Form der *Pacific Electric Railway* (PE), die im Volksmund als „Red Car" (im Gegensatz zur städtischen Straßenbahn, dem „Yellow Car") bezeichnet wurde. In seiner Blütezeit in den 1920er Jahren umfasste das PE-Netz etwa 1600 km Gleislänge, es erstreckte sich bis nach San Bernardino, Santa Ana und Huntington Beach. Auf vielen Strecken gab es auch Güterverkehr. Wie bei modernen Stadtbahnen lagen lange Überlandabschnitte auf eigenem Bahnkörper, während städtische Abschnitte oft straßenbündig gemeinsam mit dem motorisierten Verkehr und im Fall von Los Angeles auch mit

L.A.'s present light rail system consists of four lines. The Blue and Expo Lines are the only ones which share part of a route, the 2 km segment on Flower Street in downtown L.A. All routes, however, have been built to the same specifications, so that rolling stock is interchangeable and lines may be adjusted in the future as different routes become physically connected. With high-floor vehicles stopping exclusively at high platforms, the L.A. light rail system is rather unusual for the U.S. (the only other such system being that in St Louis) and follows the example of similar systems built in Canada some 10 years earlier, namely in Edmonton and Calgary.

Given the continuous sprawl of most of L.A.'s suburbs, with the only clear corridors defined by wide freeways and long-established railway routes, light rail was probably the best choice to eventually cover the entire vast region with a rail system. A similar system already existed in Greater Los Angeles from the late 19th Century until 1961 in the form of the Pacific Electric Railway (PE), popularly known as the 'Red Car' system (as opposed to the 'Yellow Car', the urban L.A. streetcar system). In its heyday in the 1920s, the PE network comprised some 1600 km of tracks, extending as far as San Bernardino, Santa Ana and Huntington Beach. Many routes also carried freight trains. Like on modern light rail systems, long interurban sections were on dedicated rights-of-way, while urban sections often shared roads with motorised traffic, and in the case of Los Angeles, with narrow-gauge streetcars, too. When the construction of freeways started in the 1930s, many PE routes were changed to bus operation, although the last line, that to Long Beach, withstood this trend until 1961.

Long Beach/1st Street – Blue Line auf der Schleifenfahrt an ihrem südlichen Ende in Long Beach
– *Blue Line on the loop at its southern end in Long Beach*

schmalspurigen Straßenbahnen verliefen. Mit dem Bau von Autobahnen ab den 1930er Jahren wurden viele PE-Linien auf Busbetrieb umgestellt, auch wenn die letzte Linie, nämlich die nach Long Beach, diesem Trend noch bis 1961 widerstand.

● **Blue Line** (35,7 km, 22 Stationen)

Im Vergleich zur Red Line und zur Green Line, die auch im Grundnetz der 1980er Jahre enthalten waren, war die Blue Line am einfachsten umzusetzen, da sie weitgehend der Trasse der alten *Pacific Electric* von Los Angeles nach Long Beach folgt. Auch wenn der Personenverkehr 1961 eingestellt worden war, hatte diese Strecke als Güterbahn überlebt, weshalb kein Grunderwerb erforderlich war.

Die Blue Line beginnt unterirdisch im Zentrum von Los Angeles, wo ein Turmbahnhof mitten im Geschäftsviertel unter der 7th & Flower Street ein bequemes Umsteigen zur Red/Purple Line auf der unteren Ebene ermöglicht. Der Tunnel entlang der Flower Street ist nur etwa 900 m lang und die Stadtbahn kommt südlich der 11th Street an die Oberfläche, bevor sie die Station Pico, die ursprüngliche nördliche Endstation von 1990, erreicht. Nach Unterquerung des aufgeständerten Santa Monica Freeway (I-10) biegt die Blue Line links in den Washington Boulevard, während die neue Expo Line geradeaus weiter auf der Flower Street bleibt. Auf der Flower Street liegen die Gleise auf einem eigenen Gleiskörper am östlichen Straßenrand, doch dann schwenkt die Stadtbahn in die Straßenmitte des Washington Boulevard und fährt nach Osten bis zum Long Beach Boulevard, wo sie die alte PE-Trasse Richtung Süden über Florence, Watts, Willowbrook, Compton und Carson nach Long Beach erreicht; die PE-Züge fuhren einst über den Olympic Boulevard in die Innenstadt. Etwa 700 m weiter südlich trifft ein Gütergleis auf die Blue Line, das an der Slauson Avenue von der Ost- auf die Westseite wechselt. An diesem Punkt wurde für die Blue Line ein Hochbahnhof gebaut, um Bahnübergänge an dieser Straße und an der 60th Street zu vermeiden. Eine ähnliche Lösung wurde am Firestone Boulevard gewählt, jedoch wurde hier auch die Güterbahn in Hochlage gebracht. Die Blue Line kreuzt die Green Line, die an dieser Stelle aufgeständert ist, an der Station Willowbrook (vormals Imperial/Wilmington). Hier gibt es eine Gleisverbindung zwischen den beiden Strecken. Ein weiterer Viadukt bringt die Blue Line dann über die Rosecrans Avenue nördlich der Station Compton, während im weiteren Verlauf eine 500 m lange Brücke die wichtigste Güterbahn zum Hafen entlang der Alameda Street überspannt. Nördlich des Del Amo

LOS ANGELES Metro Rail – *Light Rail*

~110.5 km (3.5 km unterirdisch | *underground*)
(+ 31.2 km im Bau | *under construction*)
67 Haltestellen | *stations* (+ 15 im Bau | *under construction*)

14 July 1990: Pico – Anaheim St (31.4 km)
04 Sept 1990: Long Beach loop (3.1 km)
15 Feb 1991: Pico – 7th St/Metro Center (1.2 km)
12 Aug 1995: Norwalk – Redondo Beach (31.5 km)
26 July 2003: Union Station – Sierra Madre Villa (22 km)
15 Nov 2009: Union Station – Atlantic (9.3 km)
28 Apr 2012: Pico – La Cienega/Jefferson (10.5 km)
20 June 2012: La Cienega/Jefferson – Culver City (1.5 km)
+ Farmdale
2015: Sierra Madre Villa – Azusa/Citrus (17.6 km)
2016: Culver City – Colorado/4th St (10.6 km)
2019: 7th St/Metro Center – 1st/Central (3 km)

● *Blue Line* (35.7 km, 22 stations)

Compared to the Red and Green Lines also included in the initial Metro Rail network designed in the 1980s, the Blue Line was the easiest to implement as it largely follows the alignment of the old Pacific Electric line from Los Angeles to Long Beach, which, although passenger service was discontinued in 1961, had survived as a freight corridor, and therefore no land acquisition was required.

The Blue Line starts underground in downtown L.A., where a convenient +-shaped interchange station was built in the heart of the commercial area beneath 7th & Flower Streets, with the Red/Purple Line on the lower level. The tunnel along Flower Street is only some 900 m long, and trains surface just south of 11th Street before arriving at Pico station, the original 1990 northern terminus. After passing under the elevated Santa Monica Freeway (I-10), the Blue Line turns left into Washington Boulevard, while the new Expo Line continues straight along Flower Street. On Flower Street the tracks are on the east side of the road on a private right-of-way, but they change to the centre on Washington Boulevard east to Long Beach Boulevard, where the trains pick up the old PE alignment south to Long Beach (PE trains used to run downtown via Olympic Boulevard), passing through Florence, Watts, Willowbrook, Compton and Carson. Some 700 m further south, a freight track joins the Blue Line route, switching sides from east to west at Slauson Avenue, where an elevated station was built for the Blue Line to avoid a level crossing at that road and 60th Street. A similar solution was chosen at Firestone Boulevard, where the freight line was also raised. At Willowbrook (formerly known as Imperial/Wilmington), the Blue Line intersects with the Green Line, which is elevated at this point; there is a track link between the two lines. Another viaduct then takes the Blue Line over Rosecrans Avenue north of Compton station, while further down the line a 500 m bridge spans

Wardlow

7th Street/Metro Center

Boulevard liegt der gleichnamige Hochbahnhof. Nach Überqueren des Long Beach Freeway (I-710) und einer Güterbahn auf einem hohen Viadukt ist unterhalb der Betriebshof der Blue Line sichtbar. Südlich der Station Willow Street verlässt die Blue Line die Eisenbahntrasse und erreicht den Mittelstreifen des Long Beach Boulevard. An der 9th Street wechseln die beiden Gleise die Seiten und die Stadtbahn fährt Richtung Süden geradeaus weiter bis zur 1st Street, wo sie rechts in die Long Beach Transit Mall einbiegt; die zweigleisige Endstation verfügt über einen Mittelbahnsteig. Die Blue Line kehrt Richtung L.A. über die Pacific Avenue und die 8th Street zurück. Bis auf die in nur einer Richtung bedienten Haltestellen entlang der Schleife in Long Beach und der Endstation 7th St/Metro Center haben alle Stationen Mittelbahnsteige. Auch wenn für die Blue Line mehrere wichtige Bauwerke errichtet wurden, existiert noch immer eine große Anzahl an Bahnübergängen, was zu zahlreichen tödlichen Unfällen führt, weshalb weitere Maßnahmen wie der voll kreuzungsfreie Ausbau gefordert wurden.

Die heutige Blue Line war einst nur als südlicher Teil einer langen Nord-Süd-Strecke geplant. Sie wird nun schließlich unterirdisch durch die Innenstadt verlängert, um eine Verbindung mit der Gold Line in Little Tokyo herzustellen. Das jetzt als ‚Regional Connector' bezeichnete Projekt wurde wegen des Tunnelbauverbots von 1998 aufgeschoben, aber derzeit rechnet man mit einem Baubeginn im Jahr 2013.

Die Blue Line wird meist mit 3-Wagen-Zügen bedient und verkehrt von 5:00 bis 24:00 Uhr (am Wochenende bis 2:00 Uhr), tagsüber alle 12 Minuten und während der Hauptverkehrszeiten bis Del Amo oder Willow alle 6 Minuten.

across the main harbour freight line built along Alameda Street. Del Amo is another elevated station just north of the road of that name. After passing the Long Beach Freeway (I-710) and crossing a freight line on a high flyover, the Blue Line's maintenance yard is visible below. Just south of Willow Street station, the Blue Line leaves the railway alignment and enters the median of Long Beach Boulevard. At 9th Street, the two tracks switch sides, and southbound trains continue straight ahead to 1st Street, where they turn right into the Long Beach Transit Mall; the terminus has two tracks with an island platform. The Blue Line heads back to L.A. via Pacific Avenue and 8th Street. Except for the unidirectional stops on the Long Beach loop and the 7th St/Metro Center terminus, all stations have island platforms. Despite several important structures built for the Blue Line, many level crossings still exist, resulting in numerous fatal accidents. Further measures like full grade separation have therefore been called for.

Planned to be just the southern part of a long north-south route, the Blue Line will finally be extended underground through the downtown area to link up with the Gold Line at Little Tokyo. Now dubbed the 'Regional Connector', this vital link was deferred by the 1998 tunnelling ban, but its construction is now planned to start in 2013.

In operation from 05:00 to 24:00 (until 02:00 on weekends), the Blue Line mostly uses 3-car trains, which come every 12 minutes during daytime hours, and every 6 minutes during peak times (but only as far as Del Amo or Willow).

Long Beach (Pacific Avenue)

Long Beach (Transit Mall)

Hawthorne/Lennox – Green Line-Station auf dem Mittelstreifen der Autobahn I-105 (Century Freeway)
– *Green Line station in the median strip of I-105 (Century Freeway)*

● **Green Line** (31,5 km, 14 Stationen)

Im Gegensatz zu den anderen Stadtbahnlinien, die neben unterirdischen und aufgeständerten Abschnitten auch ebenerdige mit Bahnübergängen aufweisen, ist die Green Line völlig kreuzungsfrei und erfüllt somit die Kriterien einer echten „U-Bahn" bzw. „Metro", allerdings verwendet sie die gleichen Fahrzeuge wie die anderen Stadtbahnlinien und wird auch über Oberleitung mit Fahrstrom versorgt.

Die Green Line wurde zusammen mit einer Ost-West-Autobahn, dem Century Freeway (I-105), geplant. Sie erreicht den Mittelstreifen dieser Schnellstraße östlich der Station Aviation/LAX und folgt diesem bis zur Endstation Norwalk, die in ein Autobahndreieck (I-105 & I-605) eingebettet ist. Eine 4 km lange Ostverlängerung zur Metrolink-Station Norwalk/Santa Fe Springs wurde wiederholt vorgeschlagen, aber dies würde teilweise den Bau eines Tunnels erfordern. Der Autobahnabschnitt liegt streckenweise in einem breiten Einschnitt, ebenerdig oder aufgeständert. Der Stationsabstand zwischen Long Beach Boulevard und Lakewood beträgt 6,7 km, obwohl die Strecke durchgehend durch bebautes Gebiet führt. An der Station Willowbrook kann man zur Blue Line auf der unteren Ebene umsteigen, am Harbor Freeway zu den Express-Bussen der Silver Line. Während die Autobahn nach Westen entlang des südlichen Rands des Flughafens von Los Angeles (LAX) weiterführt, taucht die Green Line unter den südlichen Fahrspuren hindurch, bleibt aber weiterhin auf einem Hochbahnviadukt und erreicht die Station Aviation/LAX. Westlich dieser Station ist im Gleisbett eine Vorleistung für einen ursprünglich vorgese-

● *Green Line* (31.5 km, 14 stations)

Unlike the other light rail lines, which besides underground and elevated sections also feature surface routes with level crossings, the Green Line is completely grade-separated and thus qualifies as a 'metro' line; however, it uses the same rolling stock as the other LRT lines, and has an overhead power supply system.

The Green Line was designed together with the east-west Century Freeway (I-105). It runs in the freeway median from just east of Aviation/LAX station all the way to Norwalk, where it terminates embedded in the freeway interchange (I-105 & I-605). A 4 km eastern extension to Norwalk/Santa Fe Springs Metrolink station has been proposed, but this would require some tunnelling. The freeway section includes segments in a wide trench, at grade and on viaducts. The station distance between Long Beach Boulevard and Lakewood is quite long at 6.7 km, although the area between them is all built up. Interchange to the Blue Line is available at Willowbrook on the lower level, while at Harbor Freeway one can change to the express buses of the Silver Line. While the freeway continues west along the southern edge of L.A.'s International Airport (LAX), the Green Line dives under the eastbound road lanes, though remaining on an elevated structure at Aviation/LAX station. Upon leaving this station for Redondo Beach, a stub built for a previously planned extension to the airport is visible. The future Crenshaw Line may eventually be connected to the Green Line at this point. The western part of the Green Line is completely elevated,

Redondo Beach

Douglas

henen Abzweig zum Flughafen erkennbar. Die jetzt geplante Crenshaw Line könnte an dieser Stelle an die Green Line angeschlossen werden. Der westliche Abschnitt der Green Line verläuft durchgehend als Hochbahn, erst nach Südwesten entlang des Atwood Way, dann in Richtung Süden über der Nash Street durch eine Mischung aus Wohn- und Gewerbegebieten, bevor sie nach Südosten schwenkt und die Trasse einer Güterbahn erreicht, die bis hinunter zum Hafen von Long Beach führt. Eine 3 km lange Verlängerung der Green Line entlang dieser Strecke bis zum Einkaufszentrum South Bay Galleria oder weiter ist im Gespräch, genießt aber derzeit keine Priorität.

Die gesamte 31,5 km lange Green Line wurde im Jahr 1995 in einem Stück eröffnet. Meist fahren nur 2-Wagen-Züge, während der frühen Morgenstunden und am späten Abend sogar nur Einzelwagen. Sie bedienen die gesamte Strecke von 4:00 Uhr bis etwa Mitternacht (Freitag und Samstag nachts bis 2:00 Uhr) während der Hauptverkehrszeiten alle 7-8 Minuten, sonst alle 15 Minuten. Da sie keine städtischen Zentren direkt erschließt, verkehrt die Green Line weit unter ihrem eigentlichen Potenzial als Tangentiallinie.

Wenn etwa im Jahr 2018 die 13,5 km lange **Crenshaw Line** fertig gestellt ist, kann die Green Line abwechselnd den Redondo Beach-Ast und den LAX-Knoten an der Station Aviation/ Century bedienen, von wo aus nach derzeitigen Planungen ein Peoplemover die Fluggäste zu den einzelnen Terminals bringen soll. Die Crenshaw Line könnte den Abschnitt der Green Line westlich von Aviation/LAX auch völlig übernehmen. In einer späteren Bauphase soll die Crenshaw Line nach Norden zum zukünftigen U-Bahnhof Wilshire/La Brea der Purple Line erweitert werden.

following Atwood Way southwest and Nash Street southwards through a mix of housing and industrial estates before swinging southeast to join the freight corridor that runs all the way south to Long Beach. A 3 km extension along this route to the South Bay Galleria shopping mall or beyond has been proposed, but is not a priority at present.

The 31.5 km Green Line was opened in its entirety in 1995. Usually, only 2-car trains (single units during early mornings and late evenings) operate the full length from 04:00 until around midnight (extended until 02:00 Fri & Sat nights), every 7-8 minutes during rush hour and every 15 minutes during off-peak times. As it does not serve any major urban centres directly, the Green Line has been performing far below its potential as a tangential line.

Once the 13.5 km Crenshaw Line has been completed in around 2018, Green Line trains may alternately serve Redondo Beach and the LAX hub at Aviation/Century from where a people mover is projected to carry passengers to individual terminals. The Green Line section west of Aviation/LAX station may also be fully integrated into the Crenshaw Line. In a later stage, the Crenshaw Line may be extended north to Wilshire/La Brea station on the future Purple Line extension.

Hawthorne/Lennox – "Companions" (Mineko Grimmer, 1995)

Norwalk

Allen – Gold Line-Station auf dem Mittelstreifen der Autobahn I-210 (Foothill Freeway)
– Gold Line station in the median strip of I-210 (Foothill Freeway)

● **Gold Line** (31,3 km, 21 Stationen)

Der nördliche Teil der heutigen Gold Line wurde ursprünglich als Teil der blauen Nord-Süd-Linie konzipiert. Als aber der Bau der unterirdischen Strecke durch die Innenstadt in ferne Zukunft rückte, wurde die Pasadena-Linie als eigenes Projekt vorgezogen. 1992 wurde die Trasse der *Atchison, Topeka and Santa Fe Railway*, auf der einst der „Southwest Chief" nach Chicago oder der „Desert Wind" nach Las Vegas und Salt Lake City fuhren, gekauft, nachdem diese Züge über Fullerton umgeleitet worden waren. An der Union Station wurden die Gleise 1 und 2 an *Metro* abgetreten, so dass für Amtrak und Metrolink noch zehn Stumpfgleise übrig blieben. Beim Verlassen der Union Station erreicht die Gold Line eine

● *Gold Line (31.3 km, 21 stations)*

The northern leg of today's Gold Line was initially conceived as part of the north-south Blue Line. With the construction of the underground downtown portion lying in the distant future, the Pasadena line was brought forward as a separate project. In 1992, the Atchison, Topeka and Santa Fe Railway right-of-way, which once carried the "Southwest Chief" to Chicago and the "Desert Wind" to Las Vegas and Salt Lake City, was purchased after these trains had been rerouted via Fullerton. At Union Station, tracks 1 and 2 were ceded to Metro, leaving ten terminal tracks for Amtrak and Metrolink services. Upon leaving Union Station, Gold Line trains climb a 1.2 km viaduct which spans over Main and Alameda

South Pasadena (Mission Street)

Chinatown

Southwest Museum

Mariachi Plaza

1,2 km lange Hochbahnstrecke, die die Main und Alameda Street überspannt und auf der die Station Chinatown liegt. Wieder ebenerdig kommt sie auf die alte *Santa Fe*-Trasse, der sie bis zur derzeitigen Endstation Sierra Madre Villa folgt. Vor Überqueren der Fernbahngleise und des Los Angeles River zweigt ein Gleis zum Betriebshof der Gold Line ab. Die ehemalige Bahntrasse erlaubt eine schnelle Fahrt Richtung Norden, außer auf einem 1 km langen Abschnitt westlich der Station Highland Park entlang des Marmion Way, wo die Züge die Geschwindigkeit reduzieren müssen, da die Gleise hier in einem eher städtischen Umfeld direkt neben den Fahrbahnen liegen. Um ein Überqueren der Gleise zwischen den Straßenkreuzungen zu verhindern, wurde zwischen den Gleisen ein Zaun errichtet. Nach Überquerung des Arroyo Seco-Tals auf einer Brücke erreicht die Gold Line die kleine Stadtgemeinde South Pasadena, dessen einzige Station bis 2011 Mission hieß. Im eigentlichen Pasadena wurde im Innenstadtbereich

Streets and holds the elevated Chinatown station. Back at ground level, they pick up the old Santa Fe alignment, which they follow to their present terminus at Sierra Madre Villa. Before crossing the mainline tracks and the Los Angeles River on a bridge, a track diverges and leads to the Gold Line maintenance yard. The former railway route allows a fast journey north, except for a 1 km section west of Highland Park station along Marmion Way, where trains have to reduce speed due to a more urban environment with road lanes directly next to the tracks. To prevent people from crossing the tracks between road intersections, a fence was installed between the tracks. After crossing the Arroyo Seco valley on a bridge, trains enter the small community of South Pasadena, whose only station used to be called Mission until 2011. Once in Pasadena proper, there is a shallow 400 m tunnel in the downtown area, followed by the partly built-over Memorial Park station. Shortly after, a 200 m tunnel is needed to allow trains to enter the median of the Foothill Freeway (I-210), which they follow to the terminus. Except for this freeway section, the northern Gold Line features many level crossings, which like on the Blue Line, are protected by automatic barriers.

The Gold Line Foothill Extension, now under construction, will allow trains to continue 17.6 km further east to Azusa by 2015, mostly along the old Santa Fe corridor, and in a future stage another 19.2 km, running through the cities of Glendora, San Dimas, La Verne and Pomona to Montclair.

Although the East L.A. corridor was once envisaged to be an eastern extension of the Red Line, several reasons, such as low population density and general objections to subway construction, led to its construction as a light rail line

East L.A. Civic Center

Soto

Mariachi Plaza

Atlantic

ein 400 m langer, flach liegender Tunnel errichtet, darauf folgt die teilweise überbaute Station Memorial Park. Dann fährt die Gold Line durch einen 200 m langen Tunnel und erreicht den Mittelstreifen des Foothill Freeway (I-210), dem sie bis zur Endstation folgt. Abgesehen von diesem Autobahnabschnitt weist die nördliche Gold Line viele Bahnübergänge auf, die jedoch wie auf der Blue Line durch automatische Schranken gesichert sind.

Derzeit ist die „Gold Line Foothill Extension" im Bau, womit die Gold Line bis 2015 17,6 km nach Osten bis Azusa meist entlang der alten *Santa Fe*-Trasse verlängert wird. Später soll eine weitere 19,2 km Verlängerung durch die Städte Glendora, San Dimas, La Verne und Pomona bis nach Montclair folgen.

Der East L.A.-Korridor war einst für eine Osterweiterung der Red Line vorgesehen, doch mehrere Gründe, wie eine niedrige Bevölkerungsdichte und allgemeine Einwände gegen den U-Bahn-Bau, führten schließlich dazu, dass diese Strecke als Stadtbahn gebaut wurde. Da bislang keine Innenstadtverbindung zur Verfügung steht, war es nur logisch, die neue Strecke an der Union Station mit der Pasadena-Linie zu verknüpfen. Über den Santa Ana Freeway (US 101) und die Commercial Street wurde ein Viadukt errichtet, der die Züge zur Station Little Tokyo/Arts District bringt, von wo aus sie auf einer eigenen Trasse in Straßenmitte der 1st Street nach Osten fahren. Kurz vor einer weiteren Kreuzung mit dem Santa Ana Freeway fährt die Gold Line in einen 2,6 km langen Doppelröhrentunnel unter den Boyle Heights mit den zwei U-Bahnhöfen Mariachi Plaza

instead. With no downtown route available, it was logical to connect it to the Pasadena line, which used to terminate at Union Station. A viaduct was built over the Santa Ana Freeway (US 101) and Commercial Street to take trains down to Little Tokyo/Arts District station, from where they continue eastwards on a reserved lane in the middle of 1st Street. Just before meeting the Santa Ana Freeway again, they descend into a 2.6 km bored tunnel under Boyle Heights with two underground stations at Mariachi Plaza and Soto. Via Indiana Street, they switch from 1st to 3rd Street upon entering the City of East Los Angeles, which has three surface stations east of I-710. Unlike the northern leg, the East L.A. section has conventional tramway signals which follow the general traffic light cycle at intersections.

At present, the Gold Line is isolated from the other light rail lines. The construction of the planned 'Regional Connector' will link it to the Blue and Expo Lines at 7th St/Metro Center, allowing two long cross-region lines, one north-south from Azusa to Long Beach, and the other east-west from East L.A. to Santa Monica.

The Gold Line is mostly served by two-car trains from 04:00 until midnight (until 02:00 Fri & Sat nights) every 6 minutes during rush hour, and every 12 minutes during off-peak hours.

MIND AWAKE AREA

Soto

Expo/Crenshaw – Expo Line auf dem Weg Richtung Culver City | Expo Line train on its way to Culver City

und Soto ein. Über die Indiana Street schwenkt die Trasse dann von der 1st auf die 3rd Street und erreicht die Stadt East Los Angeles, wo sich drei oberirdische Haltestellen östlich der I-710 befinden. Im Gegensatz zum Nordast der Gold Line hat der East L.A.-Abschnitt herkömmliche Straßenbahnampeln, die dem allgemeinen Ampelzyklus folgen.

Bislang ist die Gold Line von den anderen Stadtbahnlinien isoliert. Der geplante Bau des ‚Regional Connector' wird es ermöglichen, die heute an der Station 7th St/Metro Center endende Blue Line und Expo Line mit den Ästen der Gold Line zu zwei langen Durchmesserlinien zu verknüpfen, eine in Nord-Süd-Richtung von Azusa bis Long Beach und eine in Ost-West-Richtung von East L.A. bis Santa Monica.

Die heutige Gold Line wird meist mit Doppeltraktionen von 4:00 Uhr bis Mitternacht (Freitag & Samstag nachts bis 2:00 Uhr) betrieben, während der Hauptverkehrszeiten alle 6 Minuten und sonst alle 12 Minuten.

● **Expo Line** (14,1 km, 12 Stationen)
Die jüngste Ergänzung des Stadtbahnnetzes von L.A. war der erste Abschnitt der Expo Line, ein Name, der sich vom Exposition Boulevard ableitet, dem die Linie größtenteils folgt. Dabei handelt es sich um eine Trasse der *Pacific Electric Railway*, nämlich deren Santa Monica Air Line, die hier von 1909 bis 1953 fuhr. Die Expo Line teilt sich den ersten Abschnitt ab der Endstation 7th Street/Metro Center in der Innenstadt von L.A. mit der Blue Line, folgt dann der Flower Street weiter nach Süden parallel zum Harbor Freeway bis zum Jefferson Boulevard, wo sie in einen kurzen, 380 m langen Tunnel unter dem Exposition Boulevard und der Figueroa Street einfährt. Die Trasse verläuft dann weiter nach Westen meist ebenerdig, aber um

● *Expo Line* (14.1 km, 12 stations)
The latest addition to the L.A. light rail system is the first segment of the Expo Line, a name derived from the fact that it runs primarily along Exposition Boulevard, a corridor occupied by the Pacific Electric Railway's Santa Monica Air Line from 1909 to 1953. The Expo Line shares the first section from the 7th St/Metro Center terminus in downtown L.A. with the Blue Line, then follows Flower Street all the way south, alongside the Harbor Freeway, to Jefferson Boulevard, where it enters a short 380 m tunnel to pass under Exposition Boulevard and Figueroa Street. The route then continues west mostly at grade, but to avoid busy level crossings, short viaducts were built over La Brea Avenue, La Cienega Boulevard and Washington/National Boulevards, resulting in three elevated stations (including the current terminus Culver City). The stations have similar designs but are enhanced with individual tile artwork. The street-level stops have side platforms, sometimes staggered, while the elevated stations feature island platforms.

The Expo Line runs from 05:00 to midnight (until 02:00 Fri & Sat nights) every 12 minutes for most of the day.

The second phase of the Expo Line (10.6 km) has been under construction since summer 2012, with completion set for 2015. This extension also takes advantage of the disused PE corridor, using it all the way to Santa Monica. From the present terminus, a viaduct will continue west to span over Venice Boulevard; elevated stations will be built at Sepulveda Blvd and Bundy Drive, and bridges at the road intersections at Pico & Gateway Blvds, Centinela Avenue and Cloverfield & Olympic Boulevards to avoid level crossings. The line will terminate only three blocks from the Santa Monica beaches.

Culver City

Expo/Crenshaw

Expo/La Brea

Expo/La Brea

Expo Park/USC

Expo Park/USC > Jefferson/USC

Nippon Sharyo: in ursprünglicher Farbgebung | *in original livery*

Bernhard Kußmagk, 1996

Nippon Sharyo #145: in heutiger Farbgebung | *in current livery*

verkehrsreiche Bahnübergänge zu vermeiden, wurden kurze Viadukte über die La Brea Avenue, den La Cienega Boulevard sowie über den Washington Boulevard und National Boulevard gebaut, wodurch auch drei Hochbahnhöfe (einschließlich der derzeitigen Endstation Culver City) entstanden. Alle Stationen verfügen über ein ähnliches Design und sind mit individuellen Fliesenkunstwerken versehen. Die ebenerdigen Stationen haben Seitenbahnsteige, die manchmal versetzt angeordnet sind, während die Hochbahnhöfe Mittelbahnsteige aufweisen.

Die Expo Line verkehrt von 5:00 Uhr bis Mitternacht (Freitag und Samstag nachts bis 2:00 Uhr) in der Regel ganztags alle 12 Minuten.

Die zweite Phase der Expo Line (10,6 km) ist seit Sommer 2012 im Bau und soll im Jahr 2015 fertig gestellt sein. Diese Verlängerung nutzt auch durchgehend die ehemalige PE-Trasse bis Santa Monica. Von der heutigen Endstation wird ein Viadukt Richtung Westen den Venice Boulevard überspannen. Hochbahnhöfe werden am Sepulveda Boulevard und Bundy Drive gebaut, weitere Brücken zur Vermeidung von Bahnübergängen werden an den Kreuzungen am Pico & Gateway Boulevard, an der Centinela Avenue und am Cloverfield & Olympic Boulevard errichtet. Die Linie endet dann nur drei Häuserblocks von den Stränden von Santa Monica entfernt.

Ⓜ Stadtbahnfahrzeuge

Der gegenwärtige Stadtbahnwagenpark umfasst drei verschiedene Typen, die zwar bestimmten Linien zugeordnet sind, aber auf allen vier Linien eingesetzt werden können. Um diese Austauschbarkeit zu gewährleisten, haben alle einen ähnlichen Aufbau: Sie sind 26,5 m lang (Ansaldo-Wagen 27,4 m), 2,65 m breit, 3,5 m hoch. Die Fußbodenhöhe liegt 990 mm über Schienenoberkante. Die verschiedenen Typen sind in der Gestaltung des Innenraums kaum zu unterscheiden. Die Stromversorgung erfolgt mit 750 V Gleichstrom über Oberleitung.

1) Die japanische Firma **Nippon Sharyo** lieferte in den Jahren 1989-1990 54 Gelenkwagen vom Typ P865 (100-153) für die Eröffnung der Blue Line. Die Flotte wurde in den Jahren 1994-1995 mit 15 Fahrzeugen (154-168) des ähnlichen Typs P2020 erweitert. Diese Wagen sind im Betriebshof Long Beach beheimatet und daher in der Regel auf der Blue und Expo Line im Einsatz.

2) Der Typ P2000 von **Siemens** wurde für den automatischen Fahrbetrieb auf der Green Line entwickelt. Davon wurden insgesamt 52 Gelenkwagen (201-250, 301-302) zwischen 1996 und 1999 ausgeliefert. Da 34 Fahrzeuge momentan auf der Green Line ausreichen, werden die übrigen auf der Blue und Expo Line eingesetzt. Die letzten Siemens-Wagen wurden im April 2012 per Lkw von der Gold Line in den Betriebshof der Blue Line überführt.

Ⓜ *Light Rail Rolling Stock*

Metro's present light rail fleet includes three different types, which, although generally assigned to specific lines, can be used on any of the four lines. To guarantee this interchangeability, they all have similar dimensions and setups: 26.5 m long (Ansaldo - 27.4 m), 2.65 m wide, 3.5 m high and with a floor height of 990 mm above the top of the rail. The interior designs of the three types are very similar. 750 V dc is supplied via an overhead catenary.

*1) **Nippon Sharyo** of Japan delivered 54 articulated cars of type P865 (100-153) in 1989-1990 for the opening of the Blue Line. The fleet was increased by 15 cars (154-168) of the similar type P2020 in 1994-1995. These cars are assigned to the Long Beach yard, and are therefore normally used on the Blue and Expo Lines.*

*2) Designed for automatic driving, the P2000 class was manufactured by **Siemens** for the Green Line. A total of 52 articulated vehicles (201-250, 301-302) were delivered between 1996 and 1999. With 34 of them providing enough capacity on the Green Line, the rest are now in service on*

Nippon Sharyo #115

Siemens #218

AnsaldoBreda #730

3) Die 50 Gelenkwagen vom Typ P2550 (701-750) wurden zwischen 2006 und 2011 bei **AnsaldoBreda** angeschafft und sind nun auf der Gold Line konzentriert. Eine Option für weitere AnsaldoBreda-Wagen wurde nicht gezogen.

4) Für künftige Erweiterungen bestellte *Metro* 28 Fahrzeuge bei **Kinkisharyo**, die 2014-2015 ausgeliefert werden. Es besteht eine Option über weitere 50 Fahrzeuge.

Der Stadtbahn stehen drei Betriebshöfe zur Verfügung: im Norden von Long Beach entlang des südlichen Abschnitts der Blue Line, in Lawndale nahe der westlichen Endstation der Green Line sowie nördlich von Chinatown an der Gold Line. Weitere Anlagen sind in der Nähe der Station Olympic/26th Street in Santa Monica auf der westlichen Expo Line-Verlängerung und östlich der Station Monrovia auf der Gold Line Foothill-Erweiterung vorgesehen.

the Blue and Expo Lines. The last Siemens cars were transferred by truck from the Gold Line to the Blue Line depot in April 2012.

3) The 50 articulated cars of type P2550 (701-750) purchased from AnsaldoBreda between 2006 and 2011 are concentrated on the Gold Line. An option for more Ansaldo-Breda cars was not taken up.

4) For future extensions, Metro ordered 28 vehicles from Kinkisharyo for delivery in 2014-2015, with an option for another 50 cars.

Three facilities are available for Metro's light rail fleet: in North Long Beach along the southern Blue Line, in Lawndale near the Green Line's western terminus, and north of Chinatown on the Gold Line. New yards are planned near Olympic/26th Street station in Santa Monica on the western Expo Line extension, and east of Monrovia station on the Gold Line's Foothill extension.

Siemens

AnsaldoBreda

⦿ ANGELS FLIGHT

Einige der höchsten Gebäude von L.A. stehen mitten im Stadt-zentrum auf dem Bunker Hill, einer kleinen, aber steilen Anhöhe. Die Standseilbahn ‚Angels Flight' wurde 1901 von der Ecke Hill & 3rd Street bis zur Olive Street in einer einst noblen Gegend errichtet. Sie musste 1969 einer Stadterneuerung weichen, wurde aber schließlich im Jahr 1996 einen halben Häuserblock weiter südlich wieder aufgebaut und verbindet jetzt, nachdem sie infolge eines schweren Unfalls von 2001 bis 2011 wieder außer Betrieb war, den nordöstlichen Ausgang des U-Bahnhofs Pershing Square mit der California Plaza. Sie ist 91 m lang, hat eine Steigung von 33% und eine Fahrt kostet 0,50 $.

Some of L.A.'s tallest buildings stand on the top of a small, but steep elevation known as Bunker Hill, right in the centre of the city. Located at the time in an exclusive neighbour-hood, the Angels Flight funicular was built in 1901 from Hill & 3rd Streets to Olive Street. Dismantled in 1969 as part of an urban renewal project, it was eventually rebuilt in 1996 half a block south, and now, after another long closure between 2001 and 2011 following a serious accident, it leads from near the northeastern exit of the Pershing Square subway station to California Plaza. It is 91 m long, negotiates a 33% gradient and costs $0.50 to ride.

Tw 500 am nördlichen Endpunkt nahe der Anlegestelle für Kreuzfahrtschiffe | *Car no. 500 at the northern terminus near the cruise ship terminal*

◉ PORT OF LOS ANGELES WATERFRONT RED CAR LINE

Auf einer 2,5 km langen Strecke in San Pedro, an der Südspitze von Los Angeles, bieten zwei Fahrzeuge, die nach dem Typ 500 der *Pacific Electric* von 1909 gebaut wurden, einen Einblick in den Schienenverkehr von L.A. vor einigen Jahrzehnten. Sie verkehren seit 2003, allerdings nur nachmittags von Freitag bis Sonntag, auf einer ehemaligen *Pacific Electric*-Trasse, die auch von Güterzügen genutzt wird. Außerdem kann der restaurierte *Pacific Electric*-Wagen Nr. 1058 von 1907 für Sonderfahrten gebucht werden.

On a 2.5 km line in San Pedro, at the southern tip of Los Angeles, two replica cars patterned after the 1909 Pacific Electric 500-class interurban vehicles offer an insight into what urban transport was like in L.A. several decades ago. They have been running since 2003, but only Friday to Sunday afternoons, on a former Pacific Electric right-of-way, which is also used by freight trains. In addition, Pacific Electric car no. 1058 from 1907 was restored, and can now be chartered for special occasions.

Seit 2. Mai 2008 fahren zwei Straßenbahnwagen auf einer kurzen Ringlinie in der „Americana At Brand"-Mall in Glendale. Die Fahrzeuge wurden von Gomaco Trolley im Stil der offenen Brill-Wagen gebaut. Der vordere Wagen, Nr. 1717, wird durch eine Batterie angetrieben, der zweite ist zeitweise als Beiwagen in Betrieb.

In ähnlicher Weise pendelt eine offene Doppeldecker-Tram auf einer 350 m langen Strecke zwischen „The Grove", einer Mall in der Westside von Los Angeles, und dem bekannten Farmers Market.

On 2 May 2008, two streetcars started running on a short loop at the "Americana At Brand" mall in Glendale. Built by Gomaco Trolley, the cars were modelled after open-style Brill cars, with the leading car no. 1717 powered by a battery and the second, when in service, functioning as a trailer.

Similarly, a double-deck open streetcar shuttles on a 350 m track between "The Grove", a mall in the Westside of L.A., and the famous Farmers Market.

Canoga

Ⓜ BUSWAYS

Ursprünglich als Verlängerung der Red Line geplant, wurde die 31 km lange **Orange Line** schließlich als exklusive Bustrasse (*Busway*) auf einer ehemaligen *Pacific Electric*-Trasse gebaut, auf der seit 1952 kein Personenverkehr mehr stattfand. Die Strecke ist völlig ebenerdig und hat daher mehrere Straßenkreuzungen. Die Orange Line wurde am 29. Oktober 2005 von North Hollywood bis zum Warner Center eröffnet und am 30. Juni 2012 nach Chatsworth verlängert. Ein 2 km langer Abschnitt zwischen Canoga und dem Warner Center verläuft im Mischverkehr. Die 18 m langen *Metro Liner*-Busse fahren in der Hauptverkehrszeit alle 4 Minuten, sonst alle 10 Minuten abwechselnd nach Chatsworth und zum Warner Center.

Auf dem Netzplan der Metro Rail ist auch die 42 km lange **Silver Line** eingezeichnet, die jedoch keine eigene Busspur aufweist, sondern die HOV-Fahrspuren (*High Occupancy Vehicle*) auf dem San Bernardino Freeway I-10 (El Monte Busway, 18 km) und dem Harbor Freeway I-110 (Harbor Transitway, 18 km) mitnutzt. Durch die Innenstadt fahren die Express-Busse auf normalen Straßen. Es gibt zwei Stationen auf der Autobahn auf dem östlichen und fünf auf dem südlichen Abschnitt. Zur Green Line kann man an der Station Harbor Freeway umsteigen und eine Haltestelle liegt in der Nähe der Union Station. Die Silver Line fährt alle 5-8 Minuten in der HVZ, sonst alle 15 Minuten. Anders als bei der Orange Line gilt hier ein besonderer Fahrpreis!

Initially planned as an extension of the Red Line, the 31 km **Orange Line** *was eventually built as a dedicated busway along a former Pacific Electric right-of-way on which passenger service had stopped in 1952. The route is entirely at grade and therefore has several road intersections. It was opened from North Hollywood to Warner Center on 29 October 2005 and extended to Chatsworth on 30 June 2012. The 2 km section between Canoga and Warner Center runs in mixed traffic. The 18 m Metro Liner buses run every 4 minutes during rush hour and every 10 minutes during off-peak hours, with every other bus going to Chatsworth.*

Also shown on the Metro Rail map is the 42 km **Silver Line**, *which does not use a dedicated busway, but the HOV (high-occupancy vehicle) lanes on the I-10 San Bernardino Freeway (El Monte Busway, 18 km) and I-110 Harbor Freeway (Harbor Transitway, 18 km). On the section through downtown, the express buses have to use normal roads. There are two freeway stations on the eastern portion, and five on the southern. Convenient transfer to the Green Line is available at Harbor Freeway station, and there is also a stop near Union Station. Silver Line buses operate every 5-8 minutes in rush hour, and every 15 minutes during off-peak hours, and unlike on the Orange Line, a special fare is payable!*

Balboa

Getty Center

GETTY CENTER TRAM

Das Getty Center ist ein privates Kunstmuseum in den Hügeln oberhalb von Brentwood im Stadtbezirk West Los Angeles. Dieser Ort, der einen herrlichen Blick über das Becken von Los Angeles bietet, ist nur mit einem vollautomatischen, seilgezogenen Peoplemover erreichbar. Die von Luftkissen getragenen Züge verbinden den direkt an der I-405 liegenden Parkplatz mit dem im Dezember 1997 eröffneten Museum. Die Gesamtlänge der Bahn beträgt 1080 m. Sie liegt größtenteils auf einem Viadukt und ist im Grunde einspurig, jedoch mit einem zweispurigen Abschnitt in der Mitte, wo sich die beiden Züge begegnen können.

The Getty Center is a private art museum located in the hills above Brentwood in West L.A. To access the site, which provides a splendid view of the L.A. basin, a fully automatic, cable-hauled people mover supported by an air cushion was built between the car park just off the I-405 and the museum, which opened in December 1997. The total length of the fixed guideway system is 1080 m, most of which lies on an aerial structure and is basically single-lane, but there is a double-lane section in the middle where trains can pass each other.

Downtown Burbank

METROLINK

Metrolink betreibt ein ca. 610 km langes Netz mit sieben Vorortbahnlinien und 55 Stationen. Das Zugangebot unterscheidet
sich deutlich von Linie zu Linie: Während auf der San Bernardino Line über El Monte wochentags 21 Züge in jede Richtung
verkehren, sogar tagsüber zwischen den Hauptverkehrszeiten,
bieten andere wie die Riverside Line (über Ontario) oder die 91
Line (nach Riverside über Fullerton) nur 4-5 Züge pro Tag und
meist nur in der Hauptlastrichtung. Bis auf die Inland Empire-
Orange County Line, die 8-mal täglich im Südosten eine Tan-
gentialverbindung herstellt, gehen alle Linien strahlenförmig
von der Union Station in Los Angeles aus. Die Metrolink-Züge
müssen sich in der Regel die stark befahrenen Gleise der
Güterbahnen teilen, auf denen außerdem noch Amtrak-Züge
verkehren, wobei letztere außer auf der Strecke nach San
Diego eher selten sind. Nicht nur das Fehlen eigener Gleise,
sondern auch der Engpass am Kopfbahnhof Union Station lassen derzeit kaum ein besseres Angebot zu. Die Union Station
soll daher umgebaut werden, indem drei Gleise neu verlegt
werden, die in den 1970er Jahren, als kaum noch Personenverkehr stattfand, entfernt wurden. Außerdem sollen vier der
zehn bestehenden Stumpfgleise zu Durchgangsgleisen verlängert werden, um sie an die nach Süden verlaufenden Gleise in
der Nähe des U-Bahn-Betriebshofs anzuschließen.

Metrolink setzt typische Wendezüge mit diesel-elektrischen
Lokomotiven und Doppelstockwagen ein. Die Fahrpreise
richten sich nach der Entfernung und reichen von 5,25 $ bis
24,50 $. Ein ,Weekend Pass' für beliebig viele Fahrten ist für
10,00 $ erhältlich.

*Metrolink operates a roughly 610 km network of seven com-
muter rail lines with 55 stations. Service differs significantly
from line to line as far as frequencies are concerned: while
the San Bernardino Line via El Monte has 21 trains in each
direction on weekdays, some even during daytime off-peak
hours, others like the Riverside Line (via Ontario) or the 91
Line (to Riverside via Fullerton) only offer 4-5 trains a day,
mostly in the peak direction. All the lines radiate from L.A.'s
Union Station, except the Inland Empire-Orange County Line,
which eight times a day provides a tangential service in the
southeastern area. Metrolink trains share busy tracks with
freight trains as well as Amtrak services, the latter being
rather infrequent except on the San Diego route. The lack of
dedicated tracks and the bottleneck at the terminal Union
Station currently prevent the service from being expanded.
Union Station will therefore be rebuilt by restoring three
tracks dismantled in the 1970s when hardly any passenger
trains were dispatched there, and by extending four of the
ten existing stub-end tracks to convert them into run-
through tracks, which will link up with the southbound lines
near the Metro Red Line's maintenance yard.*

*Metrolink uses typical push-pull trains with diesel-electric
locomotives and double-deck carriages. Fares are based on
distance and range from $5.25 to $24.50. An unlimited-ride
weekend pass is available at $10.00.*

*Metrolink operation began on 26 October 1992 on the
Ventura County, Antelope Valley and San Bernardino Lines.
The service was then gradually expanded until 2002. Initially*

Oceanside

Oceanside

Der Metrolink-Betrieb begann am 26. Oktober 1992 auf der Ventura County, Antelope Valley und San Bernardino Line. Das Netz wurde dann bis 2002 stufenweise erweitert. Es wurde anfangs von Amtrak betrieben, dann 2005 für fünf Jahre von Veolia übernommen, bis Amtrak im Juli 2010 wieder als Betreiber zurückkehrte.

Metrolink untersteht der *Southern California Regional Rail Authority* (SCRRA), die 1991 von den fünf Counties (Los Angeles, Orange, Riverside, San Bernardino und Ventura) der Metropolregion Los Angeles gegründet wurde. Die Orange County Line erreicht in Oceanside auch das San Diego County, wo sie auf den Coaster von San Diego trifft (siehe S. 125).

operated by Amtrak, Veolia took over for five years in 2005 before Amtrak returned as the operator in July 2010.

Metrolink is governed by the Southern California Regional Rail Authority (SCRRA), formed in 1991 by the five counties which make up the Los Angeles metropolitan region: Los Angeles, Orange, Riverside, San Bernardino and Ventura Counties. The Orange County Line also reaches San Diego County in Oceanside, where it meets San Diego's Coaster (see page 125).

L.A. Union Station

L.A. Union Station

L.A. Union Station

Hazard Center – neuer Siemens S70-Wagen auf der Green Line, kurz bevor diese ins Stadtzentrum verlängert wurde.
– new Siemens S70 car on the Green Line shortly before it was extended into the city centre.

SAN DIEGO, CA

San Diego liegt in der südwestlichen Ecke der Vereinigten Staaten, direkt am Pazifischen Ozean und nur ein paar Meilen nördlich der mexikanischen Grenze. Mit einer Fläche von 842 km² ist das Stadtgebiet, in dem 1,3 Mio. Menschen leben, ziemlich groß. Die Metropolregion erstreckt sich entlang der Küste nach Norden bis Oceanside und ins Landesinnere bis Escondido und schließt auch Städte wie Chula Vista, National City, Carlsbad, El Cajon, Vista, San Marcos, Encinitas und La Mesa ein. Dieses Gebiet entspricht weitgehend den besiedelten Regionen des San Diego County, das rund 3 Mio. Einwohner hat. Jenseits der mexikanischen Grenze leben in Tijuana und dessen Nachbarstädten noch einmal etwa 1,5 Mio. Menschen. San Diego besitzt einen natürlichen Hafen, der einen der wichtigsten Stützpunkte der US-Marine beherbergt.

Trotz seiner abgeschiedenen Lage ist San Diego bequem mit der Bahn von Los Angeles aus (ca. 200 km) erreichbar: Amtraks „Pacific Surfliner" verkehrt 11-mal täglich zwischen den beiden Städten (Fahrzeit ca. 3 Stunden, einige Züge fahren weiter Richtung Norden nach San Luis Obispo). Dazu kommen die Orange County Line der Metrolink von Los Angeles (siehe S. 114), die in Oceanside auf den Coaster aus San Diego trifft.

Der öffentliche Nahverkehr im San Diego County wird von MTS (*Metropolitan Transit System*) und NCTD (*North County Transit District*) abgewickelt, die ein einfaches gemeinsames Tarifsystem haben. Eine einfache Fahrt auf der Stadtbahn (Trolley) kostet 2,50 $ und ein ‚Regional Day Pass' für alle Busse, den Trolley und sogar den Sprinter nur 5,00 $. Ein ‚RegionPlus Day Pass' für 12,00 $ umfasst auch Premium-Express-Busse und den Coaster-Pendlerzug. Tickets gibt es in Papierform oder als Smartcard namens ‚Compass Card'.

San Diego is located in the southwestern corner of the United States, directly on the Pacific Ocean and only a few miles north of the Mexican border. With an area of 842 km2, the city is rather large and has a population of 1.3 million. The urban sprawl of the metropolitan area extends all the way north along the coast to Oceanside and inland to Escondido, and includes cities like Chula Vista, National City, Carlsbad, El Cajon, Vista, San Marcos, Encinitas and La Mesa. This area largely matches the populated regions of San Diego County, which is home to some 3 million people. The urbanised region actually continues across the Mexican border into Tijuana and its neighbouring towns, which together have a population of 1.5 million. A natural harbour, San Diego is home to one of the most important U.S. Navy bases.

Despite its remote location, San Diego is easily accessible by rail from Los Angeles (approx. 200 km): Amtrak's "Pacific Surfliner" runs 11 times a day between the two cities (approx. 3 hours; some trains continue north to San Luis Obispo). This offer is complemented by some commuter rail trains: Metrolink's Orange County Line from Los Angeles (see p. 114) and San Diego's Coaster meet in Oceanside.

Public transport in San Diego County is provided by MTS (*Metropolitan Transit System*) and NCTD (*North County Transit District*) which share a simple fare system. A single ride on the light rail (Trolley) system is $2.50, and a Regional Day Pass good for all buses, the Trolley and even the Sprinter is just $5.00. A RegionPlus Day Pass sold at $12.00 also includes premium express buses and the Coaster commuter railway. Tickets are available in paper or on the Compass Card smartcard.

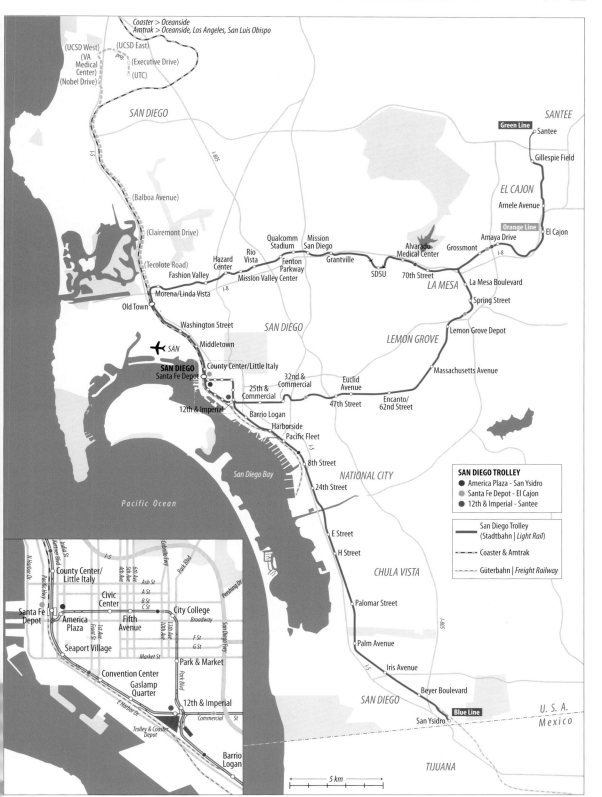

Coaster > Oceanside
Amtrak > Oceanside, Los Angeles, San Luis Obispo

(UCSD West)
(VA Medical Center)
(Nobel Drive)

(UCSD East)
proj.
(Executive Drive)
(UTC)

SAN DIEGO

SANTEE

Green Line
Santee

Gillespie Field

EL CAJON

Arnele Avenue

Orange Line
El Cajon

Amaya Drive

(Balboa Avenue)

(Clairemont Drive)

Qualcomm Stadium
Mission San Diego

Alvarado Medical Center

Grossmont

I-8

(Tecolote Road)

Hazard Center
Rio Vista

Fenton Parkway
Grantville

SDSU

70th Street

LA MESA

La Mesa Boulevard

Fashion Valley
Mission Valley Center

Morena/Linda Vista

Old Town

Spring Street

Washington Street

SAN DIEGO

LEMON GROVE

Lemon Grove Depot

✈ SAN

Middletown

SAN DIEGO
Santa Fe Depot

County Center/Little Italy

Massachusetts Avenue

32nd & Commercial

25th & Commercial

Euclid Avenue

12th & Imperial

Barrio Logan

47th Street

Encanto/62nd Street

Harborside
Pacific Fleet

8th Street

San Diego Bay

NATIONAL CITY

24th Street

Pacific Ocean

SAN DIEGO TROLLEY
● America Plaza - San Ysidro
● Santa Fe Depot - El Cajon
● 12th & Imperial - Santee

San Diego Trolley
(Stadtbahn | Light Rail)
Coaster & Amtrak
Güterbahn | Freight Railway

E Street

H Street

CHULA VISTA

Palomar Street

County Center/Little Italy

Civic Center

Santa Fe Depot

America Plaza

Fifth Avenue

City College

Broadway

Seaport Village

Convention Center
Gaslamp Quarter

Park & Market

12th & Imperial

Trolley & Coaster Depot

Barrio Logan

Palm Avenue

Iris Avenue

Beyer Boulevard

SAN DIEGO

Blue Line

San Ysidro

U.S.A.
Mexico

TIJUANA

5 km

Santee – SD100-Hochflurbahn gekuppelt mit einer S70-Niederflurbahn | *SD100 high-floor vehicle coupled with a S70 low-floor car*

◉ SAN DIEGO TROLLEY

Bei ihrer Inbetriebnahme im Juli 1981 war die moderne Stadt-bahn von San Diego die erste ihrer Art in den USA, nur die kanadischen Städte Edmonton (1978) und Calgary (Mai 1981) waren in Nordamerika früher am Start. San Diego hatte bereits in den 1960er Jahren begriffen, dass Autobahnen nicht der ein-zige Weg zur Lösung der Verkehrsprobleme sein konnten, und dachte sogar einige Zeit an den Bau eines BART-ähnlichen Schnellbahnsystems. Aber keiner der vielen Vorschläge wurde umgesetzt, bis Hurrikan Kathleen im September 1976 in der Region tobte und wichtige Teile der alten *San Diego & Arizona Eastern Railroad* (SD&AE), die San Diego direkt mit den östlichen Landesteilen verband, zerstörte. Die SD&AE Desert Line war im Jahr 1919 eröffnet worden und führte über mexi-kanisches Gebiet nach El Centro. Der Personenverkehr war bereits im Jahr 1951 eingestellt worden, aber der Güterverkehr spielte noch eine wichtige Rolle. Das gesamte Netz der damals im Besitz der *Southern Pacific* befindlichen SD&AE wurde im August 1979 vom MTDB (*Metropolitan Transit Development Board*, dem Vorgänger der heutigen MTS) aufgekauft, was eine schnelle und kostengünstige Realisierung einer Stadtbahn ermöglichte. Auf denselben Gleisen sollte gleichzeitig in den Nachtstunden auch wieder Güterverkehr stattfinden.

Das im September 2012 veränderte Stadtbahnnetz besteht aus drei farblich gekennzeichneten Trolley-Linien, die auf Netz-plänen und Hinweisschildern auch durch Symbole dargestellt werden:
Blue Line: America Plaza – San Ysidro (Welle)
Orange Line: Santa Fe Depot – El Cajon (Sonne)
Green Line: 12th & Imperial – Santee (Palme)

Opened back in July 1981, San Diego pioneered the introduc-tion of modern light rail service in the U.S., having been preceded in North America only by the Canadian cities of Edmonton (1978) and Calgary (May 1981). San Diego had ac-tually realised back in the 1960s that freeways could not be the only solution for transport problems, and for some time even considered the construction of a BART-like rapid transit system. But none of the many proposals made any progress until Hurricane Kathleen raged in the region in September 1976 and destroyed important parts of the old San Diego & Arizona Eastern Railroad (SD&AE), which was San Diego's direct link to the eastern parts of the country. Opened in 1919, the SD&AE's Desert Line ran to El Centro via Mexican territory. Although passenger service had ceased in 1951, freight operation remained an important business. Owned at the time by Southern Pacific, the entire SD&AE network was purchased by MTDB (Metropolitan Transit Development Board, the predecessor of today's MTS) in August 1979, al-lowing a fast and affordable implementation of the initial light rail service while reestablishing freight service on the same tracks at night.

The Trolley network, which was reconfigured in Septem-ber 2012, consists of three colour-coded lines, also identified on maps and signs by symbols:
Blue Line: America Plaza – San Ysidro (wave)
Orange Line: Santa Fe Depot – El Cajon (sun)
Green Line: 12th & Imperial – Santee (palm tree)
The Trolley system features every possible type of light rail alignment, from street-running on marked-off lanes in the

Santa Fe Depot – U2-Hochflurbahn vor dem prächtigen Hauptbahnhof auf dem Weg Richtung Innenstadt
– U2 high-floor train in front of the magnificent railway station, on its way into the city centre

Das Trolley-Netz weist alle möglichen Arten von Stadtbahntrassierungen auf, von straßenbündigen abmarkierten Abschnitten in der Innenstadt über alte Eisenbahntrassen auf den ersten beiden Linien bis hin zu schnellbahnartigen Neubaustrecken mit langen Hochbahnabschnitten und sogar einem kurzen Tunnel auf der neueren Green Line. Anders als bei später eröffneten Betrieben, die kurze Hochbahnsteige bauten, um gehbehinderten Fahrgästen den Einstieg zu erleichtern, wurden in San Diego die älteren Fahrzeuge mit Rollstuhlliften ausgestattet.

Derzeit wird auf der Blue und Orange Line ein Modernisierungsprogramm durchgeführt, die Haltestellenausstattung wird verbessert, die Bahnsteige werden für die neuen Niederflur-Fahrzeuge leicht angehoben und die alten Schienen und technische Ausrüstung erneuert.

SAN DIEGO Trolley

82.7 km (1.2 km unterirdisch | *underground*)
53 Haltestellen | *stations*

26 July 1981: Santa Fe Depot – San Ysidro (via City College
20 Mar 1986: 12th & Imperial – Euclid Avenue
          – San Diego Square [Haltestelle aufgelöst | *Stop eliminated*]
    1986: + E Street
14 May 1989: Euclid Avenue – Spring Street
25 June 1989: Spring Street – El Cajon
30 June 1990: America Plaza – 12th & Imperial (via Gaslamp Quarter)
   July 1992: America Plaza – Santa Fe Depot – County Center/Little Italy
28 Aug 1995: El Cajon – Santee
16 June 1996: County Center/Little Italy – Old Town
23 Nov 1997: Old Town – Mission San Diego
    2000: + Fenton Parkway
10 July 2005: Mission San Diego – Grossmont

downtown area, to old railway formations on the first two lines, to new high-speed structures on long elevated sections, and even an underground segment on the newer Green Line. Unlike the later systems, which added short high-floor platforms to allow disabled passengers to board trains with ease, San Diego's older vehicles are equipped with wheelchair lifts.

A Trolley renewal programme is currently underway on the Blue and Orange Lines with the aim to improving station amenities, raising platforms to take full advantage of the new low-floor trains, and replacing old rails and technical equipment.

The Trolley runs from about 05:00 to about 01:00, with trains every 15 minutes for most of the day; the Blue Line operates every 7-8 minutes during rush hour.

● **Blue Line** *(22.7 km, 18 stations)*
The 'South Line' to the Mexican border was built in less than two years. The old freight line was rehabilitated and electrified, but initially remained mostly single-track, with only three passing loops along the 22.7 km corridor. This constraint was soon overcome and the entire line had been doubled by February 1983. The Blue Line runs alongside San Diego's extensive port facilities, through National City and Chula Vista before returning to suburbs also belonging to San Diego just north of the international border. The terminus is located next to the checkpoint.

In the city centre, tracks were laid along Park Boulevard and C Street, with the terminus for 'Centre City'-labelled trains located on the eastern side of Santa Fe Depot, approximately where today's America Plaza station is. In 1986,

Old Town Transit Center

America Plaza – jetzt Endstation für die Blue Line
– now the Blue Line terminus

Die Stadtbahnen verkehren von etwa 5:00 bis etwa 1:00 Uhr, den ganzen Tag meist alle 15 Minuten, nur auf der Blue Line während der Hauptverkehrszeiten alle 7-8 Minuten.

● **Blue Line** (22,7 km, 18 Haltestellen)
Die ‚South Line' zur mexikanischen Grenze wurde in weniger als zwei Jahren gebaut. Die alte Güterbahnstrecke wurde saniert und elektrifiziert, blieb aber zunächst meist eingleisig mit nur drei Ausweichen entlang der 22,7 km langen Strecke. Diese Engpässe wurden bald behoben und die gesamte Linie war ab Februar 1983 zweigleisig. Die Blue Line führt entlang der weitläufigen Hafenanlagen von San Diego, dann durch National City und Chula Vista, bevor sie dann zu San Diego gehörende Vororte nördlich der Landesgrenze erreicht. Die Endstation befindet sich direkt am Grenzübergang.

In der Innenstadt wurden die Gleise entlang des Park Boulevard und der C Street verlegt. Die Endstation für Züge mit dem Fahrtziel ‚Centre City' lag auf der Ostseite des Santa Fe-Bahnhofs, etwa da, wo heute die Station America Plaza liegt. Im Jahr 1986 wurde der Abschnitt auf der C Street zwischen der 2nd und 6th Avenue für den Individualverkehr gesperrt und eine ursprüngliche Haltestelle zwischen 8th und 9th Avenue aufgelassen.

Im Jahr 1992 wurde die ‚South Line' um die Ecke von America Plaza ins Santa Fe Depot selbst verlängert, wo sie die beiden Gleise direkt neben dem Bahnhofsgebäude nutzt. Die Züge fuhren jedoch weiter nach Norden, um an der Station County Center zu wenden. Von 1996 bis zur Linienumstellung am 2. September 2012 setzte die Blue Line ihre Fahrt Richtung Old Town fort, heute wendet sie auf dem nördlichen Gleis in der Station America Plaza.

four blocks on C Street between 2nd and 6th Avenues were closed to private vehicles, and an original stop between 8th and 9th Avenues was eliminated.

In 1992, the ‘South Line' was extended around the corner from America Plaza into the Santa Fe Depot, where it stopped on the two tracks closest to the station building. To reverse, however, trains had to run further north to County Center station. From 1996 until a line reconfiguration on 2 September 2012, the Blue Line continued north to Old Town, but now it turns back on the northern track at America Plaza.

● *Orange Line* (27.7 km, 19 stations)
With the immediate success of the ‘South Line', an ‘East Line' soon started to be planned. It mostly follows the alignment of the old SD&AE Santee branch and thus retains a certain interurban feel. For financial reasons, it was opened in stages over a 10-year period. It was generally double-track from the beginning, but the three narrow bridges over major roads which were inherited were doubled later. The route diverges from the South Line at 12th & Imperial station near the Trolley workshops and runs east along Commercial Street on a marked-off centre lane to 32nd Street, from where a dedicated right-of-way is available. A horseshoe curve allows the trains to lose some altitude before heading express through two cemeteries and over I-805 to the original 1986 terminus at Euclid Avenue. The line then runs along the northern side of Imperial Avenue, which becomes Lemon Grove Avenue as the trains leave San Diego. At Lemon Grove Depot, a replica of the old station building was erected. The bridge over Martin Luther King Jr Freeway marks the border between Lemon Grove and La Mesa. With the doubling of

Old Town – Green Line & Blue Line & Coaster (Aug 2012)

Fifth Avenue (C Street) – Orange Line & Blue Line

San Ysidro – Endstation der Blue Line direkt an der mexikanischen Grenze – *Blue Line terminus directly at the Mexican border*

Fashion Valley – Hochbahnstrecke im Mission Valley – *elevated route through Mission Valley*

● Orange Line (27,7 km, 19 Haltestellen)

Nach dem sofortigen Erfolg der ‚South Line' begann bald die Planung einer ‚East Line'. Sie folgt meist der Trasse der alten SD&AE-Nebenbahn nach Santee und hat deshalb den Charakter einer Überlandstraßenbahn. Aus finanziellen Gründen wurde sie in Etappen über einen Zeitraum von 10 Jahren eröffnet. Sie war von Anfang an größtenteils zweigleisig, bis auf drei schmale Brücken über Hauptverkehrsstraßen, die erst später ausgebaut wurden. Die Route zweigt von der South Line an der Station 12th & Imperial in der Nähe des Betriebshofs ab und verläuft nach Osten entlang der Commercial Street auf einer abmarkierten Spur in Straßenmitte bis zur 32nd Street, von wo aus ein eigener Bahnkörper vorhanden ist. Auf einer hufeisenförmigen Kurve verlieren die Züge etwas an Höhe, bevor sie durch zwei Friedhöfe und über die I-805 die ursprüngliche Endstation Euclid Avenue von 1986 erreichen. Die Linie verläuft dann entlang der Nordseite der Imperial Avenue, die zur Lemon Grove Avenue wird, sobald die Stadtbahn San Diego verlässt. An der Station Lemon Grove Depot wurde ein Nachbau des alten Bahnhofsgebäudes errichtet. Die Brücke über den Martin Luther King Jr Freeway markiert die Grenze zwischen Lemon Grove und La Mesa. Mit dem zweigleisigen Ausbau dieser Brücke 1993 wurde auch der folgende Abschnitt begradigt, um höhere Geschwindigkeiten zuzulassen. Spring Street war für einige Wochen Endstation, bevor die Strecke durch das Zentrum von La Mesa fertig gestellt wurde. Nach Überqueren der I-8 trifft die Orange Line auf die neuere Strecke der Green Line durch das Mission Valley. Östlich der Brücke über den Jackson Drive erschließt die Station Grossmont dann die größte Shopping Mall in den östlichen Vororten. Von hier aus folgen die Züge der Orange und Green Line auf dem Weg nach El Cajon einer ziemlich kurvenreichen Strecke.

Der folgende 6 km lange Abschnitt von El Cajon nach Norden bis Santee wurde sechs Jahre später im Jahr 1995 eröffnet. Nördlich von El Cajon führt eine Brücke über die Main Street und nördlich der Arnele Avenue überspannt ein 300 m langer Viadukt den Fletcher Parkway und die Fesler Street. Nördlich von Gillespie Field wird die Strecke schließlich eingleisig in der Mitte der Cuyamaca Street und endet zweigleisig am Einkaufszentrum Santee Trolley Square. Bis die Green Line im Jahr 2005 fertig gestellt wurde, war der gesamte Santee-Ast Teil der Orange Line. Diese wurde dann nach Gillespie Field und schließlich im September 2012 nach El Cajon zurückgenommen. Auf der gesamten ‚East Line' ist Güterverkehr möglich, auch wenn nur wenige Anschlussgleise vorhanden sind.

Bis September 2012 fuhr die Orange Line rund um die Innenstadt über die Bayside-Strecke zur Endstation 12th & Imperial, hier verkehrt heute die Green Line. Ohne eigene Kehrgleise wendet sie jetzt auf dem westlichen Gleis im Santa Fe Depot.

this bridge in 1993, the following section was straightened to allow higher speeds. Spring Street was the terminus for some weeks before the route through central La Mesa was completed. After passing over I-8, the line merges with the newer Green Line route through Mission Valley. East of the bridge over Jackson Drive, Grossmont station serves the largest shopping mall in the eastern suburbs. From here, the Orange and Green Line trains continue to El Cajon on a rather winding route.

The following 6 km section from El Cajon north to Santee opened six years later in 1995. A bridge across Main Street just north of El Cajon, and a 300 m viaduct north of Arnele Avenue that spans over Fletcher Parkway and Fesler Street both help to speed up the overall journey. Just north of Gillespie Field, the line becomes single-track in the centre of Cuyamaca Street and ends at the two-track terminus in the Santee Trolley Square shopping mall. Until the Green Line was completed in 2005, the entire Santee branch was served by the Orange Line. The service was then cut back to Gillespie Field, and eventually in September 2012 to El Cajon. The entire 'East Line' allows freight traffic, although only a few minor sidings are connected to the route.

Until September 2012, Orange Line trains used to continue around the city centre on the Bayside route down to 12th & Imperial station, a section now served by the Green Line. With no proper reversing sidings available, Orange Line trains now turn back on the western track at Santa Fe Depot.

● Green Line (38.9 km, 27 stations)

The oldest section of today's Green Line is the 2.2 km 'Bayside Extension', which was added to the network in 1990, prior to the completion of the 'East Line'. At the same time, the original terminus at Santa Fe Depot on C Street was re-

Old Town (Taylor Street) – 4-gleisiger Bahnübergang | *4-track level crossing*

Fifth Avenue – Haltestelle im Stadtzentrum | *downtown station*

SDSU – einzige unterirdische Station | *the only underground station*

● **Green Line** (38,9 km, 27 Haltestellen)

Der älteste Abschnitt der heutigen Green Line ist die 2,2 km lange ‚Bayside-Extension', die im Jahr 1990 noch vor Vollendung der ‚East Line' eröffnet wurde. Gleichzeitig wurde die ursprüngliche Endstation Santa Fe Depot auf der C Street durch die überdachte Station America Plaza neben dem höchsten Gebäude der Stadt ersetzt. Die Bayside-Route führt von hier nach Süden entlang der alten *Santa Fe*-Gütergleise zum MTS-Hauptquartier und Betriebshof an der Kreuzung 12th & Imperial. Bis 2012 war dieser Abschnitt Teil der Orange Line.

1992 folgte die Strecke vom Santa Fe Depot bis Old Town entlang der Ostseite der *Santa Fe*-Eisenbahn, was eigentlich der erste Abschnitt einer geplanten ‚North Line' werden sollte. Bis 2012 fuhr hier die Blue Line. Im Gegensatz zu den Fernbahngleisen, die auf dieser Strecke durchgehend ebenerdig liegen, wurde für den Trolley ein 600 m langer Einschnitt ausgehoben, um Bahnübergänge an der Grape und Hawthorn Street zu vermeiden. Direkt darauf folgt ein Viadukt über die Laurel Street. Nördlich der Station Old Town besteht ein viel befahrener Bahnübergang an der Taylor Street.

Die 9,8 km lange Mission Valley West-Verlängerung war die erste Strecke, die nicht entlang eines Eisenbahnkorridors gebaut wurde, sondern grob dem San Diego River und der I-8 folgt. Aufgrund der topographischen Gegebenheiten entlang dieses Tals gibt es hier mehrere Viadukte, was zu einer fast metromäßigen Trassierung führte. Östlich des Qualcomm Stadium liegt ein mittiges Kehrgleis, wo bei Großveranstaltungen Bahnen vorübergehend abgestellt werden können. Nach der Eröffnung im Jahr 1997 wurde diese neue Strecke durch die verlängerte ‚South Line' bedient.

In der zweiten Phase wurde die Mission Valley-Linie sieben Jahre später nach Osten auf einer ähnlichen Trasse verlängert, einschließlich eines 1,2 km langen Tunnels mit einer Station unter der San Diego State University (SDSU). Die Strecke mündet westlich der Station Grossmont in die bestehende ‚East Line'. Nach Fertigstellung der 9,2 km langen Mission Valley East-Verlängerung wurde die Green Line eingeführt und die Bezeichnungen für die beiden anderen Linien auch geändert. Obwohl sie eine logische Verlängerung der Blue Line darstellte, wurde die Mission Valley-Strecke als eigenständige Linie betrieben, da einige der älteren Abschnitte und Stationen noch nicht für die neuen Niederflurbahnen vom Typ S70 ausgebaut waren.

● **Zukunft des Trolley**

Seit den 1980er Jahren ist als ‚North Line' eine Verlängerung von Old Town entlang der Fernbahnstrecke und der I-5 geplant, doch sie wurde immer wieder aufgeschoben, heute rechnet man mit einem Baubeginn im Jahr 2015 und einer

placed by the covered America Plaza station, which lies next to the city's tallest building. The Bayside route then runs south alongside the old Santa Fe freight tracks to the MTS headquarters and yards at 12th & Imperial. Until 2012, the 'Bayside Extension' was part of the Orange Line.

The route from Santa Fe Depot to Old Town, running along the eastern side of the Santa Fe railway, opened in 1992. This section, which was served by the Blue Line until 2012, was meant to become the initial part of the 'North Line'. Unlike the mainline tracks, which remain at grade along this route, a 600 m segment of the Trolley alignment was put into an open trench to avoid level crossings at Grape and Hawthorn Streets, while Laurel Street was crossed by means of a viaduct. A busy level crossing remains at Taylor Street, just north of Old Town.

The 9.8 km Mission Valley West extension was the first line not to be built along a railway corridor, and instead it roughly follows the San Diego River and I-8. Due to the topographical situation along this valley, its alignment includes several viaducts, resulting in an almost metro-style route. A centre siding was built east of Qualcomm Stadium to temporarily stable trains during big events. When it opened in 1997, this new route was served by the extended 'South Line'.

In the second stage seven years later, the Mission Valley line was extended further east on a similar alignment, including a 1.2 km tunnel with a station under the San Diego State University (SDSU) campus. The route links up with the older East Line to the west of Grossmont station. Upon completion of the 9.2 km Mission Valley East extension, the Green Line was introduced and the names for the other two lines were changed. Although actually a logical extension of the Blue Line, the Mission Valley route was then operated as a separate line as some of the older segments and stations on the network were not yet ready to accommodate the new S70 low-floor trains.

● *Future of the Trolley*

Planned as the North Line since the 1980s, an extension from Old Town along the mainline rail and I-5 corridor has always been deferred, but may eventually start construction in 2015 for completion in 2018. The so-called 'Mid-Coast Corridor Transit Project' (17.6 km) will extend the Trolley (most likely the Blue Line) from Old Town to University City, home to the University of California - San Diego (UCSD). The line will diverge from the railway corridor at Gilman Drive, cross to the west side of I-5 just south of Nobel Drive, and run through the UCSD campus mostly on an elevated structure along Voigt Drive and Genesee Avenue before terminating at the Westfield UTC Transit Center.

Siemens SD100

Siemens-Duewag U2 – mit Hebevorrichtung | *with built-in lift*

Fertigstellung im Jahr 2018. Das sogenannte „Mid-Coast Corridor Transit Project" (17,6 km; wahrscheinlich als Verlängerung der Blue Line) verbindet Old Town mit der University City, dem Standort der University of California - San Diego (UCSD). Die Strecke wird den Eisenbahnkorridor am Gilman Drive verlassen, um dann südlich des Nobel Drive auf die Westseite der I-5 zu wechseln und schließlich durch den UCSD-Campus meist als Hochbahn entlang des Voigt Drive und der Genesee Avenue die Endstation am Westfield UTC Transit Center zu erreichen.

● Trolley-Wagenpark

Bei der MTS-Stadtbahn verkehren drei verschiedene Typen:

1) Zwischen 1981 und 1993 kamen insgesamt 71 Gelenkwagen vom Typ ‚U2' in fünf Lieferungen (Serie 1000) nach San Diego. Sie sind weitgehend identisch mit den ersten Stadtbahnwagen in Frankfurt am Main, die zuvor bereits nach Edmonton und Calgary in Kanada exportiert worden waren. Die Wagen für San Diego wurden von Siemens-Duewag in Düsseldorf hergestellt, aber die Endmontage erfolgte in den USA. Im Gegensatz zu den kanadischen Fahrzeugen wurden die San Diego-Wagen für einen Einstieg von niedrigen Bahnsteigen oder sogar von Schienenniveau gebaut, weshalb sie Stufen im Wageninneren sowie eine ausfahrbare Stufe für den Einstieg von der Straße haben. Um gehbehinderten Fahrgästen den Zugang zu ermöglichen, ist die erste Tür auf jeder Seite mit einem Rollstuhllift ausgestattet. Die U2-Wagen können theoretisch Züge aus bis zu 5 Wagen bilden, aber durch die Länge der Häuserblocks in der Innenstadt sind nur 3-Wagen-Züge möglich, gelegentlich fahren 4-Wagen-Züge während der Stoßzeiten oder bei Großveranstaltungen. Jedes der Zweirichtungsfahrzeuge ist 23,2 m lang und 2,65 m breit. Wie die neueren Fahrzeuge werden sie regelmäßig gewachst, um auch in der starken Sonne Südkaliforniens ihren Glanz nicht zu verlieren.

Seit 2010 wurden 25 U2-Wagen an die Metrotranvía Mendoza in Argentinien abgegeben, wo sie nun einen zweiten Frühling in ihrer alten, glänzend roten Lackierung erleben. Weitere Wagen sollen folgen.

2) Ohne die ausfahrbaren Stufen wurden die 52 Wagen vom Typ **SD100**

● Trolley Rolling Stock

The MTS fleet of light rail vehicles consists of three different types:

1) Between 1981 and 1993, a total of 71 articulated cars of type 'U2' were delivered in five batches (1000-series). They are largely identical to the first-generation Stadtbahn cars developed in Frankfurt (Germany), which had previously been exported to Edmonton and Calgary in Canada. The San Diego cars were manufactured by Siemens-Duewag in Düsseldorf, Germany, but the final assembly work took place in the U.S. Unlike the Canadian ones, the San Diego cars were designed for boarding from low platforms and even from track level, and therefore have stairwells inside plus retractable steps for street-level boarding. To allow access for disabled passengers, the first door on each side is equipped with a wheelchair lift. The U2s can theoretically form 5-car trains, although the length of the street blocks downtown limits them to 3 cars there; 4-car trains have occasionally been used during peak times and special events. Each double-ended car is 23.2 m long and 2.65 m wide. Like the newer cars, they must be waxed regularly to keep them shiny, otherwise the strong Southern Californian sun would quickly make them look dull.

Since 2010, 25 U2 cars have been transferred to the Metrotranvia in Mendoza, Argentina, where they are enjoying a second life in their old, shiny red livery; more may follow.

Siemens-Duewag U2 in Mendoza

Dirk Budach

(Serie 2000) zwischen 1993 und 1996 für die ‚East Line' geliefert, wo an allen Stationen zumindest Niedrigbahnsteige gebaut wurden. Sie sind eine Weiterentwicklung des U2 und identisch mit den ersten Fahrzeugen in Denver und Salt Lake City. Sie wurden speziell für den nordamerikanischen Markt entwickelt und komplett im Siemens-Werk in Sacramento hergestellt.

3) Im Zuge der Einführung der Green Line kamen wiederum völlig neue Fahrzeuge nach San Diego, nämlich in den Jahren 2004-05 elf Wagen des Typs **S70** „Avanto" (Serie 3000). Sie wurden auch von Siemens in Sacramento entwickelt und sind mittlerweile zu einem Standard-Fahrzeug auf dem nordamerikanischen Markt geworden. Sie sind 70% niederflurig und brauchen daher keine Rollstuhllifte mehr, auch wenn einzelne Türen mit einer ausfahrbaren Spaltüberbrückung ausgestattet sind, um Rollstuhlfahrern einen einfachen Zugang zu ermöglichen. Die S70-

Siemens S70

Wagen können zusammen mit den SD100 in einem Zugverband eingesetzt werden. Sie haben zwei Gelenke, wobei sich das mittlere Fahrwerk unter dem kurzen Mittelteil befindet. Die erste Serie war 27,4 m lang und 2,65 m breit, aber bei einer neuen Bestellung im Jahr 2009 gemeinsam mit UTA über 57 Wagen (im April 2012 erhöht auf 64) wurde eine Länge von nur 24,4 m festgeschrieben, damit sie den älteren Wagen entsprechen und als 3-Wagen-Züge in einen 72 m langen Häuserblock passen. Der erste der kürzeren S70-Wagen (Serie 4000) ist seit Oktober 2011 auf der Green Line im Einsatz. Voraussichtlich kommen die S70 im Frühjahr 2013 auch auf die Orange Line und im Sommer 2014 auf die Blue Line.

2) Delivered without retractable steps, the 52 cars of type **SD100** (2000-series) which followed between 1993 and 1996 were destined for the 'East Line', which was built with low-level platforms at all stations. They are similar to the U2s and identical to the early cars used in Denver and Salt Lake City. Especially developed for the North American market, they were entirely built at the Siemens plant in Sacramento.

3) The introduction of the Green Line also saw the introduction of a completely new vehicle, the **S70** 'Avanto', of which 11 units were delivered in 2004-05 (3000-series). They were also manufactured by Siemens in Sacramento and have since become one of the standard vehicles on the North American market. They are 70% low-floor and thus do not require a wheelchair lift, although some doors are equipped with an extractable bridge plate to allow easy access for wheelchair users. The S70s can be used together with the SD100s in a single trainset. They have two articulations, with the middle bogie sitting under the short centre module. The initial batch was 27.4 m long and 2.65 m wide, but a new order for 57 cars placed together with UTA in 2009 (increased to 64 in April 2012) specified a length of only 24.4 m to match the older stock and allow a 3-car train to fit into a 72 m street block. With the first of the shorter S70s (4000-series) in service on the Green Line since October 2011, they are expected to arrive on the Orange Line in spring 2013 and the Blue Line in summer 2014.

Als ‚Silver Line' verkehrt der PCC-Wagen Nr. 529 alle 30 Minuten im Uhrzeigersinn auf den Trolley-Gleisen rund um die Innenstadt (über die Gleisverbindung an der Station 12th & Imperial), allerdings nur dienstags und donnerstags von 9:50 bis 14:00 Uhr, sowie samstags und sonntags von 10:50 bis 15:30 Uhr. Der Fahrpreis beträgt 2,50 $.

Labelled the 'Silver Line', PCC car no. 529 runs around the Trolley's city loop (using the track link at 12th & Imperial) in a clockwise direction at limited times. It comes every 30 minutes from 09:50 to 14:00 on Tuesdays and Thursdays, and from 10:50 to 15:30 on Saturdays and Sundays. The regular fare is $2.50.

Der Oldtimer wurde ursprünglich im Jahr 1946 gebaut – nur drei Jahre bevor im April 1949 die letzten Straßenbahnen in San Diego fuhren – und nach einer sechsjährigen Restaurierung kehrte er am 27. August 2011 auf die Straßen von San Diego zurück. Fünf weitere Wagen sollen restauriert werden. Die erste elektrische Straßenbahn fuhr in San Diego 1887, aber erst 1892 wurde die *San Diego Electric Railway Company* gegründet, woraufhin dieses Verkehrsmittel die ganze Stadt eroberte.

C Street (India St) — Photo © San Diego Metropolitan Transit System

The vintage vehicle was originally built in 1946 — only three years before the last streetcars ran in San Diego in April 1949 — and after a six-year restoration period it returned to the streets of San Diego on 27 August 2011; five additional cars are scheduled for restoration. Although the first electric streetcars ran in San Diego in 1887, it was not until 1892 that the 'San Diego Electric Railway Company' was founded and this form of transport began to take over the entire city.

San Diego Santa Fe Depot
- Steuerwagen am Ende eines Pendlerzugs in der Mittagspause im Hauptbahnhof von San Diego; die Fahrgäste rechts im Hintergrund warten auf den Trolley.
- *Control trailer at the end of a commuter rail train in San Diego's main station at midday; passengers in the background wait for the Trolley.*

COASTER (Commuter Rail)

Unter der Regie des *North County Transit District* (NCTD) verkehrt die auf Pendler ausgerichtete Regionalbahn ‚Coaster' morgens sieben Mal (die letzte Fahrt immerhin erst um 11:05 Uhr!) und nachmittags vier Mal von Oceanside nach San Diego (Santa Fe Depot), Richtung Norden gibt es ein umgekehrtes Zugangebot. Am Wochenende wird die Strecke 4-mal täglich bedient. Der Sommerfahrplan enthält weitere Fahrten. Die Züge halten an sechs Zwischenstationen, darunter Old Town, ein wichtiger Umsteigepunkt für die nördlichen Stadtteile von San Diego, sowie Solana Beach und Carlsbad, zwei beliebte Badeorte. Die Strecke wird täglich auch von elf „Pacific Surfliner"-Zügen von Amtrak nach Los Angeles befahren, diese halten nur in Solana Beach, manche auch in Old Town. Obwohl sechs Metrolink-Züge Oceanside auch von Los Angeles aus erreichen, gibt es dort leider nur selten gute Anschlüsse.

Der Coaster verkehrte erstmals am 27. Februar 1995, nachdem NCTD im Jahr 1994 die Eisenbahnstrecke zwischen San Diego und Oceanside von der *Atchison, Topeka and Santa Fe Railway* (die später mit der *Burlington Northern Railroad* fusionierte und so in der *BNSF* aufging) erworben hatte. Mit dem Betrieb wurde TransitAmerica Services Inc. (TASI) beauftragt. Es werden typische Wendezüge aus diesel-elektrischen Lokomotiven und doppelstöckigen Waggons von Bombardier eingesetzt.

Governed by the North County Transit District (NCTD), the Coaster commuter railway provides seven trains from Oceanside to San Diego's Santa Fe Depot in the morning (the last leaving at 11:05!), and four in the afternoon, with an inverted service pattern in the northbound direction. Four trains a day run on weekends. Additional trains can be found in the summer timetable. The trains call at six intermediate stations, among them Old Town, a major interchange point for the northern parts of San Diego, and Solana Beach and Carlsbad, two busy seaside resorts. The route is shared with Amtrak's 11 daily "Pacific Surfliner" trains to Los Angeles. Most of them stop only at Solana Beach, but some stop at Old Town, too. Although six Metrolink trains from Los Angeles also reach Oceanside, good connections are rather scarce.

The Coaster service was first introduced on 27 February 1995, after the NCTD had purchased the railway line between San Diego and Oceanside from the 'Atchison, Topeka and Santa Fe Railway' (which later merged with the 'Burlington Northern Railroad' to become BNSF) in 1994. Day-to-day operation is carried out by TransitAmerica Services Inc. (TASI) using typical push-pull trains made up of diesel-electric locomotives and bi-level coaches from Bombardier.

Oceanside

SPRINTER (Oceanside – Escondido)

Auch wenn es sich um kein städtisches Schienenverkehrs-mittel im engeren Sinne handelt, so ist der ‚Sprinter' doch ein ziemlich einzigartiges Transportmittel in den USA (ähnlich ist nur die River Line bei Philadelphia): Er verkehrt in einem vorortähnlichem Umfeld ganztags alle 30 Minuten, von 4:00 bis 21:00 Uhr (freitags und samstags bis Mitternacht). Die Neben-strecke nach Escondido wurde von der *Atchison, Topeka and Santa Fe Railway* im Jahr 1992 gekauft. Der Ausbau begann jedoch erst 2005 und der regelmäßige Betrieb wurde schließ-lich am 9. März 2008 aufgenommen. Auch wenn die Strecke oft als „Light Rail" bezeichnet wird, fahren dort in Deutschland gefertigte Desiro VT642-Dieseltriebwagen von Siemens, wie man sie hierzulande auf vielen nicht elektrifizierten Neben-bahnstrecken sehen kann. Die Bahn wird von Veolia im Auftrag des NCTD betrieben.

In Oceanside, wo man zu Amtraks „Pacific Surfliner" nach Los Angeles bzw. San Diego sowie zur Metrolink nach Los Angeles und zum Coaster nach San Diego umsteigen kann, hat der Sprinter seine eigene Station mit zwei Stumpfgleisen neben dem zweigleisigen Fernbahnhof. Die Strecke verläuft Richtung Osten durch kontinuierlich, jedoch nicht allzu dicht bebaute Gebiete bis Escondido. Der Großteil der 35,4 km langen Strecke ist eingleisig mit längeren zweigleisigen Abschnitten, die Trasse ist größtenteils für einen zweigleisigen Ausbau vorbereitet. Da auf der Strecke außerhalb der Sprinter-Betriebszeiten auch einige breitere Güterzüge verkehren, sind die Bahnsteige etwas zurückversetzt und mit seitlichen Überbrückungen ausgestattet, die nach Betriebsende hochge-klappt werden. Neben der Endstation Oceanside ist einzig die Station Cal State San Marcos davon ausgenommen, da sie auf einem 2,7 km langen Neubauabschnitt liegt, der über den Campus der California State University - San Marcos südlich der Autobahn SR 78 führt.

Although not urban rail in the strict sense of the word, the Sprinter is a rather unique from of transport in the U.S., similar only to the River Line near Philadelphia. It operates in a suburban environment with a train every 30 minutes throughout the day from 04:00 until 21:00 (extended to midnight on Fridays and Saturdays). The Escondido branch was purchased from the 'Atchison, Topeka and Santa Fe Rail-way' in 1992, but upgrading did not start until 2005. Regular revenue service eventually began on 9 March 2008. Although sometimes referred to as 'light rail', the Sprinter uses Desiro VT642 DMUs (diesel multiple units) manufactured by Siemens in Germany, where they are seen on many secondary non-electrified regional lines. The trains are operated for NCTD by Veolia.

At Oceanside, where transfer is provided to Amtrak's "Pacific Surfliner" to Los Angeles and San Diego as well as Metrolink's commuter rail trains to Los Angeles and the Coaster to San Diego, the Sprinter has its own 2-stub sta-tion adjacent to the 2-track mainline station. It runs east to Escondido through continuously, though not too densely built-up suburbs. Most of the 35.4 km route is single-track with lengthy double-track sections, allowing a regular serv-ice; most single-track sections were prepared to accommo-date a second track in the future. Due to the wider freight trains the line carries when there is no passenger service, the station platforms had to be set back from the tracks, and side extensions which are folded up when passenger service finishes were installed. Besides the Oceanside terminus, the only exception is Cal State San Marcos station, which lies on a newly-built 2.7 km diversion route for the California State University - San Marcos campus on the south side of State Route 78.

Oceanside

Escondido

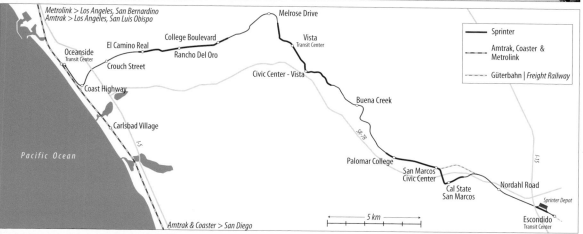

Metrolink > Los Angeles, San Bernardino
Amtrak > Los Angeles, San Luis Obispo

Oceanside
Transit Center

El Camino Real

Crouch Street

Coast Highway

Carlsbad Village

Pacific Ocean

I-5

College Boulevard

Rancho Del Oro

Melrose Drive

Vista
Transit Center

Civic Center - Vista

Buena Creek

SR-78

Palomar College

San Marcos
Civic Center

Cal State
San Marcos

Nordahl Road

I-15

Sprinter Depot

Escondido
Transit Center

Amtrak & Coaster > San Diego

5 km

Sprinter

Amtrak, Coaster &
Metrolink

Güterbahn | Freight Railway

Siemens Desiro

Escondido

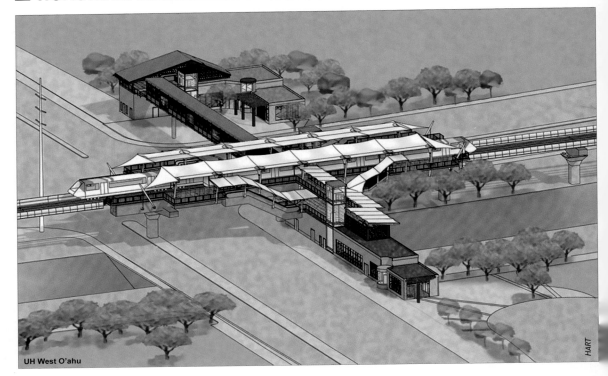

UH West O'ahu

HONOLULU, HI

Honolulu ist die Hauptstadt von Hawaii und befindet sich auf der Insel O'ahu (1545 km²), der mit etwa 950.000 Einwohnern meist bevölkerten aller Hawaii-Inseln. Etwa ein Drittel der Inselbevölkerung lebt in der Hauptstadt selbst. Honolulu liegt 3850 km südwestlich von San Francisco, der nächst gelegenen Stadt auf dem amerikanischen Festland.

Derzeit wird der öffentliche Nahverkehr auf O'ahu nur mit Bussen abgewickelt. Die häufigen Staus in den dicht bebauten Gebieten der Insel haben Politiker immer wieder dazu veranlasst, ein schienengebundenes Verkehrsmittel vorzuschlagen, doch wurde daraus nie etwas, bis die Bevölkerung der Insel schließlich bei den Wahlen im Jahr 2008 das neueste Projekt mit knapper Mehrheit guthieß.

Man entschied sich für eine völlig kreuzungsfreie Bahn mit herkömmlicher Stahlrad-auf-Stahlschiene-Technologie, jedoch mit vollautomatischem, fahrerlosem Betrieb. Die gesamte HART-Linie (<u>H</u>onolulu <u>A</u>uthority <u>R</u>apid <u>T</u>ransportation) wird als Hochbahn ausgeführt und von den westlichen Vororten Kapolei, Waipahu und Pearl City über den Flughafen in die Innenstadt von Honolulu führen und im Einkaufsviertel rund um das Ala Moana Center enden. Die Stützen werden meist im Mittelstreifen von Hauptverkehrsstraßen errichtet, nämlich auf dem Farrington Highway, dem Kamehameha Highway, der Ualena Street, dem Dillingham Boulevard, dem Nimitz

Honolulu is the capital of Hawaii and located on the island of O'ahu (1545 km2), the most populated of the Hawaiian Islands with some 950,000 inhabitants, a third of which live within the state capital's boundaries. Honolulu lies 3850 km southwest of San Francisco, the nearest city on the American mainland.

At present, public transport on O'ahu only consists of buses, but congestion in the densely built-up areas of the island has repeatedly inspired politicians to propose some sort of rapid transit system. None of the proposals had prospered, however, until the island's population approved the latest one by a narrow margin in the 2008 elections.

The final choice was for a completely grade-separated rail system with conventional steel-wheel-on-steel-rail technology, but with fully automatic driverless operation. The entire HART (<u>H</u>onolulu <u>A</u>uthority <u>R</u>apid <u>T</u>ransportation) line will be elevated, and will run from the western suburbs of Kapolei, Waipahu and Pearl City via the airport to downtown Honolulu before terminating in the shopping district around Ala Moana Center. The supporting pillars will mostly be placed in the median of major roads, notably Farrington Highway, Kamehameha Highway, Ualena Street, Dillingham Boulevard, Nimitz Highway, Halekauwila Street, Queen Street and Kona Street.

The following stations will become major transit centres and/or park-and-ride stations: East Kapolei (P+R), UH West O'ahu (TC & P+R), West Loch (TC), Pearl Highlands (TC & P+R) and Aloha Stadium (TC & P+R).

The initial line, the construction of which was launched in February 2011, will open in stages, starting with the westernmost segments. The first support columns were erected on undeveloped land in the East Kapolei area in spring 2012. Future extensions may bring the metro line to other parts of

HONOLULU Rail Transit

32 km (im Bau | under construction)
21 Bahnhöfe | stations (im Bau | under construction)

2015: Kapolei – Aloha Stadium
2017: Aloha Stadium – Middle Street
2019: Middle Street – Ala Moana Center

Highway, der Halekauwila Street, der Queen Street und der Kona Street.

Die folgenden Stationen werden wichtige Umsteigepunkte zum Busverkehr (TC) und/oder Park-&-Ride-Anlagen: East Kapolei (P+R), UH West O'ahu (TC & P+R), West Loch (TC), Pearl Highlands (TC & P+R) und Aloha Stadium (TC & P+R).

Die erste Linie, deren Bau im Februar 2011 begann, wird in Etappen beginnend mit den westlichsten Abschnitten in Betrieb gehen. Die ersten Stützpfeiler wurden im Frühjahr 2012 auf unbebautem Terrain in East Kapolei errichtet. In Zukunft könnte die Metrolinie in weitere Gebiete im Westen von O'ahu sowie nach Salt Lake erweitert werden, außerdem ist im Osten eine Verlängerung vom Ala Moana Center zur UH Manoa mit einem Abzweig nach Waikiki möglich.

Die Züge werden ab 4:00 Uhr bis Mitternacht während der Hauptverkehrszeiten alle drei Minuten, sonst tagsüber alle sechs Minuten und abends alle 10 Minuten fahren. Eine Fahrt auf der ganzen Linie dauert 42 Minuten. Die Metro wird voll in das bestehende Bustarifsystem bei kostenfreiem Umsteigen integriert und es soll keine Zugangssperren geben.

40 Zwei-Wagen-Züge und das Betriebssystem werden von der italienischen Firma Ansaldo geliefert, die im Jahr 2002 ein ähnliches System in der dänischen Hauptstadt Kopenhagen errichtet hat. Die Energiezufuhr der klimatisierten Züge erfolgt über eine seitliche Stromschiene. Der Metro-Betriebshof ist in der Nähe der Station Leeward Community College vorgesehen.

West O'ahu and to Salt Lake, and at the eastern end from Ala Moana Center to UH Manoa with a branch to Waikiki.

Trains will operate from 04:00 to midnight, every three minutes during peak travel times, every six minutes during the day and every 10 minutes in the evenings. A trip along the entire line will take 42 minutes. The rail system will be fully integrated with the existing bus network with a flat fare and free transfers using the proof-of-payment system.

40 two-car trains and the control system will be supplied by Ansaldo of Italy, who implemented a similar system in the Danish capital Copenhagen in 2002. The air-conditioned trains will be powered by a third rail. The vehicle maintenance and storage facility will be located near Leeward Community College station.

West Loch

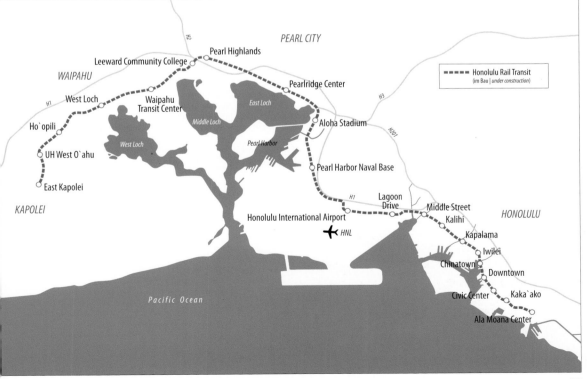

Convention Center > LVH – nach Süden fahrende Bahn mit dem Stratosphere Tower rechts im Hintergrund
– southbound train with the Stratosphere Tower in the background on the right

LAS VEGAS, NV

Las Vegas, die weltweite Hauptstadt des Glücksspiels, liegt an der Südspitze des Staates Nevada, in einer eher wüstenähnlichen Region etwa 450 km (mit dem Auto) nordöstlich von Los Angeles. Die eigentliche Stadt (352 km²) hat 584.000 Einwohner, während rund 2 Millionen Menschen in der Metropolregion leben, die ganz zum Clark County gehört.

Auch wenn es immer wieder gefordert wird, fährt durch Las Vegas seit 1997 kein Amtrak-Zug mehr, nachdem der „Desert Wind" von Salt Lake City nach Los Angeles eingestellt worden

Las Vegas, the gambling capital of the world, is located at the southern tip of the state of Nevada in a rather desert-like region some 450 km (by car) northeast of Los Angeles. The city proper (352 km2) has a population of 584,000, with roughly 2 million in the metropolitan area, all of which belongs to Clark County.

Although a rail connection has often been demanded, Las Vegas has not been served by Amtrak trains since 1997, when the "Desert Wind" from Salt Lake City to Los Angeles was discontinued. A project to build a new high-speed line to L.A., the XpressWest, is at an early stage of planning.

Considering the size of the city and the number of visitors it receives, Las Vegas' transportation system is very limited, consistsing mostly of bus routes. The only fixed-guideway systems are the 6 km monorail and several smaller 'trams' designed to carry tourists from their hotels to one of the casinos. At the airport, there is a people mover that links the two main terminals.

MGM Grand > Bally's/Paris L.V. (Harmon Ave)
– die Züge tragen meist Vollwerbung.
– most trains are covered with full adverts.

Bally's/Paris Las Vegas – Zugang durch das Casino
– *entrance through the casino*

war. Ein Projekt zum Bau einer neuen Hochgeschwindigkeitsstrecke Richtung Los Angeles, des XpressWest, befindet sich
in einer frühen Planungsphase.

Angesichts der Größe der Stadt und der Menge an Besu-
chern ist der Nahverkehr in Las Vegas sehr unterentwickelt
und wird hauptsächlich mit Bussen abgewickelt. Die einzigen
Bahnsysteme sind die 6 km lange Monorail sowie mehrere
kleinere ‚Trams', deren Funktion vor allem darin liegt, die
Touristen von ihren Hotels in eines der Casinos zu bringen. Am
Flughafen gibt es außerdem einen Peoplemover zwischen den
beiden Hauptterminals.

● Las Vegas Monorail
Die Einschienenbahn sollte einmal das Hauptverkehrsmittel
auf dem „Strip"-Korridor werden, doch ist sie seit ihrer Inbetriebnahme im Jahr 2004 nicht mehr verlängert worden. Die
heutige Linie beginnt am nördlichen Ende des Las Vegas Strip,
jenes Boulevards mit den riesigen Hotels, Einkaufszentren
und verschiedenen Vergnügungseinrichtungen. Die nördliche
Endstation liegt in der Nähe des Stratosphere Tower, noch
ca. 3 km von der alten Downtown rund um die Fremont Street
und dem jetzt geschlossenen Bahnhof entfernt. Die Strecke
verläuft zunächst nach Süden entlang der Paradise Road
zum Hilton Hotel und zum Convention Center, bevor sie dann
nach Westen in die Sands Avenue einbiegt und in die Nähe
des Las Vegas Boulevard kommt, ohne diesen jemals wirklich
zu erreichen. Die Trasse liegt nämlich größtenteils an der
Rückseite der großen Hotels und Spielcasinos, von denen
man einige durchlaufen muss, um zu den einzelnen Stationen
zu gelangen. Die südliche Endstation befindet sich östlich des
MGM Grand, eines der größten Hotelkomplexe der Welt.

Die Las Vegas Monorail verkehrt von 7:00 bis 2:00 Uhr
(3:00 Uhr am Wochenende) meist alle 5-6 Minuten. Eine
einfache Fahrt kostet 5,00 $, während eine Tageskarte, die
allerdings nur für die Monorail gilt, für 12,00 $ zu haben ist!

Die heutige Monorail-Strecke ging aus einer kurzen, 1,1 km
langen Monorail hervor, die im Juni 1995 als Verbindung
zwischen dem MGM und Bally's eröffnet worden war. Die Züge
fahren auf 66 cm breiten parallelen Betonbalken durchschnitt-
lich 9 m über dem Boden, wobei der höchste Punkt mit 18 m
über einem Fußgängersteg am Las Vegas Convention Center

LAS VEGAS Monorail

5.9 km
7 Bahnhöfe | *stations*

15 July 2004: Sahara – MGM Grand

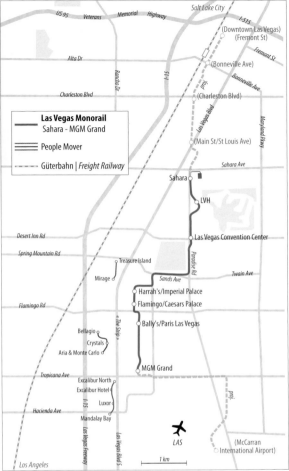

Las Vegas Monorail
Sahara – MGM Grand

People Mover

Güterbahn | *Freight Railway*

● *Las Vegas Monorail*
*Once planned to become the backbone of public transport
along the Strip corridor, the Las Vegas Monorail has not been
extended since it opened in 2004. The present line starts at
the northern end of the Las Vegas Strip (the row of high-rise
hotels, shopping malls and leisure facilities on Las Vegas
Boulevard) near the Stratosphere Tower, about 3 km short
of the city's downtown area around Fremont Street and the
now-closed railway station. It first runs south along Paradise
Road to serve the Hilton Hotel and the Convention Center,
before turning west on Sands Avenue and approaching the Las
Vegas Boulevard, which it never actually reaches as its route
is aligned mostly at the back of major hotels and gambling
parlours, through many of which passengers have to walk to
reach the stations. The southern terminus is located at the
east side of MGM Grand, one of the largest hotel complexes
in the world.*

*The Las Vegas Monorail operates from 07:00 to 02:00
(03:00 on weekends), with trains passing every 5-6 minutes
for most of the day. A single ride costs $5.00, while a day
pass for exclusive use on the monorail is $12.00!*

*Today's monorail route incorporates a short 1.1 km mono-
rail opened in June 1995 to link MGM and Bally's. The trains
run on 66 cm wide parallel concrete beams lying on average
9 m above the ground, with the highest point of 18 m being
reached above the Las Vegas Convention Center pedestrian*

Convention Center

Harrah's/Imperial Palace – Bahnsteig | *platform*

zu finden ist. Der Fahrweg ist ähnlich wie beim ALWEG-System, das in Seattle in Betrieb ist (siehe Seite 14).

Eine Nordverlängerung um 3,5 km mit vier Stationen entlang der Main Street bis Downtown Las Vegas war von Anfang an geplant, wurde aber später wegen fehlender Finanzierung auf Eis gelegt.

Eine Südverlängerung zum McCarran International Airport war ebenfalls von Anfang an vorgesehen, aber auch wenn sie weiterhin geplant ist, sind keine Fortschritte zu beobachten, wohl auch wegen des Widerstands von Taxi- und Limousinenunternehmen, aber vor allem wegen der finanziellen Schwierigkeiten der privaten Betreiberfirma.

● Monorail-Fahrzeuge

Die Monorail-Flotte besteht aus neun vierteiligen Zügen, die aus M-VI-Wagen (INNOVIA Monorail 200) von Bombardier gebildet werden. Diese basieren auf den Zügen der Disney World Monorail in Florida. Sie sind klimatisiert, 42 m lang, 2,65 m breit und bieten 72 Sitzplätze. Die vier Abschnitte sind nicht durchgehend begehbar, da zwischen ihnen die Radaufhängung untergebracht ist, die aus einem tragenden angetriebenen Reifen in der Mitte und zwei seitlichen Führungsreifen unter dem Gelenk besteht. Trotz des fahrerlosen Betriebs ist ein Blick aus dem vorderen bzw. hinteren Fenster nicht möglich. Die Stromversorgung mit 750 V Gleichstrom erfolgt über eine Stromschiene. Der Monorail-Betriebshof liegt in der Nähe der nördlichen Endstation Sahara. Bombardier Transportation ist für den Betrieb und die Wartung der Züge sowie für das automatische Zugsteuerungssystem zuständig.

walkway. The guideway is similar to the ALWEG system in operation in Seattle (see page 14).

A 3.5 km northern extension with four stations along Main Street to Downtown Las Vegas had been planned from the beginning, but was later put on hold due to a lack of funding.

A southern extension to McCarran International Airport has also been envisaged from the beginning, but although still planned, has not made any progress. This is due partly to objections brought forward by taxi and limousine companies, but mostly to the private operator's financial troubles.

● Monorail Rolling Stock

The monorail fleet consists of nine four-car trains made up of Bombardier M-VI (INNOVIA Monorail 200) cars, which are based on the Disney World Monorail trains in Florida. They are climate-controlled, 42 m long, 2.65 m wide and contain 72 seats. The four sections are not interconnected, due to the type of suspension system used, which consists of a centre load tyre that carries and moves the train, and two guide tyres placed under the articulations. Despite the driverless operation, a view out the front or rear windows is not possible in the end sections. 750 V dc is supplied via a power rail. The monorail fleet is stored and maintained in a facility near the northern terminus Sahara. Bombardier Transportation is responsible for operating and maintaining the trains and the automatic train control system.

Convention Center – Bahnsteigtüren | *platform screen doors*

Nicht durchgängig begehbare Wagen | *carriages not interconnected*

Mandalay Bay Tram

Neben der Las Vegas Monorail gibt es in dieser Stadt noch drei kleinere Peoplemover, die alle innerhalb von Hotelanlagen liegen, jedoch für jedermann frei zugänglich sind:
1) Die **Mirage – Treasure Island Tram** sieht aus wie eine alte Standseilbahn, nutzt aber eine ähnliche Technologie wie die beiden anderen „Trams", d.h. mit Gummireifen, die auf Metallbalken laufen. Sie ist etwa 350 m lang und wurde zusammen mit dem Treasure Island Resort am 27. Oktober 1993 eröffnet.
2) Die **CityCenter Tram** ist der neueste Peoplemover in Las Vegas. Er verbindet das Einkaufs- und Entertainment-Center Crystals im Herzen des neuen CityCenter-Areals mit dem Aria und Monte Carlo im Süden und dem Bellagio im Norden. Die 640 m lange Hochbahn, die am 1. Dezember 2009 eröffnet wurde, verwendet die Cable Liner-Technologie von Doppelmayr Cable Car (DCC), mit zwei gummibereiften Zügen, die auf einer aufgeständerten modularen Stahlfachwerkkonstruktion verkehren. Jeder Zug fährt auf seiner eigenen Bahn.
3) Die **Mandalay Bay Tram** wurde am 9. April 1999 in Betrieb genommen und verbindet das Excalibur und Luxor mit dem Mandalay Bay am südlichen Ende des Strip. Die 850 m lange Bahn nutzt dieselbe Doppelmayr-Technologie wie die neuere CityCenter Tram.

Besides the Las Vegas Monorail, the city has three smaller people mover systems, all within resort complexes but freely accessible to anyone:
1) The **Mirage – Treasure Island Tram** *appears to be a vintage funicular, but it is technologically similar to the other two 'tram' systems, with rubber tyres running on metal beams. It is about 350 m long, and opened together with the Treasure Island resort on 27 October 1993.*
2) The **CityCenter Tram** *is the newest people mover in Las Vegas. It links the Crystals shopping and entertainment centre in the heart of the new CityCenter resort with the Aria and Monte Carlo to the south and the Bellagio to the north. The 640 m elevated system, which opened on 1 December 2009, uses Cable Liner technology from Doppelmayr Cable Car (DCC), with two rubber-tyred trains running parallel on an elevated modular steel truss guideway. Each unit operates on its own track.*
3) The **Mandalay Bay Tram**, *opened on 9 April 1999, links the Excalibur, Luxor and Mandalay Bay resorts at the southern end of the Strip. The 850 m line uses the same Doppelmayr technology as the newer CityCenter Tram.*

Mirage – Treasure Island Tram

CityCenter Tram

19th Ave/Camelback > Montebello/19th Ave – Zugbegegnung südlich der heutigen Endstelle im Nordwesten – *trains meeting south of the current northwestern terminus.*

PHOENIX, AZ

Phoenix ist die Hauptstadt des Bundesstaates Arizona und mit rund 1,5 Mio. Einwohnern auf einer Fläche von 1.338 km^2 auch dessen größte Stadt. Der Großraum von Phoenix, der den Beinamen „Tal der Sonne" trägt und zu den am schnellsten wachsenden Ballungszentren in den USA zählt, ist die Heimat von 4,2 Mio. Menschen und umfasst Städte wie Chandler, Gilbert, Glendale, Mesa, Peoria, Scottsdale, Surprise und Tempe im Maricopa und Pinal County.

Phoenix ist die größte Stadt in den USA, die nicht per Bahn erreichbar ist. Der nächste Amtrak-Bahnhof befindet sich in Maricopa, 55 km südlich von Phoenix, wo der „Sunset Limited" (New Orleans – Los Angeles) und der „Texas Eagle" (Chicago – Los Angeles) hält. Langfristig könnte die geplante Hochgeschwindigkeitsstrecke von Los Angeles nach Las Vegas bis Phoenix verlängert werden.

Der öffentliche Nahverkehr, d.h. Stadtbahn und Busse, in und um Phoenix werden von *Valley Metro* betrieben. Eine Einzelfahrt kostet 1,75 $ (ohne Umsteigen) und eine Tageskarte nur 3,50 $ (5,25 $ beim Kauf im Bus)!

Im Jahr 2012 betreibt *Valley Metro* erst eine einzige Stadtbahnlinie. Die Züge fahren von 4:40 bis 23:20 Uhr, tagsüber alle 12 Minuten, am frühen Morgen und nach 18:30 Uhr alle 20 Minuten. Samstags verkehrt die Stadtbahn alle 15 Minuten und sonntags alle 20 Minuten. Am Freitag- und Samstagabend wird der Betrieb bis 2:30 Uhr ausgedehnt. Eine Fahrt von einem Ende zum anderen dauert 65 Minuten.

Phoenix is the capital of Arizona as well as the state's largest city with a population of approximately 1.5 million in an area of 1,338 km2. The Phoenix metropolitan area, nicknamed the "Valley of the Sun" and one of the fastest growing in the U.S., is home to 4.2 million people and includes cities like Chandler, Gilbert, Glendale, Mesa, Peoria, Scottsdale, Surprise and Tempe in Maricopa and Pinal Counties.

Phoenix is the largest city in the U.S. not accessible by train. The closest Amtrak station is at Maricopa 55 km south of Phoenix, which is served by the "Sunset Limited" (New Orleans – Los Angeles) and the "Texas Eagle" (Chicago – Los Angeles). In the long term, the planned high-speed rail line from Los Angeles to Las Vegas may be extended to Phoenix.

Public transport, i.e. light rail and a bus service, in and around Phoenix is provided by Valley Metro. A single ride costs $1.75 (no transfer), and an unlimited-ride day pass is available at just $3.50 ($5.25 if bought on buses)!

As of 2012, Valley Metro operates a single light rail line, with trains running from 04:40 until 23:20 every 12 minutes during daytime hours, and every 20 minutes early mornings and after 18:30. On Saturdays, trains operate every 15 minutes and on Sundays every 20 minutes. On Friday and Saturday nights, service is extended until 02:30. A trip from end to end takes 65 minutes.

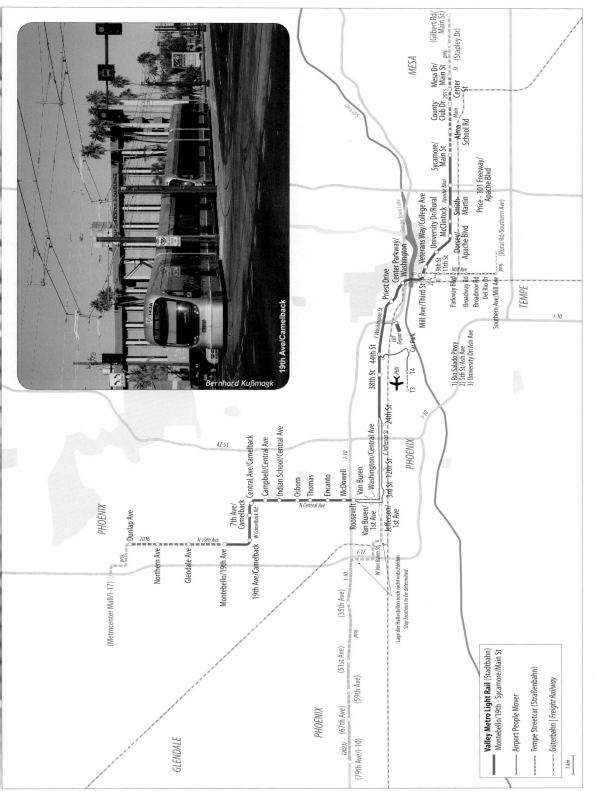

19th Ave/Camelback

Bernhard Kußmagk

Montebello/19th Avenue

Bernhard Kußmagk

● Valley Metro Light Rail

Die Stadtbahn von Phoenix gehört zu den neueren in den USA. Die erste Linie lässt einige typische Merkmale der anderen amerikanischen Stadtbahnen vermissen, wie die Nutzung alter Eisenbahntrassen (außer einem kurzen Stück im Zentrum von Tempe) oder eine Trassierung im Mittelstreifen von Schnellstraßen. Die Stadtbahn von Phoenix ähnelt vielmehr einer modernen Straßenbahn in Europa. Sie verkehrt durchweg auf einer eigenen Trasse in der Mitte städtischer Straßen, wobei die Gleise in eine Betonfahrbahn eingebettet sind. Es gibt zahlreiche, nur durch Ampeln gesteuerte Bahnübergänge. Die zwei einzigen größeren Bauwerke, die speziell für die Stadtbahn errichtet wurden, sind eine eigene Brücke über den Tempe Town Lake (einen vom Salt River gespeisten Stausee) parallel zu einer bestehenden Eisenbahnbrücke südlich der Haltestelle Center Parkway/Washington in Tempe sowie eine kurze Brücke parallel zum Red Mountain Freeway auf der Zufahrt zum Betriebshof.

Die heutige Stadtbahnlinie wurde 2009 eröffnet und beginnt an der Montebello Avenue auf der 19th Avenue. Sie verläuft erst nach Süden und biegt bald nach Osten in die West Camelback Road ein, um kurz darauf in Richtung Süden auf der North Central Avenue, der Haupt-Nord-Süd-Achse der Stadt, in

Phoenix's light rail system is one of the newest in the U.S. Its starter line lacks some typical features seen in other American cities, like the use of old railway corridors (except for a short segment in downtown Tempe) or alignments in the median of freeways. Phoenix's line bears more resemblence to a European-style modern tram line, running on a reserved, double-track right-of-way in the centre of urban roads, with tracks embedded in concrete, and numerous level crossings only controlled by traffic lights. The only two major structures built for the light rail system are a dedicated bridge over Tempe Town Lake (a reservoir fed by the Salt River),

E Jefferson Street (8th St)

Bernhard Kußmagk

PHOENIX Valley Metro Light Rail

31.4 km (+ 4.4 km im Bau | *under construction*)
28 Haltestellen | *stations* (+ 4 im Bau | *under construction*)

01 Jan 2009: Montebello/19th Avenue – Sycamore/Main Street
2015: Sycamore/Main Street – Mesa Drive/Main Street

Priest Drive/Washington Street

Central Ave/Camelback

die Innenstadt zu fahren. Kurz bevor die Stadtbahn das eigentliche Zentrum erreicht, schwenkt das nach Süden führende Gleis in die North 1st Avenue, während das Gleis Richtung Norden auf der North Central Avenue bleibt. Letzteres biegt dann nach Osten in die East Washington Avenue, die alle kreuzenden Straßen in einen Nord- und einen Südabschnitt unterteilt, während das nun nach Osten führende Gleis in der East Jefferson Street liegt. Die beiden Gleise verbleiben fast 4,5 km in den zwei parallel verlaufenden Straßen und treffen schließlich an der 26th Street auf der East Washington Avenue wieder aufeinander. Sie folgen dieser Straße dann bis zur Überquerung des Salt River in Tempe. Am Südufer verläuft die Route entlang des East Veterans Way, der South Terrace Road und schließlich des East Apache Boulevard, der in Mesa in die East Main Street übergeht.

Alle Haltestellen sind ähnlich gestaltet und weisen meist Mittelbahnsteige auf, jedoch spiegeln individuelle Kunstwerke die Umgebung der Station wider.

Von der derzeitigen Endstelle Sycamore Street ist eine geradlinige Verlängerung entlang der Main Street bis zum Mesa Drive im Bau (4,4 km), die Fertigstellung ist für das Jahr 2015 vorgesehen. Diese Strecke soll später bis zur Gilbert Road (3 km) erweitert werden.

which lies parallel to an existing railway bridge just south of Center Parkway/Washington station in Tempe, and a short bridge parallel to the Red Mountain Freeway to access the LRT maintenance facility.

The present route, opened in 2009, starts at Montebello Avenue on 19th Avenue, runs south, then turns east into W Camelback Road before again heading south into the city centre on N Central Avenue, the city's primary north-south artery. Just before getting into downtown proper, the southbound track switches onto N 1st Avenue, while the northbound track stays on N Central Avenue. The latter then turns east into E Washington Avenue, which divides the intersecting streets into north/south sections, while the track which is now eastbound follows Jefferson Street. The two tracks remain on parallel streets for almost 4.5 km before reuniting at 26th Street on E Washington Avenue, which they stay on all the way to the Salt River crossing in Tempe. On the south bank, the route gets aligned along E Veterans Way, S Terrace Road and finally E Apache Boulevard, which becomes E Main Street in Mesa.

The stations all have a similar design, mostly with island platforms, but are enhanced with individual artwork reflecting their respective surroundings.

From the present terminus at Sycamore Street, a straight extension along Main Street to Mesa Drive is under construction (4.4 km) for completion in 2015. This route is planned to be further extended to Gilbert Road (3 km).

Montebello/19th Avenue

Veterans Way/College Ave

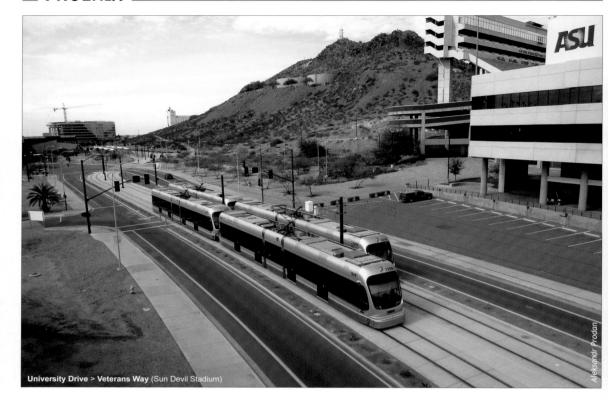

University Drive > Veterans Way (Sun Devil Stadium)

Aleksandr Prodan

⦿ Zukunft des Schienennahverkehrs in Phoenix

Neben der Verlängerung in Mesa, die bereits im Bau ist, soll im Jahr 2013 eine Nordverlängerung von der Montebello Avenue bis zur Dunlap Avenue in Angriff genommen werden (5 km; 2016). In einer zweiten Phase soll die Stadtbahn schließlich nach Nordwesten entlang der Dunlap Avenue, der North 25th Avenue und der West Mountain View Road weiterfahren, um in der Nähe der Metrocenter Mall zu enden (2,5 km; 2026).

Eine wesentliche Vergrößerung des Netzes soll mit der 17,5 km langen Weststrecke erreicht werden. Diese wird auf der Washington bzw. Jefferson Street nach Westen bis zur 18th Avenue, dann nach Norden bis zur Van Buren Street und wieder nach Westen bis zur Autobahn I-17 führen. Nach Norden am Westrand der I-17 verlaufend wird sie die I-10 erreichen, auf deren Mittelstreifen sie dann westwärts weiterführen soll. Etwa an der 47th Avenue soll sie auf die Nordseite schwenken und schließlich an der 79th Avenue enden (2023).

Langfristige Pläne beinhalten auch einen Abzweig Richtung Glendale sowie eine neue Strecke entlang des Piestewa Freeway-Korridors (AZ-51).

Neben den ehrgeizigen Plänen für den Stadtbahnausbau wird bis 2016 in Tempe eine klassische, 4,2 km lange Straßenbahnlinie gebaut. Sie verläuft größtenteils in Nord-Süd-Richtung entlang der Mill Avenue, nur im Zentrum von Tempe, wo Anschluss zur Stadtbahn besteht, wird das Gleis Richtung Süden in der parallelen Ash Avenue verlegt.

⦿ *Phoenix Urban Rail Future*

Besides the Mesa extension already underway, in 2013 the construction of a northern extension from Montebello Avenue to Dunlap Avenue (5 km by 2016) is scheduled to start. The second phase will eventually take the light rail service northwest along Dunlap Avenue, N 25th Avenue and W Mountain View Road to terminate near the Metrocenter Mall (2.5 km by 2026).

A significant expansion of the system will be achieved with the 17.5 km Phoenix West extension, which will travel west on Washington / Jefferson Streets to 18th Avenue, then north to Van Buren Street and west to the I-17 freeway. Heading north along the western edge of I-17, it will reach I-10. From here, Valley Metro's light rail line will boast a freeway alignment within the median to about 47th Avenue, and then along the north side of I-10 up to 79th Avenue (2023).

Long-term plans include branches towards Glendale and along the Piestewa Freeway corridor (AZ-51).

Besides the ambitious plans for light rail expansion, a conventional 4.2 km streetcar line will be built in Tempe by 2016. Running mostly north-south along Mill Avenue, the southbound track will be laid on the parallel Ash Avenue in downtown Tempe, where interchange with the Light Rail line will be provided.

Mark Kavanagh

Innenraum eines Kinkisharyo-Wagens
– *Interior of a Kinkisharyo car*

● Stadtbahnfahrzeuge

Valley Metro verfügt über eine Flotte von 50 Zweirichtungsfahrzeugen, die von Kinkisharyo hergestellt wurden. Die elektrische Ausrüstung wurde von Faiveley und das Antriebssystem von Elin EBG beigesteuert. Die Stadtbahnen sind ähnlich wie die in San Jose und Seattle aufgebaut, nämlich 27,7 m lang, 2,65 m breit und mit einem losen Fahrwerk unter dem kurzen Mittelteil und jeweils angetriebenen Drehgestellen unter den hochflurigen Endabschnitten. Die sechsachsigen Doppelgelenkfahrzeuge sind 70% niederflurig (355 mm/889 mm). Wegen der hohen Anzahl an Bahnübergängen wurden sie mit einziehbaren, abgedeckten Kupplungen ausgerüstet, Energie absorbierende Stoßfänger erhöhen die Sicherheit zusätzlich. Normalerweise sind 2-Wagen-Züge im Einsatz, die Bahnsteige sind allerdings für 3-Wagen-Züge ausgelegt.

Der Stadtbahnbetriebshof befindet sich östlich des Flughafens, etwa auf Höhe der 51st Street in Phoenix.

● *Light Rail Rolling Stock*

Valley Metro owns a fleet of 50 double-ended light rail vehicles manufactured by Kinkisharyo. The electrical equipment was supplied by Faiveley, and the propulsion system by Elin EBG. The trams are similar to those in San Jose and Seattle, in that they are 27.7 m long, 2.65 m wide, and have a trailer bogie under the short middle section and two powered bogies under the raised end sections. The 6-axle, double-articulated vehicles are 70% low-floor (355 mm/889 mm). Especially designed for operation on routes with a lot of level crossings, the couplers can be folded and hidden, while energy-absorbing bumpers increase safety, too. Normally, 2-car trains are in service, although the platforms are laid out to accommodate 3-car trains.

The LRT maintenance facility is located east of the airport, with the access tracks diverging from the line near 51st Street in Phoenix.

Photo © Phoenix Sky Harbor International Airport

PHX Sky Train™

Ab dem Frühjahr 2013 wird die Stadtbahn mit dem Phoenix Sky Harbor International Airport (Terminal 4) über einen aufgeständerten, 2,7 km langen kostenlosen Peoplemover verknüpft sein. Die gummibereiften fahrerlosen Züge, 18 Fahrzeuge vom Typ INNOVIA APM 200 von Bombardier, werden alle paar Minuten von der Stadtbahnhaltestelle 44th Street zum Flughafen fahren und unterwegs am Langzeitparkplatz halten. Auf dem letzten Abschnitt vor dem Terminal liegt der Viadukt etwa 30 m über dem Boden, damit auch große Flugzeuge weiterhin die Rollbahn darunter nutzen können. 10 Jahre lang wird Bombardier für den Betrieb und die Wartung des Systems verantwortlich sein. Eine 1,1 km lange Erweiterung zum Terminal 3 soll im Frühjahr 2015 folgen.

From spring 2013, the light rail line will be linked to Phoenix Sky Harbor International Airport (Terminal 4) via a free, elevated 2.7 km people mover. The rubber-tyred driverless trains, 18 INNOVIA APM 200 vehicles built by Bombardier, will run every few minutes from the 44th Street LRT station to the airport, stopping also at the long-term car park. On its approach to the terminal building, the viaduct rises to about 30 m above the ground, allowing large aircraft to use the taxiway beneath. For 10 years, Bombardier will be responsible for the operation and maintenance of the system. A 1.1 km extension to Terminal 3 is planned to follow in early 2015.

Old Pueblo Trolley (University Avenue & 4th Avenue)

Bernhard Kußmagk, 2009

TUCSON, AZ

Mit 526.000 Einwohnern in der Stadt und rund einer Million im Großraum ist Tucson das zweitgrößte Ballungsgebiet in Arizona. Es liegt rund 170 km südöstlich von Phoenix und ca. 100 km von der mexikanischen Grenze entfernt. Im Gegensatz zu Phoenix hält in Tucson drei Mal pro Woche der Amtrak-Zug „Sunset Limited" (New Orleans – Los Angeles), wobei einige Wagen von San Antonio direkt nach Chicago fahren („Texas Eagle").

● Old Pueblo Trolley

Die letzte der ursprünglichen Straßenbahnen fuhr im Jahr 1930 durch Tucson. 63 Jahre später, am 17. April 1993, kehrte dieses Verkehrsmittel in Form einer Oldtimer-Straßenbahn mit eingeschränktem Betrieb an einigen Wochentagen in die Stadt zurück, teilweise auf einem originalen, freigelegten Gleis auf dem University Boulevard und teilweise auf einem neuen Gleis entlang der 4th Avenue nach Süden bis zu einem Wagenschuppen an der 8th Street. Die Strecke war eingleisig in Straßenmitte mit einer Ausweiche auf der 4th Avenue zwischen 4th Street und University Boulevard. Der Betrieb wurde anfangs mit dem Birney-Wagen Nr. 10 bestritten, der für die *Pacific Electric Railway* gebaut worden war und vom Orange Empire Railway Museum geleast wurde. Dazu kam Triebwagen Nr. 255 von der *Hankai Electric Tramway* in Osaka. Dieser wurde 1995 in seinen ursprünglichen Zustand von 1953, als er in Kyoto unterwegs war, zurückversetzt und trägt jetzt die Nummer 869. Der Wagenpark wurde später mit Fahrzeugen aus Brüssel (der zweiachsige Wagen Nr. 1511 von 1936) und Toronto (PCC-Wagen Nr. 4608 von 1951) erweitert. Die ursprüngliche Strecke wurde 2009 weiter nach Süden unter den *Union Pacific*-Bahngleisen zu einer Schleife näher an der Innenstadt verlängert.

Der Oldtimer-Betrieb wurde am 8. Oktober 2011 eingestellt, um die Strecke zu einer modernen Straßenbahn ausbauen zu können.

With a population of 526,000 in the city and approximately 1 million in the metropolitan area, Tucson is Arizona's second largest conurbation. It lies some 170 km southeast of Phoenix and about 100 km from the Mexican border. Unlike Phoenix, Tucson is served three times a week by Amtrak's "Sunset Limited" (New Orleans – Los Angeles), with some carriages going directly to Chicago from San Antonio ("Texas Eagle").

● Old Pueblo Trolley
The last of the original streetcars ran through Tucson in 1930. 63 years later, on 17 April 1993, they returned to the city in the form of a heritage streetcar line with limited service on some weekdays, partly on original uncovered track on University Boulevard, and partly on new track south along 4th Avenue to a carbarn on 8th Street. The route was single-track in the middle of the road, with a passing loop on 4th Avenue between 4th Street and University Boulevard. Service was initially provided by the Birney-type car no. 10, built for Pacific Electric Railway and leased from the Orange Empire Railway Museum, plus car no. 255, acquired from the Hankai Electric Tramway in Osaka. The latter was restored in 1995 to its original 1953 Kyoto look, and renumbered 869. The fleet was later enlarged with vehicles from Brussels (two-axle car no. 1511 from 1936) and Toronto (PCC car no. 4608 from 1951). In 2009 the initial route was extended south under the UP railway tracks to a loop closer to downtown.

Service on the Old Pueblo Trolley was discontinued on 8 October 2011 to allow for its upgrading to modern streetcar standard.

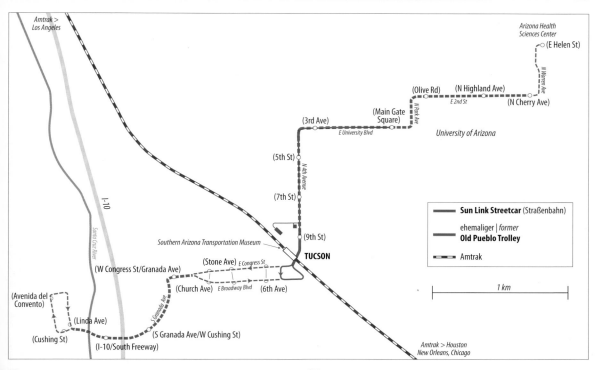

● Sun Link Streetcar

Der Bau einer modernen Straßenbahn begann im April 2012, die Fertigstellung ist für Ende 2013/Anfang 2014 geplant. Die 6,3 km lange Strecke ersetzt die frühere Old Pueblo Trolley-Route, die gleichzeitig an beiden Enden verlängert wird, nach Osten durch den Bereich der University of Arizona und nach Westen in ein Entwicklungsgebiet westlich der I-10 im Stadtteil Mercado. Das wichtigste Bauwerk ist die Luis G. Gutierrez Bridge über den Santa Cruz River. Bis auf das östliche Ende und die Schleife im Westen ist die Strecke zweigleisig, wobei in der Innenstadt durch parallel verlaufende Straßen gefahren wird.

Acht Fahrzeuge vom Typ 200 von United Streetcar werden tagsüber im 10-Minuten-Takt verkehren. Diese wurden mit einer speziellen Klimaanlage für Städte im Süden ausgerüstet, ansonsten ähneln sie den Fahrzeugen, die nach Portland geliefert werden. Sie sind 20,13 m lang und 2,46 m breit, die Fußbodenhöhe beträgt über den Endabschnitten 780 mm und im mittleren Abschnitt 350 mm. Sie benötigen 750 V Gleichstrom.

● *Sun Link Streetcar*

The construction of a modern streetcar line began in April 2012, with expected completion in late 2013/early 2014. The 6.3 km route will replace the former Old Pueblo Trolley route, with new extensions at each end, both east through the University of Arizona area, and west towards a new development west of I-10 in the Mercado district. The single most important purpose-built structure will be the Luis G. Gutierrez Bridge over the Santa Cruz River. Except for the eastern end of the line and the western loop, the route will be double-track, with parallel running through the downtown area.

Eight United Streetcar 200 vehicles will provide a 10-minute daytime service. They are specifically manufactured with increased cooling capacity for cities with hot climates. Other than that they will be similar to the cars being delivered to Portland, 20.13 m long and 2.46 m wide, with a floor height of 780 mm above the end sections and 350 mm in the middle section. They use a 750 V dc power supply.

United Streetcar 200 (Source: unitedstreetcar.com)

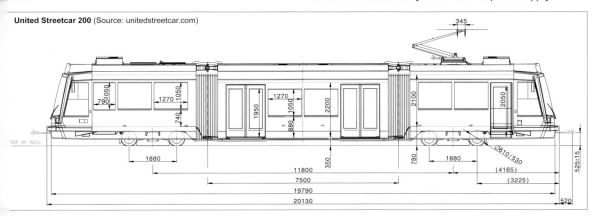

Courthouse – Umsteigepunkt am südlichen Rand der Innenstadt
– *transfer point at the southern edge of the city centre*

SALT LAKE CITY, UT

Salt Lake City ist die Hauptstadt des Bundesstaates Utah und auch dessen größte Stadt, auch wenn die Stadt selbst nur knapp 190.000 Einwohner zählt (282,5 km²). Im Salt Lake County, das in etwa dem durchgehend bebauten Gebiet entspricht und Städte wie South Salt Lake, Sandy, West Jordan und West Valley City einschließt, leben etwa 1 Mio. Menschen. Die Stadtbahn erschließt das gesamte County. Über 2 Mio. Menschen, also mehr als zwei Drittel der Bevölkerung von Utah, sind in einem 150 km langen Nord-Süd-Streifen von Ogden bis Provo zu Hause. Die als Wasatch Front bekannte Region wird im Osten durch die Wasatch Mountains und im Westen durch den Great Salt Lake, die Oquirrh Mountains und den Utah Lake begrenzt.

In Salt Lake City hält der tägliche Amtrak-Zug „California Zephyr" auf seinem Weg von Chicago über Denver und Sacramento nach Emeryville (bei San Francisco).

Der öffentliche Nahverkehr entlang der gesamten Wasatch Front wird von UTA (*Utah Transit Authority*) betrieben und umfasst Busse, Stadtbahn (TRAX) sowie eine Regionalbahnlinie (FrontRunner). Während eine Einzelfahrt mit lokalen Bussen und Stadtbahnen 2,35 $ (mit Umsteigen) kostet, ist eine Tageskarte für 5,75 $ erhältlich. Fahrpreise für den FrontRunner richten sich nach der Entfernung, reichen von 2,35 $ bis 8,95 $ (Ogden – Provo) und erlauben das Umsteigen auf TRAX bzw. Lokalbusse. TRAX und Busse sind in der Innenstadt zwischen Salt Lake Central, Library und Courthouse kostenlos.

Salt Lake City is the capital of the state of Utah as well as its largest city, despite a population of just 190,000 within the city limits (282.5 km2). However, about 1 million people live in Salt Lake County, which roughly coincides with the contiguously built-up area served by the light rail system and includes several other cities, among them South Salt Lake, Sandy, West Jordan and West Valley City. About 2 million people, accounting for more than two-thirds of Utah's population, live in a 150 km north-south corridor between Ogden and Provo, known as the Wasatch Front, a region bordered on the east by the Wasatch Mountains, and on the west by the Great Salt Lake, the Oquirrh Mountains and Utah Lake.

Salt Lake City is a stop on Amtrak's daily "California Zephyr" operating between Chicago and the San Francisco Bay Area via Denver and Sacramento.

Public transport along the entire Wasatch Front is provided by UTA (Utah Transit Authority), and includes buses, light rail (TRAX) and regional rail (FrontRunner). While a single fare for local buses and light rail is $2.35 (including transfer), a day pass is available at $5.75. FrontRunner one-way fares range from $2.35 to $8.95 (Ogden - Provo), depending on the distance travelled, and include transfer to TRAX or local buses. Riding TRAX and buses is free in the downtown area between Salt Lake Central, Library and Courthouse stations.

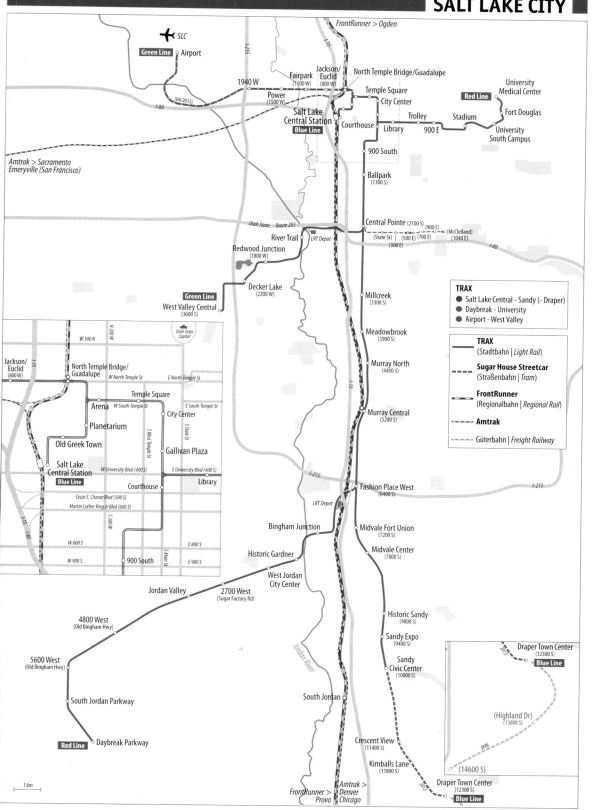

✈ SLC

Green Line Airport

FrontRunner > Ogden

I-215

1940 W

Fairpark (1100 W)

Jackson/ Euclid (800 W)

North Temple Bridge/Guadalupe

University Medical Center

Power (1500 W)

Temple Square

City Center

Red Line

Fort Douglas

Salt Lake Central Station

Blue Line

Courthouse

Library

Trolley

Stadium

University South Campus

900 E

900 South

Amtrak > Sacramento Emeryville (San Francisco)

I-80

Ballpark (1300 S)

Utah State Route 201

LRT Depot

Central Pointe (2100 S)

(900 E)

(McClelland) (1040 E)

River Trail

(State St) (500 E) (700 E)

(300 E)

I-80

Redwood Junction (1800 W)

Green Line

Decker Lake (2200 W)

Millcreek (3300 S)

West Valley Central (3600 S)

Meadowbrook (3900 S)

Murray North (4400 S)

Murray Central (5200 S)

I-15

I-215

Fashion Place West (6400 S)

LRT Depot

Bingham Junction

Midvale Fort Union (7200 S)

Midvale Center (7800 S)

Historic Gardner

West Jordan City Center

Jordan Valley

2700 West (Sugar Factory Rd)

Historic Sandy (9000 S)

4800 West (Old Bingham Hwy)

Sandy Expo (9400 S)

Jordan River

Sandy Civic Center (10000 S)

5600 West (Old Bingham Hwy)

South Jordan Parkway

Red Line Daybreak Parkway

South Jordan

Crescent View (11400 S)

Kimballs Lane (11800 S)

FrontRunner > Provo

Amtrak > Denver Chicago

Draper Town Center (12300 S)

Blue Line

Inset map (upper right):

TRAX
- ● Salt Lake Central - Sandy (- Draper)
- ● Daybreak - University
- ● Airport - West Valley

──	**TRAX** (Stadtbahn | *Light Rail*)
- - -	**Sugar House Streetcar** (Straßenbahn | *Tram*)
──	**FrontRunner** (Regionalbahn | *Regional Rail*)
─·─	**Amtrak**
─ ─	Güterbahn | *Freight Railway*

Inset map (lower left):

Jackson/ Euclid (800 W)

North Temple Bridge/ Guadalupe

Utah State Capitol

W 300 N

M 00 E N

W North Temple St

E North Temple St

Temple Square

Arena

W South Temple St

E South Temple St

Planetarium

S West Temple St

S State St

City Center

Old Greek Town

Gallivan Plaza

Salt Lake Central Station

Blue Line

W University Blvd (400 S)

E University Blvd (400 S)

Courthouse

Library

Cesar E. Chavez Blvd (500 S)

Martin Luther King Jr Blvd (600 S)

M 300 E

I-15

I-80

W 800 S

E 800 S

900 South

S Main St

W 900 S

E 900 S

Inset map (lower right):

Draper Town Center (12300 S)

Blue Line

(Highland Dr) (13800 S)

proj.

(14600 S)

1 km

Sandy Civic Center – Siemens SD160

Arena (ex-Delta Center) – UTDC-Wagen | *UTDC car* (ex San Jose)

Maurits van den Toorn

⬡ TRAX Light Rail

Das Stadtbahnnetz von Salt Lake City besteht aus drei farblich gekennzeichneten Linien, die in den Fahrplantabellen mit den Liniennummern 701 (blau), 703 (rot) und 704 (grün) geführt werden. Im Jahr 1999 war TRAX (kurz für „Transit Express") die letzte der modernen Stadtbahnen in den USA, die mit Hochflurfahrzeugen in Betrieb genommen wurde, während nur ein Jahr später die *Hudson-Bergen Light Railway* in New Jersey mit teilweise niederflurigen Wagen von Kinkisharyo an den Start ging und von Siemens gebaute Niederflurbahnen bereits seit zwei Jahren in Portland im Einsatz waren.

Das TRAX-Netz ist eine typische Stadtbahn mit meist abmarkierten straßenbündigen Abschnitten im Stadtzentrum und weitgehend eigenen Trassen durch die Vororte, jedoch ebenerdig und mit zahlreichen Bahnübergängen, die allerdings mit automatischen Schranken gesichert sind, so dass hohe Fahrgeschwindigkeiten möglich sind. Das gesamte TRAX-Netz ist heute zweigleisig, nachdem auch zwei vorher eingleisige Brücken auf der ursprünglichen Linie ausgebaut wurden. Die Stadtbahn verkehrt von 5:30 Uhr bis etwa Mitternacht (sonntags von 10:00 bis 21:00 Uhr!), montags bis freitags alle 15 Minuten, samstags und sonntags alle 20 Minuten.

● **Blue Line** (31 km, 24 Haltestellen)
Die erste Stadtbahnlinie von Salt Lake City umfasste eine Strecke von 23,9 km von der Innenstadt (die ursprüngliche Endstelle Arena neben dem alten Bahnhof der *Union Pacific* hieß damals Delta Center) nach Süden bis Sandy. Während die Gleise durch die Innenstadt in Straßenmitte (South Temple Street, Main Street, 700 South und 200 West Street) auf einer

The UTA light rail system currently consists of three colour-coded routes, also identified on timetables by the line numbers 701 (blue), 703 (red) and 704 (green). Only opened in 1999, TRAX (short for 'Transit Express') was the last modern U.S. light rail system to be brought into service using high-floor cars. Just one year later, New Jersey's Hudson-Bergen Light Railway was launched with partly low-floor vehicles from Kinkisharyo, and Siemens-built low-floor trains had already been inroduced in Portland two years earlier.

The TRAX network can be described as a typical light rail system, with street-running sections on mostly marked-off lanes in the city centre. In suburban areas, the routes are largely segregated, though at grade and with numerous level crossings, which are nonetheless equipped with automatic barriers allowing high travel speeds. The entire TRAX network is now double-tracked, after the expansion of two single-track bridges on the original line. TRAX operates from 05:30 until around midnight (Sundays 10:00-21:00!), with trains every 15 minutes from Monday to Friday, and every 20 minutes on Saturdays and Sundays.

● **Blue Line** (31 km, 24 stations)
The initial TRAX line connects between downtown (the original terminus Arena, next to the old Union Pacific Station, was formerly named Delta Center) and Sandy, a distance of 23.9 km. While operating in the middle of downtown streets (South Temple St, Main Street, 700 South and 200 West) in reserved lanes, there is a short 700 m street-running section used by all three lines just south of 900 South station. Just north of Ballpark station, TRAX joins an old railway right-of-way UTA had purchased from Union Pacific (UP Provo Branch) in the early 1990s. TRAX follows this railway corridor all

City Center – Siemens SD100 + SD160

SALT LAKE CITY – TRAX (Light Rail)

71.4 km (2013)
50 Haltestellen | *stations* (2013)

04 Dec 1999: Arena – Sandy Civic Center (23.9 km)
15 Dec 2001: Gallivan Plaza – Stadium (3.6 km)
29 Sept 2003: Stadium – University Medical Center (2.5 km)
19 Sept 2005: + 900 South
28 Aug 2006: + Sandy Expo
27 April 2008: Arena – Salt Lake Central Station (1.4 km)
07 Aug 2011: Central Pointe – West Valley Central (7.9 km)
Fashion Place West – Daybreak Parkway (17 km)
April 2013: Arena – Airport (9.4 km)
2013: Sandy Civic Center – Draper Town Center (5.7 km)

Library – Siemens S70

besonderen Fahrbahn liegen, gibt es südlich der Station 900 South einen kurzen, 700 m langen straßenbündigen Abschnitt, der von allen drei Linien befahren wird. Nördlich der Haltestelle Ballpark trifft TRAX auf eine alte Eisenbahntrasse (UP Provo Branch), die UTA in den frühen 1990er Jahren von der *Union Pacific* gekauft hatte, und folgt dieser hinunter bis Sandy, ab 2013 bis Draper und später sogar darüber hinaus. Damit der Einstieg auch für Menschen mit eingeschränkter Mobilität möglich ist, mussten alle Stationen mit kurzen Hochbahnsteigen ausgestattet werden, die mit den ersten Türen jedes Zuges übereinstimmen (zusätzlich klappt der Fahrer manuell eine Überbrückung aus).

Im Jahr 2008 wurde die ursprüngliche Strecke 1,4 km von Arena zu einem neuen Nahverkehrsknoten, der Salt Lake Central Station, verlängert, wo die Amtrak-Züge bereits seit 1999 hielten, nachdem sie vom nahe gelegenen Rio Grande-Bahnhof hierher verlegt worden waren. Im Süden wird die Blue Line derzeit um 5,7 km bis Draper verlängert.

● **Red Line** (37,7 km, 25 Haltestellen)
Nach dem Erfolg der Sandy-Linie und mit den Olympischen Winterspielen 2002 vor der Tür wurde im Jahr 2000 mit dem Bau des ersten, 3,6 km langen Abschnitts der 'University Line' begonnen. Diese zweigt von der Sandy-Linie nördlich der Haltestelle Courthouse ab und verläuft in Straßenmitte des University Boulevard bis zum Rice-Eccles Stadion. Auch wenn in der Regel ein eigener Gleiskörper zur Verfügung steht, wird das Stadtbahngleis an mehreren Kreuzungen von links abbiegenden Autos befahren, was zu Beeinträchtigungen führen kann. Seit 2003 fahren die TRAX-Bahnen entlang des South Campus Drive hinauf zum Gelände der University of Utah und enden nach weiteren 2,5 km am Medical Center; die Strecke bietet eine schöne Aussicht auf die Wasatch Mountains und

the way to Sandy, and in the future further south to Draper (2013) and possibly beyond. To allow boarding for people with reduced mobility, every station had to be equipped with short high-level platforms lining up with the first doors of each train (additionally requiring a bridge plate operated manually by the driver).

In 2008, the original route was extended 1.4 km from Arena to a new intermodal hub called Salt Lake Central Station, which Amtrak trains had been using since being moved from the nearby Rio Grande Station in 1999. At its southern end, the Blue Line is currently being extended by 5.7 km to Draper.

● ***Red Line*** *(37.7 km, 25 stations)*
With the success of the Sandy Line and the 2002 Winter Olympic Games coming up, the first 3.6 km section of the University Line was started in 2000. It branches off the Sandy Line north of Courthouse to operate in the median of University Boulevard up to the Rice-Eccles Stadium; though generally on a reserved right-of-way, left-turning traffic occupies an LRT track at several intersections, a potential source of delay. Since 2003, TRAX trains have been climbing through the University of Utah campus to reach the Medical Center (2.5 km), providing pleasant views of the Wasatch Mountains and the valley below. In the city centre, the 'University Line' as well as the 'North-South Line' used to terminate at Delta Center (now Arena).

The southern leg of the current Red Line, the 17 km Mid-Jordan extension, was built as a key element of the ambitious Frontlines 2015 project. It diverges from the Sandy Line at Fashion Place West in Midvale, runs under I-15 and the Union Pacific and FrontRunner tracks to Provo, and passes by the original LRT maintenance facility, before picking up

Arena

University South Campus

das davorliegende Tal. Die ‚University Line' hatte ihren innerstädtischen Endpunkt wie die ‚North-South-Line' damals am Delta Center (jetzt Arena).

Der südliche Ast der heutigen Red Line, die 17 km lange ‚Mid Jordan Line', wurde als ein wichtiges Element des ehrgeizigen Ausbauprojekts ‚Frontlines 2015' gebaut. Sie zweigt von der Sandy-Linie bei Fashion Place West in Midvale ab, verläuft dann unter der I-15 und den Gleisen der *Union Pacific* sowie des Frontrunner nach Provo hindurch, vorbei am älteren TRAX-Betriebshof, erreicht schließlich die alte Güterbahntrasse (D&RGW Bingham Branch), die UTA von UP erworben hatte, und folgt dieser bis kurz vor der Station 5600 West. Der letzte Abschnitt nach Süden bis Daybreak verläuft durch bislang unbebautes Gebiet, hier werden in Zukunft weitere Wohnungen entstehen.

● **Green Line** (23,9 km, 18 Haltestellen)
Als zweites Projekt der ‚Frontlines 2015' wurde die 7,9 km lange ‚West Valley Line' gleichzeitig mit der ‚Mid Jordan Line' eröffnet. Sie zweigt von der Nord-Süd-Linie südlich der Station Central Pointe in der Stadt South Salt Lake ab, folgt dann einer alten Güterbahn auf ihrem Weg unter den zahlreichen Fahrspuren der I-15, um dann auf einem neu erbauten Viadukt die Fern- und Regionalbahngleise zu überqueren. Ein zweites Brückenbauwerk umgeht eine Kreuzung mit der 900 West östlich des zweiten TRAX-Betriebshofs. Westlich davon überspannt eine weitere Brücke den Jordan-Fluss, bevor die Stadtbahn für 500 m in eine eher städtische Umgebung entlang der Winston Street mit der Haltestelle River Trail gelangt. Sie folgt dann dem Jordan-Fluss nach Süden, schwenkt nach Westen entlang eines Kanals und erreicht schließlich Decker Lake, wo sich

the former D&RGW Bingham Branch, a freight rail alignment UTA purchased from UP. The line follows this right-of-way through West Jordan to just east of 5600 West station. The last section south to Daybreak cuts through undeveloped land that will contain future phases of this large master-planned community.

● *Green Line* (23.9 km, 18 stations)
As the second Frontlines 2015 project, the 7.9 km West Valley extension was opened on the same day as the Mid-Jordan extension. It diverges from the north-south trunk line just south of Central Pointe in the city of South Salt Lake and follows an old freight line on its way under the numerous I-15 lanes and ramps. TRAX then climbs a purpose-built viaduct over the mainline UP tracks and crosses a second bridge over 900 West adjacent to the second LRT facility. To its west, yet another bridge spans across the Jordan River, bringing the line into a more urban environment for 500 m along Winston Street, stopping at River Trail. It then follows the Jordan River south, turns west along a canal, and reaches Decker Lake adjacent to a hockey arena and events center. Via 3100 South (the bridge over I-215 was widened on the southern side) and Constitution Boulevard, the Green Line arrives at West Valley Central, next to the city hall. The 2011 extensions were built without the short high-level platforms and can therefore only be served by the new S70 rolling stock.

In April 2013, the Green Line will be extended with a northern leg to Salt Lake City International Airport. This extension was initially planned as part of an east-west line from the University to the Airport, but timing and funding

West Jordan City Center

West Valley Central

Fort Douglas – mit Blick auf die Wasatch Front | *with a view over the Wasatch Front*

eine Hockey-Arena und Veranstaltungshalle befinden. Über die 3100 South (die Brücke über die I-215 wurde auf der Südseite verbreitert) und den Constitution Boulevard kommt die Green Line ins Zentrum von West Valley City. Die Verlängerungen von 2011 wurden ohne die kurzen Hochbahnsteige gebaut, weshalb auf diesen Linien nur die neuen Fahrzeuge vom Typ S70 zum Einsatz kommen.

Im April 2013 wird die Green Line um einen nördlichen Ast zum Flughafen ergänzt. Ursprünglich sollte das der westliche Ast einer Ost-West-Linie vom Flughafen zur Universität werden, er wurde dann aber aufgrund der hohen Kosten und des Zeitdrucks vor den Olympischen Spielen zurückgestellt und schließlich erst im November 2007 im Rahmen der ‚Frontlines 2015' genehmigt. Die frühere Straßenbrücke über die Bahn-

in the period running up to the Olympics only allowed the eastern half of the project to be built. The western half was eventually approved in November 2007 as one of the Frontlines 2015 projects. The previously existing bridge carrying North Temple Street over the railway tracks was demolished and replaced with a new viaduct (now one block shorter on the east side) for road traffic and light rail, including a station directly above the new FrontRunner station, thus providing convenient interchange between the two rail systems. The Airport extension follows the median of North Temple Street until it becomes Old State Route 186, which it flanks on the northern side on its way to the airport. The Airport station is located at the end of one of the terminals, just a few steps away from the check-in counters.

Salt Lake Central – Nahverkehrsdrehscheibe | *transportation hub*

Fort Douglas > University Medical Center

Siemens SD160

Siemens S70

gleise entlang der North Temple Street wurde abgerissen und eine neue, jetzt auf der Ostseite einen Block kürzere wurde für den Autoverkehr und die Stadtbahn errichtet, einschließlich einer Haltestelle direkt über dem auf bestehender Strecke eingefügten FrontRunner-Bahnhof, so dass man bequem zwischen beiden Bahnen umsteigen kann. Die ‚Airport Line' verläuft im Mittelstreifen der North Temple Street bis zur Old State Route 186, an deren Nordseite sie dann den Flughafen erreicht, wo sich die Endhaltestelle nur wenige Schritte von den Check-in-Schaltern entfernt befindet.

● TRAX-Wagenpark
UTA besitzt drei verschiedene Typen von Stadtbahnfahrzeugen, auch wenn derzeit nur zwei davon im Linienverkehr eingesetzt werden. Während der Olympischen Winterspiele 2002 halfen mehr als 20 Wagen aus Dallas aus, um den Massenandrang zu bewältigen.

1) 23 Gelenkwagen vom Typ **SD100** und 17 vom Typ **SD160** stammen von Siemens-Duewag. Sie sind weitgehend identisch, nur dass die von 2001 bis 2003 in zwei Serien gelieferten SD160 statt der ursprünglichen Gleichstrommotoren über Drehstrommotoren verfügen und statt der Falttüren nun Schwenkschiebetüren haben. Beide Typen sind 24,8 m lang und 2,65 m breit. Da diese Hochflurfahrzeuge kurze Hochbahnsteige benötigen, werden sie nur noch auf der Blue Line eingesetzt.

2) Um dem Wagenmangel Abhilfe zu verschaffen, wurden 2003 29 Gebrauchtwagen von der Santa Clara VTA in San Jose übernommen, da man dort die gesamte Flotte durch neue Niederflurfahrzeuge ersetzte. Diese Wagen stammen von UTDC aus Kanada und sind derzeit im Depot abgestellt.

3) Für die umfangreiche Netzerweiterung bestellte UTA im Jahr 2008 77 Wagen des Typs S70 von Siemens in Sacramento. Das erste Fahrzeug wurde im Jahr 2010 ausgeliefert. Die gleichen, 70% niederflurigen Fahrzeuge mit einer Länge von 24,4 m laufen nun auch in San Diego, während etwas längere Versionen in anderen Städten der USA zu sehen sind. Im Gegensatz zu den Wagen in Portland haben sie an beiden Enden Fahrerkabinen und können daher auch einzeln eingesetzt werden. Es besteht eine Option auf 180 weitere Fahrzeuge.

Auf der Red und Green Line kommen in der Regel 2-Wagen-Züge des Typs S70 zum Einsatz, während auf der Blue Line mit 3-Wagen- (und sogar 4-Wagen-)Züge der älteren Typen unterwegs sind. Alle Stationen sind lang genug für 4-Wagen-Züge.

Es gibt zwei Betriebshöfe, der erste liegt an der Nord-Süd-Linie in der Nähe der Station Fashion Place West und ein neuerer auf dem West Valley-Ast in der Nähe der Haltestelle River Trail.

● TRAX Rolling Stock
UTA owns three different types of light rail vehicles, although only two are now in regular service. During the 2002 Winter Olympics, more than 20 cars from Dallas helped to cope with the heavy crowds.

*1) 23 **SD100** and 17 **SD160** articulated vehicles were manufactured by Siemens-Duewag. They are largely identical, although the SD160 delivered in two batches in 2001 and 2003 feature ac motors and have sliding doors as opposed to the original dc motors and folding doors of the original 1998 stock. Both are 24.8 m long and 2.65 m wide. As these high-floor cars require special high-level boarding platforms, they are now used only on the Blue Line.*

*2) Short on rolling stock, UTA took the opportunity to purchase 29 used cars from San Jose in 2003, when Santa Clara VTA replaced its entire fleet with low-floor vehicles to allow level boarding for everyone. These cars were built by **UTDC** in Canada and are currently stored in the depot.*

*3) In view of major extensions, UTA ordered 77 cars of type **S70** from Siemens in Sacramento in 2008, with the first car being delivered in 2010. The same 70% low-floor cars with a length of 24.4 m also run in San Diego, while slightly longer versions can now be seen in other U.S. cities. Unlike the Portland cars, they are double-ended and can therefore also operate as single units. The order includes an option for 180 additional cars.*

On the Red and Green Lines 2-car trains of type S70 are normally used, while on the Blue Line, 3-car (and even 4-car) trains of the older types are in service. The stations are all long enough for 4-car trains.

There are two storage and maintenance facilities, the first just off the north-south line near Fashion Place West, and a second on the West Valley branch near the River Trail stop.

Siemens S70
– Trotz Niederflureinstieg steht Rollstuhlfahrern eine Hilfsrampe zur Verfügung.
– *despite low-floor access, an auxiliary ramp is available for wheelchair users.*

Salt Lake Central

Layton

🚊 FrontRunner

Seit dem 26. April 2008 betreibt UTA auch eine Regionalbahnlinie, den FrontRunner, der nach der Bergkette Wasatch Front
benannt ist, an der er entlang läuft. Der FrontRunner wird
offiziell zwar als „Commuter Rail" bezeichnet, bietet aber im
Gegensatz zu anderen so bezeichneten Bahnen einen regelmäßigen Betrieb den ganzen Tag, also nicht nur für typische
Pendler. Die Züge fahren an Wochentagen stündlich (während
der Hauptverkehrszeiten in der Hauptlastrichtung alle 30 Minuten). Samstags herrscht nun ein 90-Minuten-Takt, sonntags
gibt es bislang jedoch keine Züge.

Die erste, nicht elektrifizierte Linie verlief von Salt Lake City
60 km nach Norden bis Ogden eingleisig mit einigen Begeg-
nungsabschnitten auf einer eigenen, neben den Gütergleisen
der *Union Pacific* exklusiv für den FrontRunner angelegten
Trasse. Es gab ursprünglich fünf Zwischenstationen, bis am
10. Dezember 2012 die Station North Temple Bridge/Guadalu-
pe mit baldiger Umsteigemöglichkeit auf die TRAX Green Line
eingefügt wurde. Zwischen September 2008 und September
2011 fuhren einzelne HVZ-Züge 10 km weiter nach Norden bis
Pleasant View, hier allerdings im Mischbetrieb mit Güterzügen.
Im Dezember 2012 wurde auf diesem Abschnitt wieder eine
Fahrt täglich in den Fahrplan aufgenommen.

Gleich nach Inbetriebnahme der Nordstrecke begann UTA
im August 2008 mit dem Bau einer 71 km langen Südstrecke
nach Provo, die am 10. Dezember 2012 mit sieben Stationen
eröffnet wurde. Eine Umsteigemöglichkeit zu den TRAX-Linien
besteht an der Station Murray Central.

Der FrontRunner-Betrieb wird mit Wendezügen durchgeführt, die aus MotivePower MPXpress-Lokomotiven und
Bombardier-Doppelstockwaggons sowie einigen modernisier-
ten Comet I-Waggons von NJT (*New Jersey Transit*) bestehen.

*Since 26 April 2008, UTA has also operated a regional rail
line, the FrontRunner, named after the Wasatch Front it runs
along. Although officially referred to as 'commuter rail', the
FrontRunner offers regular service throughout the day, not
just for commuters, with trains running hourly on weekdays
(although every 30 minutes during peak hours in the peak
direction). Intervals between trains are 90 minutes on Saturdays, and there are no trains on Sundays.*

*The initial non-electrified line ran from Salt Lake City
60 km north to Ogden on a new single track with some passing loops laid alongside the UP freight tracks for exclusive
use by the FrontRunner. There were five intermediate stations until 10 December 2012, when North Temple Bridge/
Guadalupe station was added (as a future transfer to the
TRAX Green Line). A rather limited peak-only service was
also provided in mixed operation with freight trains on
a 10 km northern extension to Pleasant View starting in
September 2008. It was discontinued in September 2011, but
resumed in December 2012 with one peak trip in each direction per day.*

*In August 2008, right after the northern line was brought
into service, UTA broke ground on a 71 km seven-station
southern extension to Provo, which opened on 10 December
2012. Interchange with TRAX is provided at Murray Central.*

*The FrontRunner service is provided with diesel-powered
push-pull trains using MotivePower MPXpress locomotives and
Bombardier bi-level carriages, plus some refurbished single-
deck Comet I cars from NJT (New Jersey Transit).*

Sugar House Streetcar

Seit Mai 2012 baut UTA ihre erste Straßenbahnstrecke.
Ausgehend von der bestehenden TRAX-Station Central
Pointe an der 2100 South wird sie nach Osten entlang der
ehemaligen Sugar House-Eisenbahnzweiglinie der D&RGW
bis zur McClelland Street, westlich des Highland Drive,
verlaufen. Die 3,2 km lange Strecke mit sieben Haltestellen
soll im Dezember 2013 eröffnet werden. Die Straßenbahnen
werden alle 20 Minuten fahren, ein Takt, der von der überwiegend eingleisigen Trassierung mit einer einzigen Ausweiche
auf halber Strecke bestimmt wird. Mögliche Trassen für eine
Erweiterung Richtung Osten werden derzeit untersucht.

*Construction began on UTA's first streetcar line in May
2012. Starting from the existing TRAX Central Pointe
station at 2100 South, it will run eastward along the abandoned D&RGW Sugar House Branch to McClelland Street,
just west of Highland Drive. The 3.2 km line with seven
stops will open in December 2013, with streetcars running
every 20 minutes. The headway is limited by the line's
predominantly single-track alignment, with a single passing
loop midway along the line. Various alternatives for an
eastern extension are being studied.*

Littleton/Mineral – Siemens SD100

DENVER, CO

Die Hauptstadt des Bundesstaates Colorado wird auch „Mile High City" genannt, da sie auf einer Höhe von 1600 m über dem Meeresspiegel in einer eher flachen Gegend, den High Plains, am Ostrand der Rocky Mountains liegt. Die eigentliche Stadt (396 km²) hat 620.000 Einwohner, im Ballungsraum leben jedoch rund 3 Mio. Menschen. Dazu gehören Städte wie Boulder, Broomfield, Thornton, Arvada, Aurora, Golden, Lakewood, Englewood und Littleton in den Counties Jefferson, Adams und Arapahoe.

In Denver macht der tägliche Amtrak-Zug „California Zephyr" auf seinem Weg von Chicago über Salt Lake City nach Emeryville (bei San Francisco) Halt.

Für den öffentlichen Nahverkehr im Großraum von Denver ist RTD (*Regional Transportation District*) zuständig. RTD betreibt momentan nur Busse und Stadtbahnen, doch eine S-Bahn befindet sich bereits im Bau. Obwohl es sich um einen einzigen Betreiber handelt, ist das Tarifsystem eher kompliziert. Die Fahrpreise richten sich bei der Stadtbahn nach der Entfernung und bei den Bussen nach der Art des Angebots (local/express/regional). Einzelfahrten auf der Stadtbahn kosten (mit Umsteigen zu den Bussen) 2,25 $ (1-2 Zonen), 4,00 $ (3 Zonen) und 5,00 $ (alle Zonen), entsprechend sind Tageskarten für 6,75/11,50/14,00 $ erhältlich, was Denver bezüglich Nahverkehr zu einer der teuersten Städte in den USA macht.

Denver, the capital of the state of Colorado, is nicknamed the 'Mile High City' as it is located at an altitude of 1600 m in a rather flat region known as the High Plains, just east of the Rocky Mountains. The city proper (396 km2) has a population of 620,000, with some 3 million people living in the larger Denver metropolitan area, which contains cities like Boulder, Broomfield, Thornton, Arvada, Aurora, Golden, Lakewood, Englewood and Littleton in Jefferson, Adams and Arapahoe Counties.

Denver is a stop on Amtrak's daily "California Zephyr" on its way from Chicago to Emeryville (for San Francisco) via Salt Lake City.

Public transport in the Denver Metro Area is provided by RTD (*Regional Transportation District*), which currently operates buses and light rail and is developing a suburban rail service as well. Although there is just the single operator, the fare system is rather complex, with distance-based fares on the light rail system, and bus fares depending on the type of service (local/express/regional). Single rides on light rail trains (including free transfer to buses) are $2.25 (1-2 zones), $4.00 (3 zones) and $5.00 (all zones); accordingly, day passes are available at $6.75/$11.50/$14.00, making Denver one of the most expensive transit systems in the U.S.

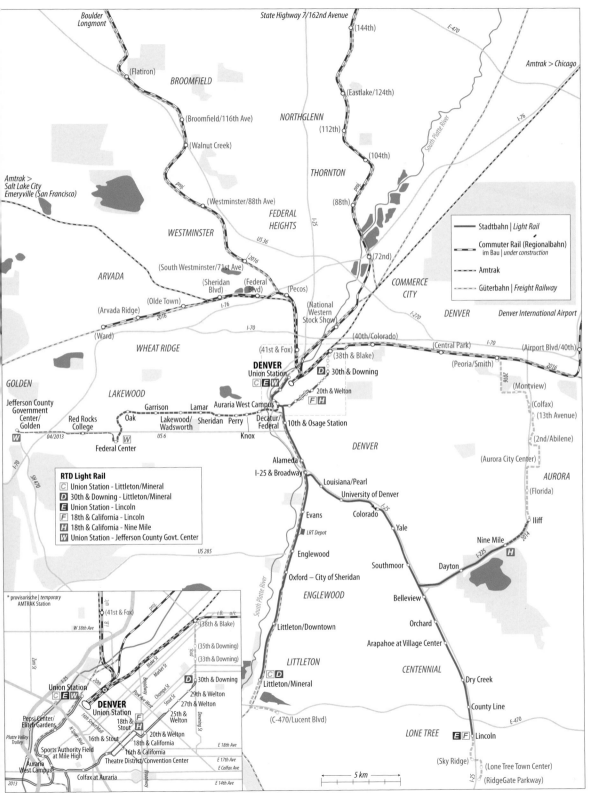

Colfax at Auraria – kurzer Hochbahnsteig | *short high-level platform*

Colorado

◉ RTD Light Rail

Das heutige Stadtbahnnetz von Denver besteht aus fünf durch Buchstaben und Farben gekennzeichnete Linien, eine sechste, die Linie W zum Jefferson County Government Center, kommt im Jahr 2013 hinzu. Neben Sacramento ist Denver die einzige Stadt im Westen der USA, wo der Betrieb noch ausschließlich mit Hochflur-Fahrzeugen, die an Niedrigbahnsteigen halten, durchgeführt wird. Im Gegensatz zu Salt Lake City ist ein Wechsel zu Niederflur-Fahrzeugen auch mittelfristig nicht vorgesehen. Um trotzdem behindertengerecht zu sein, wurden alle Haltestellen mit kurzen Hochbahnsteigen ausgestattet, so dass Rollstuhlfahrer und andere Menschen mit eingeschränkter Mobilität an der vordersten Tür einsteigen können, wo der Fahrer außerdem manuell eine Überbrückung hinunterklappt.

Das Stadtbahnnetz von Denver ist ein für die USA typisches Light Rail-System, mit abmarkierten straßenbündigen Abschnitten im Stadtzentrum und einem hohen Anteil an völlig kreuzungsfreien Strecken durch die äußeren Vororte, entweder entlang von Eisenbahnkorridoren oder im Mittelstreifen bzw. entlang von Autobahnen, woraus sich hohe Reisegeschwindigkeiten ergeben. Die neue Weststrecke folgt teilweise einer alten Bahntrasse und weist mehrere Bahnübergänge auf.

Die Stadtbahn verkehrt an allen Tagen von 4:30 bis 1:00 Uhr, wobei die Linien D, E, H und W tagsüber mindestens alle 15 Minuten (abends alle 30 Min.) fahren, während die Linien C und F alle 30 Minuten während der Hauptverkehrszeiten hinzukommen.

● **D Line** (22,4 km, 17 Haltestellen)
Denvers erste Stadtbahnlinie von 1994 entspricht der heutigen Linie D. Ihre Route beginnt an einer zweigleisigen Stumpfendstelle auf der Downing Street im Stadtteil Five Points und wird sofort eingleisig, sobald sie in die Welton Street einbiegt, wo sie über einen eigenen Gleiskörper am südlichen Straßenrand verfügt. Entlang dieses 870 m langen Engpasses gibt es drei einseitige Haltestellen, keine davon jedoch mit Ausweiche. Die Strecke wird an der 24th Street zweigleisig, die Züge halten aber erst wieder an der 20th Street am nordöstlichen Rand der Innenstadt, bevor sie rechts in die 19th Street einbiegen. Einen Häuserblock weiter westlich erreichen sie das nördliche Ende einer Innenstadtschleife, auf der die Linien F und H wenden. Da es hier aber für endende Züge keine Warteposition gibt, kann es sein, dass ein 4-Wagen-Zug, wie er in der Hauptverkehrszeit eingesetzt wird, den Kreuzungsbereich blockiert. Richtung Süden fährt die Stadtbahn entlang der Stout Street, Richtung Norden auf der California Street, jeweils in entgegengesetzter Richtung zum Autoverkehr auf einer durch niedrige

The RTD light rail system currently consists of five letter and colour-coded routes, with a sixth (W) to be introduced in 2013 when the extension to Jefferson County Government Center opens. Besides Sacramento, Denver is the only city in the western U.S.A. whose light rail system is still operated exclusively with high-floor vehicles stopping at low-level platforms. Unlike Salt Lake City, a transition to low-floor rolling stock is not planned in the mid-term future. To be ADA compliant (Americans with Disabilities Act), all stations are equipped with short high-level platforms that line up with the front door of the trains, where the driver manually unfolds a bridge plate to allow wheelchair users and other people with reduced mobility to board the train.

Denver's network can be classified as a typical light rail system, with street-running sections on mostly marked-off lanes in the city centre, and a high degree of completely grade-separated routes through suburban areas, either within railroad corridors or alongside or in freeway medians, resulting in high travel speeds. The new western route partly follows a disused railway corridor and has several level crossings.

Light rail trains operate from 04:30 until 01:00 all week, with the D, E, H and W lines running every 15 minutes for most of the day (every 30 min in the evenings), while the C and F lines offer extra service every 30 minutes during peak periods.

● *D Line* (22.4 km, 17 stations)
Denver's entry into the light rail age came with what is now the D line. The 1994 route begins in a double-track stub terminus on Downing Street in the Five Points neighbourhood, but immediately becomes single-track as it turns into Welton Street on a reserved lane along the south side of the roadway; there are three single-sided stops along this

DENVER Light Rail

72.7 km (2013)
47 Haltestellen | *stations* (2013)

10 Oct 1994: 30th St & Downing – I-25/Broadway (8.5 km)
14 July 2000: I-25/Broadway – Littleton/Mineral (13.9 km)
05 Apr 2002: 10th & Osage – Union Station (2.5 km)
17 Nov 2006: I-25/Broadway – Lincoln (21.7 km)
Southmoor – Nine Mile (6.4 km)

26 April 2013: Auraria West Campus – Jefferson County Government Center/Golden (19.4 km)
2014: Nine Mile – Iliff (2.4 km)

Orchard – Siemens SD160

Bordsteine abgetrennten Spur. Die beiden Haltestellen entlang dieses Abschnitts bestehen nur aus einem gelben Streifen auf dem Bürgersteig, einem Unterstand sowie dem kurzen Hochbahnsteig am vorderen Ende, ein 4-Wagen-Zug nimmt dabei fast die gesamte Länge eines Häuserblocks ein. An der 16th Street kann man zu den kostenlosen Mall Shuttle-Bussen (siehe Kasten auf S. 155) umsteigen.

Die beiden Gleise treffen vor der überbauten Station Theatre District/Convention Center wieder aufeinander. Diese wurde am 6. Dezember 2004 eröffnet und ersetzte die ursprünglichen Haltestellen auf der Stout & 14th Street (Richtung Süden) und 14th & California Street (Richtung Norden). Die ursprüngliche Strecke verlief geradeaus zweigleisig Richtung Südwesten entlang der Stout Street, bis diese Straße 2002/03 etwas nach Westen zwar ebenerdig, aber unter das erweiterte Convention Center verlegt wurde. Nach Überqueren des Cherry Creek, des North Speer Boulevard und der Kalamath Street erreicht die Stadtbahn die Haltestelle Colfax at Auraria, die einen Campus mit mehreren Hochschuleinrichtungen erschließt.

Etwa 350 m westlich von Colfax at Auraria biegen die Züge Richtung Süden unter der jetzt aufgeständerten Colfax Avenue ab und erreichen die von RTD gekaufte Trasse der ehemaligen Eisenbahn *Denver & Rio Grande Western* (D&RGW). Entlang der gesamten Südweststrecke bis Littleton gibt es parallel noch eine viel befahrene Güterbahnstrecke, wobei die Stadtbahn zwischen Oxford und Littleton/Downtown auf einer Überführung auf die Westseite wechselt. Die ursprüngliche, 8,5 km lange Strecke endete an der Station I-25/Broadway, wo ein großer Bus/Bahn-Umsteigepunkt sowie eine Park-and-Ride-Anlage eingerichtet wurden. Eine 13,9 km lange Verlängerung nach Littleton mit nur fünf Stationen kam im Jahr 2000 hinzu. Die Strecke ist südlich von Alameda völlig

870 m bottleneck, none of which has a passing loop. The line becomes double-track at 24th Street, but trains do not stop until they reach 20th Street on the northeastern edge of the city centre. They turn right into 19th Street and travel one block west to reach the northern end of a downtown loop that is used by the F and H trains to turn back. Since there is no layover track, 4-car peak-hour trains may block the intersections. South on Stout Street and north on California Street, trains operate in the opposite direction to the road traffic, with the tracks separated from the traffic lanes by a small curb. The platforms for the two stops along this segment consist of little more than a yellow stripe painted on the sidewalk, plus a shelter and a short high-level platform at the front end; a full-length 4-car train occupies nearly the entire street block. At 16th Street, transfers can be made to the free Mall Shuttle buses (see box on p.155).

The two tracks rejoin upon entering the built-over Theatre District/Convention Center station, which opened on 6 Dec 2004 to replace the original stops on Stout & 14th (southbound) and 14th & California (northbound). The original route had a straight double-track alignment southwest along Stout Street until the latter was diverted slightly west in 2002/03 into the undercroft of the expanded Convention Center. After crossing Cherry Creek, Speer Boulevard and Kalamath Street, trains arrive at Colfax at Auraria, the stop for a campus shared by three universities and colleges.

Some 350 m west of Colfax at Auraria, trains turn south under an elevated section of Colfax Avenue to pick up an old Denver & Rio Grande Western (D&RGW) railway right-of-way purchased by RTD. A busy freight line still runs alongside the southwestern light rail route all the way to Littleton (the light rail line switches to the western side on a flyover

kreuzungsfrei, die Fahrgäste müssen jedoch an allen Haltestellen die Gleise überqueren, um den Bahnsteig zu erreichen,
weshalb die Züge sehr langsam und mit einem Warnsignal in
die Stationen einfahren. Der kreuzungsfreie Ausbau der alten
Bahnstrecke hatte bereits in den 1970er Jahren lange vor dem
Stadtbahnbau begonnen. Eine 3,8 km lange Verlängerung
bis C-470/Lucent Boulevard ist geplant. Eine 1,4 km lange
Norderweiterung wird die Linie D mit der zukünftigen S-Bahn
zum Flughafen verknüpfen.

● ● E & H Lines (28,8/24 km, 18/14 Haltestellen)

Der nördliche Ast der Line E zur Union Station hat in seiner
kurzen 10-jährigen Geschichte bereits einige Veränderungen
hinter sich. Er zweigt von der ursprünglichen Nord-Süd-Linie
westlich der Station Colfax at Auraria ab. Hier gab es anfangs
ein volles Gleisdreieck, bis im Jahr 2011 der nördliche Schenkel entfernt wurde, als auch die westlich daran anschließende
Strecke verlegt wurde, um eine neue Haltestelle Auraria West
in Verbindung mit der 2013 zu eröffnenden Weststrecke zu
bauen. Die frühere Station Auraria West lag in Ost-West-
Richtung, 100 m nördlich und parallel zur Colfax Avenue. Die
nächste Haltestelle mit einem Mittel- und zwei Seitenbahnstei-
gen liegt nur 250 m weiter nördlich und erschließt ein großes
Stadion, wo die Heimspiele der Denver Broncos, des lokalen
American Football-Teams, stattfinden. Hier trifft die Stadtbahn
wieder auf die von Norden nach Süden die Stadt durchqueren-
de Güterbahn. Die Station Pepsi Center/Elitch Gardens liegt
zwischen der gleichnamigen Veranstaltungshalle und einem
Vergnügungspark. Die 2,5 km lange Zweiglinie endet schließlich an der Union Station, eine Gegend, die derzeit eine riesige
Baustelle darstellt. Die ursprüngliche Endstelle, die sich östlich
der 16th Street in der Nähe des historischen Bahnhofsgebäudes befand, wurde über eine S-Kurve erreicht. Um den Bau
eines intermodalen Knotens mit Amtrak- und S-Bahnhof sowie
einem unterirdischen Busbahnhof zu ermöglichen, wurde die
Light Rail-Haltestelle im August 2011 etwa 300 m nach Nordwesten verschoben. Union Station wird auch die Endstation für
die Linie W, die im Jahr 2013 eröffnet wird.

Südlich von Auraria teilen sich die Linien E und H die Gleise
mit der Linie D bis I-25/Broadway, bevor sie südlich dieser
Station abzweigen (hier komplettiert ein eingleisiger südlicher
Schenkel das Gleisdreieck). Die Züge überqueren die Kentucky
Avenue und den Broadway auf einem Viadukt und erreichen
dann die Westseite der I-25. Sie folgen dieser Autobahn bis
zum South Colorado Boulevard, schwenken dann in Richtung
Süden ab und halten nach einem kurzen Tunnel an der Station
Colorado, die in einem offenen Einschnitt neben dem Colorado
Center Drive liegt. Östlich davon erreichen sie wieder die Auto-
bahn und verbleiben an ihrer Westseite bis zur Endstation der
Linie E in Lincoln. Mehrere Brücken und Unterführungen wurden

between Oxford and Littleton/Downtown). The original
8.5 km route terminated at I-25/Broadway, a large bus/rail
interchange and a park & ride facility. A 13.9 km extension to
Littleton with only five stations was added in 2000. Although
the line is completely grade-separated south of Alameda
station, passengers have to cross the tracks to access the
platforms at every station; trains therefore enter at low
speed and with a warning sound. The grade separation of the
pre-existing railway route had started back in the 1970s prior
to construction of the light rail system. A 3.8 km extension
to C-470/Lucent Boulevard is planned. A 1.4 km northern extension will close the gap between the D line and the future
East Line to the airport.

● ● E & H Lines (28.8/24 km, 18/14 stations)

The northern leg of the E Line to Union Station has already
undergone some rebuilding in its short 10-year history. It
diverges from the original north-south line west of Colfax at
Auraria station; this junction used to be a full wye, but the
northern leg was removed in 2011 when the section to the
west was also reconfigured to create a new Auraria West station in conjunction with the western extension, which opens
in 2013. The platforms of the old Auraria West station lay in
an east-west direction, 100 m north of the parallel Colfax Avenue. The next stop, with an island and two side platforms,
is only 250 m further north and serves the home stadium
of the Denver Broncos, the local American football team.
Here the light rail route aligns again with the freight line
that runs north-south through the city. Pepsi Center/Elitch
Gardens station is located between an indoor arena and an
amusement park. The 2.5 km spur finally ends at Union Station, an area under redevelopment. The original terminus
was located on the east side of 16th Street close to the old
station building and used to be reached via an S-curve. To
allow for the construction of a large intermodal hub for
Amtrak and commuter rail trains, including an underground
bus station, the light rail terminus was moved some 300 m
northwest in August 2011. Union Station will also become the
terminus for the W line when it opens in 2013.

Running south from Auraria, the E and H lines share the
D line route to I-25/Broadway before diverging just south of
this station (there is a single-track southern leg to complete
the wye junction). Trains climb a viaduct to pass over Kentucky Avenue and Broadway to align with I-25 on its western
side. They follow this freeway down to Colorado Boulevard,
where they diverge towards the south, enter a short tunnel
and stop at Colorado station, which is located in an open
trench next to Colorado Center Drive. Just to the east, the
tracks rejoin the freeway and remain on its western fringe
all the way to the E line terminus at Lincoln. Several bridges

19th Street & Stout Street – Innenstadtschleife | *downtown loop*

Theatre District/Convention Center

im Bereich von Autobahnausfahrten errichtet, was schließlich zu einer völlig kreuzungsfreien Strecke führte. Außer an den Stationen Louisiana/Pearl und Southmoor überqueren die Fahrgäste jedoch die Gleise an allen Haltestellen.

Der gesamte 21,7 km südöstliche Ast nach Lincoln, der stets von der Linie E und zu bestimmten Zeiten auch durch die Linie F bedient wird, wurde gleichzeitig mit dem 6,4 km langen Abzweig nach Nine Mile, der Endstation der Linie H, eröffnet. Dieser Ast zweigt von der I-25-Linie 1,5 km südlich von Southmoor an einem voll kreuzungsfreien Gleisdreieck ab und verläuft dann im Mittelstreifen der I-225, wo zwei Bahnhöfe mit Mittelbahnsteigen liegen. Seit Eröffnung der beiden Äste im November 2006 bis zum 3. Mai 2009 wurde eine Linie G direkt von Nine Mile nach Lincoln betrieben. Diese Linie könnte wieder auftauchen, sobald im Jahr 2016 die geplante Strecke durch Aurora bis Peoria/Smith vollendet ist, der erste 2,4 km lange Abschnitt ist derzeit im Bau (2014). Die Aurora-Erweiterung, die grob dem Korridor der I-225 folgt, wird 13 km lang sein. Von Lincoln soll eine 3,7 km lange Neubaustrecke den derzeit entstehenden Lone Tree Town Center erreichen.

● W Line (21,5 km, 15 Haltestellen)

Im April 2013 wird die ‚West Rail Line' als erstes von mehreren Projekten des ‚FasTracks'-Programms von RTD in Betrieb gehen. Die 19,4 km lange Stadtbahnverlängerung zweigt von der bestehenden Strecke zur Union Station südlich der verschobenen Station Auraria West ab. Der Verzweigung fehlt der südliche Schenkel für ein Gleisdreieck, weshalb die neue Linie W vom Westen kommend nicht direkt in Richtung Innenstadtstrecke fahren kann, sondern nur zur Union Station. Die neue Strecke führt sofort auf einen Viadukt über die UP/BNSF-Güterbahngleise und die Umatilla Street, kommt dann aber wieder auf Straßenebene zurück, um die zwölf Fahrspuren der I-25 auf einer ehemaligen Güterbahntrasse zu unterqueren. Nach einer neuen Brücke über den South Platte River folgt die Strecke bis Lakewood weitgehend dem Weg der alten *Denver, Lakewood and Golden Railway*, einer seit 1950 nicht mehr befahrenen Überlandstraßenbahn. Die Trasse wurde von RTD im Jahr 1988 gekauft. Die Strecke schlängelt sich entlang des Lakewood Dry Gulch, unterquert den Sheridan Boulevard in einem Einschnitt und erreicht schließlich die 13th Avenue auf ihrem Weg durch Lakewood. Ein Hochbahnhof wurde auf der Brücke über den Wadsworth Boulevard integriert. Ein weiterer Viadukt wurde weiter westlich über die Kipling Street errichtet, während an allen anderen kreuzenden Straßen Bahnübergänge vorhanden sind. Nach der Haltestelle Oak verlässt die

and underpasses avoid conflicts with traffic at freeway exits, which results in a completely grade-separated route. However, except at Louisiana/Pearl and Southmoor, passengers have to cross the tracks at stations.

The entire 21.7 km southeastern branch to Lincoln, served regularly by the E line and at certain times by the F line as well, was opened together with the 6.4 km spur to Nine Mile, terminus of the H line. 1.5 km south of Southmoor, this spur diverges from the I-25 line in a fully grade-separated wye junction that brings the line into the median of the I-225 freeway, along which two stations with island platforms are located. From the opening of the two branches in November 2006 until 3 May 2009, the G line operated directly between Nine Mile and Lincoln. This line may be reinstated in 2016 once the planned route through Aurora to Peoria/Smith has been built, the first 2.4 km of which is currently under construction (2014). The Aurora extension, which roughly follows the I-225 corridor, will add another 13 km to the total network length. From Lincoln, a 3.7 km extension is planned to reach the Lone Tree Town Center currently under development.

● W Line (21.5 km, 15 stations)

The West Rail Line will open in April 2013 as the first of several projects in the RTD FasTracks programme. The 19.4 km light rail extension diverges from the existing Union Station spur just south of the relocated Auraria West station. The new junction lacks the southern leg to become a full wye, with the result that W trains cannot be routed on the old cross-downtown tracks, but only to Union Station. Trains immediately climb a viaduct that takes them over the UP/BNSF freight tracks and Umatilla Street, but return to street level to dive under the twelve I-25 lanes on an alignment once occupied by a freight line. After crossing the South Platte River on a new bridge, the line largely follows the path of the original 'Denver, Lakewood and Golden Railway' to Lakewood; this interurban tram line ceased operation in 1950. The right-of-way was purchased by RTD back in 1988. The route skirts Lakewood Dry Gulch and, after passing under Sheridan Boulevard in a trench, runs along 13th Avenue through Lakewood. An elevated station was integrated into a bridge over Wadsworth Boulevard. Another viaduct was built over Kipling Street further west, whereas the other intersections with urban roads are all level crossings. After Oak station, the route diverges from the old interurban right-of-way and turns south through an industrial area to reach the Fed-

FREE MallRide

Entlang der Fußgängerzone auf der 16th Street wird zwischen der Union Station im Norden und dem Busbahnhof am Civic Center im Süden ein kostenloser Shuttle angeboten. Batteriebetriebene Busse fahren fast ununterbrochen und halten an jeder Straßenkreuzung. Dieser Service wurde im Jahr 1982 eingeführt. Seit 1999 verkehrt die zweite Generation von Bussen. Diese wurden in eigener Werkstatt hergestellt und verwenden einen Ford-Erdgasmotor zur Stromerzeugung, wobei die Batterien auch durch Einspeisung der Bremsenergie aufgeladen werden. Um Fußgänger und Fahrgäste besser im Blick zu haben, sitzen die Fahrer auf der rechten Seite des Busses.

A special shuttle bus service is operated along the pedestrianised 16th Street Mall between the Union Station hub in the north and Civic Center bus station in the south, with battery-powered buses running almost continuously and stopping at every intersecting street. The service was first introduced in 1982. The second-generation buses, which were manufactured in-house in 1999, use a Ford natural gas engine to generate power, with the batteries being recharged by regenerative braking as well. Bus drivers are seated on the right to give them a better view of pedestrian movements and boarding passengers.

16th Street Mall & Stout Street

Stadtbahn die alte Überlandstrecke, fährt nach Süden durch ein Industriegebiet und erreicht auf einer ehemaligen Bahntrasse das Federal Center. Zur Überquerung der hier autobahnähnlichen 6th Avenue musste eine 240 m lange Brücke gebaut werden. Das Federal Center beherbergt mehrere Delegationen von Bundesbehörden und ist neben einem großen Krankenhaus-Komplex ein wichtiger Arbeitgeber in dieser Gegend. Die Station Federal Center ist dreigleisig, da hier während der Hauptverkehrszeiten zwei von drei Zügen enden sollen. Die Strecke schwenkt dann nach Norden und wird eingleisig, bevor sie Richtung Westen den Union Boulevard unterquert und an die Südseite der 6th Avenue gelangt. An der einzigen Zwischenstation vor dem Streckenende, Red Rocks College, gibt es eine Ausweiche. Auf einer 470 m langen eingleisigen Überführung schwenkt die Stadtbahn auf die Nordseite der 6th Avenue, taucht unter der I-70 hindurch, überquert die Colfax Avenue und erreicht schließlich die dreigleisige Endstelle am Jefferson County Government Center in Golden (ca. 4 km vom alten Kern von Golden entfernt). Eine Fahrt von der Union Station bis zum Jefferson County Government Center dauert 35 Minuten.

eral Center, taking advantage of land once occupied by spur tracks. A 240 m bridge was built to convey the tracks to the south side of the 6th Avenue Freeway. The Federal Center, housing offices of several federal government agencies, along with an adjacent large hospital complex represent a major employment centre. Federal Center has three tracks and will become a regular terminus for two out of three trains during peak hours. After turning north, the line reduces to a single track and turns west to pass under Union Boulevard and align with the southern side of 6th Avenue. Red Rocks College, the only intermediate station before the end of the line, has a passing loop. Via a 470 m single-track flyover the line switches to the northern side of 6th Avenue, then passes under I-70 and over Colfax Avenue before reaching its 3-track terminus at Jefferson County Government Center in Golden (about 4 km short of the old town centre). A ride from Union Station to Jefferson County Government Center will take 35 minutes.

Union Station – Siemens SD160

● Stadtbahnfahrzeuge

Trotz eines Bestands von 172 Fahrzeugen ist die RTD-Flotte sehr homogen, denn es gibt nur SD100- bzw. SD160-Wagen von Siemens-Duewag. Denver nahm seine erste Linie wenige Jahre, bevor die ersten Niederflur-Fahrzeuge in den USA in Portland eingeführt wurden, in Betrieb und ist seitdem im Gegensatz zum benachbarten Salt Lake City demselben Wagentyp treu geblieben.

Zwischen 1993 und 2002 wurden in vier Serien insgesamt 49 Gelenkwagen des Typs SD100 bei Siemens in Sacramento gefertigt. Eine Weiterentwicklung stellt der Typ SD160 dar, von dem seit dem Jahr 2004 insgesamt 123 in drei Serien geliefert wurden. Letztere verfügen über Drehstrommotoren und haben 1,3 m breite Schwenkschiebetüren statt der ursprünglichen Gleichstrommotoren und Falttüren beim Typ SD100. Die SD160-Wagen erkennt man außerdem an den blauen Streifen, die zusätzlich zu den gelb-orange-roten der älteren Fahrzeuge angebracht sind. Beide Typen sind 24,8 m lang und 2,65 m breit. Sie sind meist als 3-Wagen-Züge im Einsatz, aber während der Hauptverkehrszeiten sind auch 4-Wagen-Züge zu sehen.

Der Stadtbahnbetriebshof befindet sich entlang der Strecke nach Littleton zwischen den Bahnhöfen Evans und Englewood. Bis auf 30th & Downing und Jefferson County Government Center gibt es hinter allen Endstationen Kehrgleise, die außerhalb der Hauptverkehrszeiten auch zum Abstellen von Zügen benutzt werden.

● Light Rail Rolling Stock

RTD's 172-car fleet is very homogenous, consisting only of Siemens-Duewag SD100/160 trains. Denver opened its first line a few years before Portland first introduced low-floor vehicles to the U.S., and ever since, unlike neighbouring Salt Lake City, RTD has remained faithful to the same type of car. As a result, in the western U.S. only Denver and Sacramento now operate exclusively with high-floor vehicles that stop at low-floor platforms.

Between 1993 and 2002, 49 articulated cars of the SD100 type were manufactured in four batches by Siemens at its Sacramento plant. The more advanced, but very similar SD160 type was first delivered in 2004, and since then, a total of 123 cars have been added to the fleet in three batches. They feature ac motors and have 1.3 m wide sliding doors as opposed to the dc motors and folding doors of the original SD100 stock. The SD160 cars can also be distinguished by a blue stripe added to the original yellow-orange-red stripes. Both are 24.8 m long and 2.65 m wide. They are mostly in service as 3-car trains, but 4-car sets are also deployed during peak hours.

The trains are stored and maintained at a facility located along the Littleton route between Evans and Englewood stations. Beyond all termini, except 30th & Downing and Jefferson County Government Center, there are sidings for reversing and stabling trains during off-peak hours.

Siemens SD100

Stout Street & 16th Street Mall – SD100-Wagen auf der Linie D auf dem Weg Richtung Littleton Mineral | *SD100 car on a line D service to Littleton Mineral*

● RTD Commuter Rail

Neben der neuen Linie W und den oben beschriebenen Stadtbahnerweiterungen enthält das ehrgeizige, im Jahr 2006 beschlossene ‚FasTracks'-Programm auch den Bau von vier Vorortbahnlinien, die von der völlig umgebauten Union Station in der Innenstadt von Denver ausgehen werden. Da man den Betrieb von leichten Stadtbahnfahrzeugen und schweren Güterzügen nebeneinander aus Sicherheitsgründen vermeiden wollte, fiel die Wahl bei den Nordstrecken auf ‚Heavy Rail', weshalb die Fahrgäste umsteigen werden müssen, wenn sie quer durch die Stadt fahren möchten. Das Zugangebot soll jedoch dem der Stadtbahnlinien entsprechen, d.h. tagsüber alle 15 Minuten, und da die Strecken von Anfang an elektrifiziert sein werden, kann man sie durchaus als „S-Bahn" bezeichnen.

Der Bau der 17,9 km langen ‚Gold Line' in den westlichen Vorort Arvada begann im Jahr 2012 und soll 2016 vollendet sein, genauso wie der erste 9,6 km lange Abschnitt der ‚Northwest Rail Line' bis South Westminster (davon sind 6,3 km gemeinsam mit der Gold Line) und die 36,5 km lange ‚East Rail Line' zum Flughafen von Denver (DIA). Später soll die Nordwestlinie 56 km weiter nach Boulder und Longmont verlängert werden und die 29,5 km lange ‚North Metro Line' durch Thornton dazukommen.

Für den S-Bahn-Betrieb wurden bei Hyundai Rotem elektrische Triebzüge bestellt, die der Baureihe SilverLiner V von SEPTA in Philadelphia ähnlich sein werden. Alle Bahnhöfe werden dazu mit Hochbahnsteigen gebaut.

Besides the new W line and the light rail extensions mentioned above, the ambitious FasTracks scheme approved in 2006 also includes the construction of four 'commuter rail' lines radiating from the completely rebuilt Union Station hub in downtown Denver. To avoid the operation of light rail and heavy freight trains on parallel tracks, 'heavy rail' was chosen for the northern routes, so passengers will have to change trains if they wish to continue their journeys through the city centre. The service provided will be similar to that on the existing light rail routes (every 15 minutes during daytime hours), and with the first lines to be electrified from the start, the designation 'suburban rail' would be more accurate.

The construction of the 17.9 km Gold Line to the western suburb of Arvada, the first 9.6 km segment of the Northwest Rail Line to South Westminster (6.3 km of which is shared with the Gold Line), as well as the 36.5 km East Rail Line to Denver International Airport (DIA), started in 2012 for completion set for 2016. Future plans include a 56 km extension of the Northwest Line to Boulder and Longmont, and a 29.5 km North Metro Line through Thornton.

The commuter rail lines will be operated with Hyundai Rotem EMUs (electric multiple units), similar to the SEPTA Silverliner V stock in service in Philadelphia. Stations will feature high-level platforms.

Hyundai Rotem

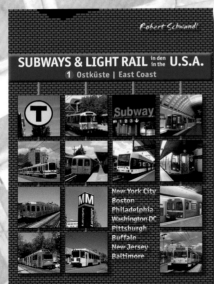
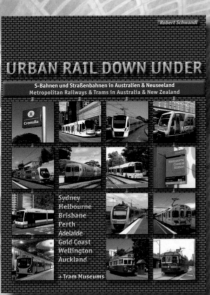

Websites & Bücher | *Websites & Books*

- Harre W. Demoro & John N. Harder: **Light Rail on the West Coast**. - *1989, Quadrant Press, NYC, ISBN 0915276496*

Seattle – www.soundtransit.org | www.seattlestreetcar.org | metro.kingcounty.gov | www.seattlemonorail.com

Portland – www. trimet.org | www.portlandstreetcar.org | gobytram.com

Sacramento – www.sacrt.com

San Francisco – www.bart.gov | www.sfmta.com | www.511.org | www.centralsubwaysf.com | www.streetcar.org | www.sfcablecar.com | www.cablecarmuseum.org

- Anthony Perles: **The People's Railway. A History of the Municipal Railway of San Francisco**. - *1981, Interurban Press, ISBN 0916274424*

- Grant Ute, ed al.: **San Francisco's Municipal Railway: MUNI** - *2011, Arcadia Publishing, ISBN 9780738575803*

- Zachary Malott, Leia Kaba: **The Streetcars of San Francisco** - *2009, ISBN 9781442188815*

San Jose – www.vta.org

Los Angeles – www.metro.net | www.metrolinktrains.com

San Diego – www.sdcommute.com | www.511sd.com | www.gonctd.com

- Gena Holle: **The San Diego Trolley**. - *1990, Interurban Press, ISBN 0916374920*

Honolulu – www.honolulutransit.org | www.ansaldohonolulurail.com

Las Vegas – www.lvmonorail.com

Phoenix – www.valleymetro.org

Tucson – www.tucsonstreetcar.com | www.rtamobility.com | www.oldpueblotrolley.org

Salt Lake City – www.rideuta.com | www.shstreetcar.com

Denver – www.rtd-denver.com

Weitere Weblinks und aktuelle Informationen finden Sie unter
More websites and updated information can be found at

UrbanRail.Net – www.urbanrail.net